STUDENT FEEDBACK QUESTIONNAIRE

SCHOOL OF FOOD AND ACCOMMODATION MANAGEMENT

HND IN HOTEL CATERING & INSTITUTIONAL MANAGEMENT

Course Evaluation 1989/90

<u>2nd year</u>

In order to assess the success or failure of Accommodation Services this year and to enable me to improve for future years, I would be grateful if you would complete this questionnaire. Please note that the replies are more useful if they are anonymous.

Thanks.

Part 1 - General impact of the Unit

Place a ✓ in the appropriate box

1. How DIFFICULT did you find the unit?

1	Very difficult
2	Fairly difficult
3	Just right
4	Fairly easy
5	Very easy

2. How INTERESTING did you find the unit?

1	Very interesting
2	Fairly interesting
3	Not very interesting
4	Of no interest at all

3. Was enough TIME allocated for the amount of work involved?

1	Not enough time
2	Just right
3	Too much time

4. To what extent have you UNDERSTOOD the unit?

1	Thoroughly
2	Fairly well
3	Partially
4	Hardly at all

5. To what extent were you clear about the AIMS of the unit?

1	Quite clear
2	Partially clear
3	Not clear at all

6. How VALUABLE have you found the unit?

1	Very valuable
2	Fairly valuable
3	Not very valuable
4	Hardly any value

7. How SATISFIED are you with this unit?

1	Highly satisfied
2	Quite satisfied
3	Not very satisfied
4	Very dissatisfied

Any other comments

Part 2 - Teaching Strategies and Techniques

Part 2 Teaching Strategies & Techniques

Was the range of teaching methods used

    satisfactory
    unsatisfactory
    no opinion

Was enough guidance and encouragement given for individual private study.

    yes
    no
    don't know

Within this subject do you prefer to work

    individually
    in groups
    don't mind
    a mixture of both

How do you rate the following teaching methods as a means of teaching Accommodation Service.
Please tick a column

	good	bad	indifferent
lectures taking own notes			
lectures with overheads			
lectures with participative h/outs			
Tutorials - discussions			
- practical sessions			
- on going projects			

Is there any teaching method not presently used for this subject that you would like to see used.

Part 3 - The Teacher

Do you agree or disagree with the following statements? Indicate the level of your agreement by ticking one box beside each statement.

The lecturer -

Strongly disagree	Disagree	Neither agree nor disagree	Agree	Strongly agree	
					Is clear and understandable in his or her explanations
					Presents material in a well organised way
					Gives a good factual coverage of the subject matter
					Identifies and stresses important aspects
					Writes legibly on the blackboard or projector
					Can be clearly heard
					Adjusts his or her pace to the needs of the class
					Stimulates students to think independently
					Is sensitive to the feelings and problems of individual student
					Encourages students to ask questions
					Answers questions satisfactorily
					Encourages students to express their own views
					Sets interesting and worthwhile tests and exercises
					Makes constructive and helpful comments on written work and practical tasks
					Is enthusiastic about his or her subject
					Points out the links between his or her subjects and related subjects
					Tries to create links between various parts of the course e.g. between lectures and laboratory exercises
					Shows the relevance of his or her subject to the work you expect to do when you qualify
					Is approachable
					Has a good sense of humour

Any other comments.

Economics
a first course
SECOND EDITION

Ian Hobday
Senior Lecturer in Economics
South Downs College of Further Education
Havant, Hampshire

Edward Arnold
A division of Hodder & Stoughton
LONDON   BALTIMORE   MELBOURNE   AUCKLAND

© 1988 Ian Hobday

First published in Great Britain 1983
Second edition 1988

British Library Cataloguing in Publication Data

Hobday, Ian
  Economics: a first course.—— 2nd ed.
  1. Economics — For schools
  I. Title
  330

  ISBN 0–7131–7751–9

Text set in 11/12 pt Plantin Medium Compugraphic
by Colset Private Limited, Singapore
Printed and bound in Great Britain for Edward Arnold, the educational,
academic and medical publishing division of Hodder and Stoughton
Limited, 41 Bedford Square, London WC1B 3DQ by Richard Clay plc,
Bungay, Suffolk

Contents

Introduction

When *Economics: a first course* was first published it successfully established itself as a book suitable for both school and college students wishing to gain examination success in introductory courses in economics. This revised edition has been written for students and teachers of economics for all the GCSE board groups and for the economics components of the various professional and vocational courses awarded by the Business and Technician Education Council (BTEC). It is also suitable for the economics sections of GCSE business studies and commerce syllabuses as well as for more vocational examinations, which include much economics, particularly the Chartered Institute of Bankers and RSA courses. The book covers all the essential topic areas and has been written with examination syllabuses in mind.

This edition has been completely updated with new photographs, diagrams and tables, which are used wherever possible to stimulate and maintain interest. Recent economic issues such as poll tax, privatisation and the Stock Exchange 'big bang' have all been dealt with. Current economic problems and issues are cited throughout the book to show the relevance of the subject to everyday life. All chapters have been completely revised to take into account recent developments. To help understanding and revision a list of checkpoints has been added to each chapter. These briefly outline the main ideas to be found within the chapter.

Examination questions in economics are now increasingly being structured so that you, the student, can show what you know rather than what you do not know. Consequently this edition includes, at the end of each chapter, multiple-choice questions and stimulus data response-type questions. Answers to the multiple-choice questions can be found at the end of the book. Students of economics at GCSE level have to produce at least one piece of coursework and this edition will prove to be an ideal reference text for this purpose.

It is hoped that this book will lead to a better understanding of economics and economic problems. It is intended that the reader will find what is written to be both an interesting educational resource and a guide to examination success.

Acknowledgements

The Publishers wish to thank the following for their permission to reproduce copyright material:

Access for their card, p. 181; Bank of England for a photograph, p. 189; Barclays Bank plc for a Barclaycard, p. 181, a Connect card, p. 203, and their logo, p. 184; British Steel for a photograph, p. 85; Christian Aid for a photograph, p. 1; Commission of the European Communities for a photograph, p. 164; Corby Industrial Development Centre, p. 68; Coutts for their logo, p. 184; *Daily Mail*, pp. 45, 126, 202 and 203; *Daily Telegraph*, pp. 50, 212 and 248; *Economics*, p. 61; *The Economist*, pp. 17, 166, 209 and 273; *Financial Times*, p. 242; *The Guardian*, pp. 50, 229 and 316; Her Majesty's Stationery Office for material from the Central Statistical Office, pp. 59 and 87, *Demographic Year Books*, p. 254, Department of Employment New Earnings Survey, *Employment Gazette*, pp. 269, 275, 289, 293 and 301, Department of Health and Social Security, p. 126, Economic Progress Report, pp. 91, 146, 205 and 318, *Economic Trends*, pp. 53 and 161, *Economic Trends*, Annual Supplement, 1985, pp. 138, 283 and 326, and 1986, pp. 156 and 157, Economic Trends and Financial Statistics, p. 312, a Government report, p. 58, Monthly Digest of Statistics, p. 266, Office of Population Censuses and Surveys, Government Actuary's Department, pp. 254, 257 and 261, Overseas Trade Statistics, p. 168, and Crown Copyright, with the permission of the Controller of HMSO, for a Treasury Bill, p. 194; *The Independent*, pp. 93, 219, 226, 230 and 311; Institute of Management Studies, pp. 31 and 33; Lloyds Bank plc for their *Economic Bulletin*, pp. 142, 158 and 213, and their logo, p. 184; Manpower Services Commission, p. 281; Midland Bank plc for a cheque card, p. 179, and their logo, p. 184; Monthly Bulletin of Statistics, United Nations, p. 254; National Westminster Bank plc for their logo, p. 184; *The Observer*, pp. 98 and 192; OECD, pp. 213, 227, 313, 319 and 320; Royal Bank of Scotland for their logo, p. 184; Statistical Office of the European Communities, p. 267; and TSB for their logo, p. 184.

1 Basic economic problems

Slums on reclamation land, Bombay, India

The central economic problem of scarcity and choice

The central economic problem can be illustrated by the diagram overleaf.

1

Consumers' → **exceed** → the **resources** (*factors of production*: land, labour,
wants   capital, enterprise) available, to produce the goods
            and services, to satisfy consumer wants.

↓

There is a **scarcity** of goods and services.

↓

Consumers have to make a **choice** about which
wants they will satisfy.

↓

This involves an **opportunity cost** because some
other choices will remain unsatisfied.

If there were enough of the goods and services which consumers wanted then
they would not need to worry about how they each got a share. Consumers do not,
for instance, count the number of times they breathe in air because there is
enough air for everybody. Air is a '**free good**', because there is no restriction on
supply and therefore it is supplied free of charge. However, most goods are
'**economic goods**' because they are relatively scarce due to the fact that the
resources available to produce these goods are scarce. By resources is meant
factors of production (land, labour, capital and enterprise) and these are limited
in supply and are said to be scarce.

On the other hand consumers' **wants** are virtually unlimited because
consumers want houses and bigger houses, clothes and more clothes, food and
better quality food. Consumer wants are unending.

Since the supply of goods and services is not adequate to satisfy the totality of
consumer wants, consumers must make a **choice**. Most consumers have a 'scale
of preferences' and will therefore choose to satisfy some wants but not other
wants. For instance, Peter Smith may be able to afford to purchase a motor car or
pay for a foreign holiday but not both. If Peter Smith decides to purchase the car
then the other want must be sacrificed, ie the foreign holiday. Every choice
involves a sacrifice or **opportunity cost**.

All economic problems arise out of the inadequacy of resources which forces on
consumers, producers and even communities, the problem of choice. Whatever
choice is made, it will involve an opportunity cost. For instance, if a community
decides to produce more hospitals and fewer schools, the increase in the number
of hospitals has an opportunity cost in terms of the number of schools forgone.

Since resources are scarce, they must be allocated in the most efficient way
possible. Countries differ over which method of allocation is most efficient.
There are *three possible economic systems*:

(a) *planned economies*: where scarce resources are allocated by the government
(b) *market economies*: where scarce resources are allocated by the market to
    satisfy consumer wants
(c) *mixed economies*: where scarce resources are allocated by a mixture of both
    government and consumer wants.

We will look at these types of economy in more detail later in this chapter.

Production

The meaning of production

The term *production* includes all those activities which create the goods and services consumers are prepared to pay for in order to satisfy human wants. The production process is not completed until the good or service is in the hands of the final consumer. For instance, the production of any good involves not only the work of miners, farmers and factory workers but also the services of bankers, solicitors, accountants, wholesalers, retailers and transporters. They are all part of the production process.

Exchange is important to production because for any activity to be productive, it must be wanted and consumers must be willing to buy the good or service. If consumers are not willing to buy the good or service, ie, to consume it, then that good or service is not part of production. All productive processes are directed towards *consumption* which is the using of goods and services to satisfy human wants.

The production process is often divided into three categories, primary production, secondary production and tertiary production (see page 29).

What is being produced?

Free goods and economic goods

In economics we are only concerned with the production of economic goods. These are goods which are scarce and consumption of them involves opportunity cost (ie, something has to be given up in order to satisfy the want for the goods). Free goods are not scarce and can be consumed without the problem of choice and opportunity cost. We have already given air as an example of a free good.

Producer goods and consumer goods

Economic goods are classified into two types. Producer (capital or investment) goods are those goods which are not wanted for their own sakes, but because they will produce other goods (ie, other capital or consumer goods). Factories, machinery, and tractors are examples of these goods. Consumer goods are goods which directly satisfy consumer wants and are wanted for their own sakes.

Durable and non-durable consumer goods

Durable consumer goods are those which have a long life and give satisfaction over a long period of time. These would include motor cars, furniture, televisions and most domestic electrical goods. Non-durable consumer goods are those which are consumed and give satisfaction for only a short period (perhaps for only a single usage). This would include food, drink and cigarettes.

Services

These are invisible and intangible but nonetheless give satisfaction to consumers. Examples include leisure activities, education, accountancy, banking and health services.

Commodities
This term includes all economic goods and services.

Merit goods, and de-merit goods
Merit goods are those which give benefits to society in their production, for example, education and health. De-merit goods cause adverse social costs (see page 10) and cause some harm in their production, such as those industries causing pollution and environmental damage.

The meaning of wealth

A community's stock of its capital and consumer goods is often referred to as its wealth. The maintenance of a community's standard of living depends on it preserving its wealth. An important aspect in this is that *gross investment* should be greater than *depreciation* (or capital consumption). Gross investment is the addition to a community's stock of capital goods whereas depreciation is the wear and tear of capital goods in the same time period. If gross investment is greater than depreciation, then a community has *net investment* and will be increasing its wealth. It can produce more consumer and capital goods which will increase the standard of living of the community. If, on the other hand, gross investment is less than depreciation then a country will have fewer capital goods and a lower national wealth and eventually a lower standard of living.

Factors of production

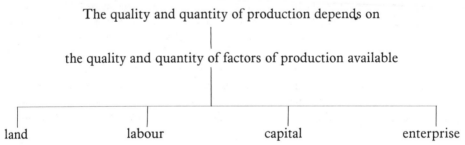

The quality and quantity of production depends on

the quality and quantity of factors of production available

land   labour   capital   enterprise

A main influence on any country's total volume of production is the quantity and quality of its productive resources. Another name, perhaps more widely used, for productive resources is **factors of production**. There are four main factors of production, *land, capital, labour* and *enterprise*.

Land

Land is used in its widest sense in economics to include all kinds of natural (as distinct from manufactured) resources, such as farm lands, mineral wealth, coal, metal ores, fishing grounds and climate. Perhaps the main service of land is the provision of space where production can take place.

The classical economists of the early nineteenth century considered land to be fundamentally different from the other factors because land is a gift of nature; supply of land is fixed and industries dependent on land are subject to the **law of**

diminishing returns. This law states that as successive units of variable factors of production (those which can be increased or decreased in supply, probably labour and capital) are added to a unit of fixed factor of production (which cannot be increased or decreased in supply, probably land), then after a certain point there will be a diminishing return – the increase in output will be less than that caused by the previous unit of variable factor. For instance, the third person may add more to output than did the second person, but if the fourth person adds less than the third person and the fifth person less than the fourth person, then diminishing returns have set in.

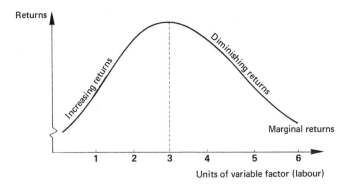

These three contentions have been criticised. The fact that land is a gift of nature is of little economic significance because human beings utilise land to make it useful. The view that land is strictly limited in supply is not quite true. Irrigation, land reclamation and better farming techniques increase crop yields and land supply. The contention that industries dependent on land are subject to the law of diminishing returns is true. However, non-land dependent industries also suffer diminishing returns. The law of diminishing returns does not only apply to land-based industries. Land is said to earn an income or reward called **rent**.

Capital
This includes a varied assortment of resources – factory buildings, tools and machinery, raw materials, partly finished goods and means of transport. These things are not required for their own sakes but to assist in the production of other commodities. Capital is not the same as money but is measured in terms of money. When we discussed capital goods we were in reality discussing capital. Capital is an important part of a community's wealth. *Social capital* is that part of a community's stock of capital which is not directly concerned with the production of goods and services but still assists the production process. This would include schools, hospitals and houses.

How is capital accumulated?
For capital to be created, a community needs to spend less on consumption and

divert resources into the production of capital goods. The act of forgoing consumption is called *saving*, but these savings have to be borrowed by entrepreneurs and used to create new capital goods. The creation of new capital goods is called *investment*. As we have already seen, if gross investment is greater than depreciation (or capital consumption) then a community's stock of capital should increase and it should become wealthier and have a higher standard of living. Capital earns an income or reward called *interest*.

Labour

By labour is meant the mental and physical human effort employed in production. There are special problems involved in labour because it has a human element. Unemployment of labour is, for example, of special concern to economists. Labour earns a reward or income called *wages*. Production is determined both by the quantity and quality of labour in a particular community.

The supply of labour
This is determined by:

(a) *The size of total population* The more people in a community then probably the greater the supply of labour.
(b) *The proportion of labour available for employment* The age composition of a population will greatly determine the size of the working population, which is that proportion of the population which is willing and able to work. In the United Kingdom, at the moment, the working population consists of all those over the age of 16 years, who are willing and able to work.
(c) *The number of hours worked by each individual* This is itself determined by the length of the working day, the length of the working week and the number of holidays. In recent years, the number of hours worked by each individual has declined with a shorter working week and more holidays. However, production has increased. This is due to greater output per worker (or *productivity*) due to better machinery and technology.
(d) *The wage level* Generally at higher wages the supply of labour increases and at lower wages the supply of labour declines. This is only a general rule because at certain high levels of wages, workers may decide to work less and enjoy more leisure, knowing that the wages they will still earn are relatively high.

The efficiency of labour
Production does not only depend on the supply of labour but also on how efficient that labour is. The efficiency of labour depends on:

(a) *The quantity and quality of social services* The healthier and happier the labour force, then the greater the probability that production will be high. In the United Kingdom the *Welfare State* provides pensions, health care, unemployment and social security benefits which should ensure that the labour force is healthy and happy.
(b) *Working conditions* Workers will work harder if the place of work is pleasant: a comfortable working environment is important in making labour more

efficient. Nobody wants to work in cold, damp or miserable conditions.
(c) *Education and training* Workers need to be well educated and well trained if they are to be efficient. Modern industry requires many skilled workers who need to be literate and well educated. In the United Kingdom schools attempt to provide a good basic education.
(d) *The efficiency of other factors of production* Labour can only work efficiently if it is combined with efficient machinery and factories and if the quality of land and enterprise is of a high standard.
(e) *Incentives* Labour will work efficiently if it has sufficient motivation. A high level of wages and job satisfaction are important considerations here. Also, the method of payment can be used to motivate workers by the use of bonuses and overtime payments.

Productivity
This is a measure of output flowing from the use of given amounts of resources. Labour productivity is usually expressed as the number of units of output produced per person per unit of time (ie, output per worker).

A high level of productivity indicates efficiency and is regarded as a significant factor in achieving economic growth (see page 140) and a higher standard of living. Indeed the United Kingdom's disappointing economic growth record up to the early 1980s is often blamed on poor levels of labour productivity.

There are several factors which influence a higher level of labour productivity.

(a) The use of more and better capital equipment increases labour productivity as old and out-of-date equipment is replaced.
(b) Improvements in organisation such as more division of labour and economies of large-scale production (see Chapter 2).
(c) A better quality labour force – better skills and better educated.
(d) Concentrating production on those industries which are already expanding and growing. Reducing the amount of labour involved in declining and contracting industries.
(e) Government policies aimed at achieving all of the other factors, for example, encouragement for investment and re-training of labour directed towards expanding industries.

Of great concern to economists is the fact that labour tends to be **occupationally and geographically immobile** (see page 278).

Enterprise
The early nineteenth century economists saw only three factors of production, but Alfred Marshall, who wrote *Principles of Economics* in 1890, saw one more factor – the **entrepreneur** (or **organiser**). It is the entrepreneur who decides what is to be produced and who makes decisions to bring the other factors of production together to produce goods and services.

Many economists say that the entrepreneur is not a separate factor of production, but is linked to labour. These economists argue that organising is required of all labour from the lowest employee to the managing director. Other economists maintain that the entrepreneur *is* a separate factor because the entrepreneur is not only concerned with organising a single piece of work but this organising covers all the factors employed. He or she also has to decide what to produce, how to produce and where to produce.

Without the entrepreneur, land, labour and capital are just masses of resources of no economic importance. It is the entrepreneur who organises them for production.

The main functions of the entrepreneur include:

(a) *Uncertainty (or risk) bearing* When an entrepreneur organises the factors of production he or she is really like a manager. What distinguishes the entrepreneur from the manager is that the entrepreneur carries the risks of production. The entrepreneur engages labour and buys raw materials and machines now, in order to produce a good which will be sold in the future. Perhaps in the mean time taste may change or a rival may produce a better or cheaper product. *Profit* (or loss) is the reward for uncertainty bearing and whoever accepts this ultimate risk is the entrepreneur. The most fundamental fact in connection with organisation, it has been said, is the meeting of uncertainty.

(b) *Management control* This would involve delegating responsibility to the right person.

(c) *How much should be produced and by what method?* Should the firm use mostly labour (labour-intensive) or mostly capital (capital-intensive)?

The entrepreneur can be an individual, the government, or a large limited company.

The costs of production

The costs of production are the monetary expenditures on the use of factors of production, on such items as labour, raw materials, power and transport. To the economist, costs are the same as *opportunity cost*. For instance if an entrepreneur hires a factor of production such as labour, then the cost of production is what has to be paid for the use of that labour, ie wages. Moreover if the entrepreneur works privately or uses personal money in the firm then this also has a cost. For instance, by being self-employed the entrepreneur has forgone a wage by not working for another firm. By using his or her own money in the firm, the entrepreneur is forgoing the interest which that money could have earned, if it was saved in a bank or building society. Thus the economist is concerned with the *real cost* of producing a good which is the same as the opportunity cost (the cost of the next best alternative which has been forgone).

Different categories of costs
Fixed costs and variable costs
Fixed costs (overheads or indirect costs) are those costs of the fixed factors of production – those resources which cannot be varied in supply in the short run, such as land. The short run is not a specified period of time and varies in length from industry to industry. For instance, the short run for fresh vegetables may be the short summer season. Whereas the short run for the steel industry may be a

period of years. Fixed costs include rent, rates, interest on loans, salaries and depreciation on capital.

Variable costs (direct or prime costs) are those costs of variable factors of production – those resources which can be varied in supply even in the short run such as labour and raw materials. Wages are a good example of a variable cost. Variable costs will increase as output increases and decrease as output decreases.

In the long run, again an unspecified period of time varying from industry to industry, all factors of production are said to become variable. This is because even the fixed factors of production such as land can be increased or decreased in supply in the long run.

This distinction between fixed costs and variable costs is important because in the short run so long as revenues (or receipts) cover variable costs, the firm will go on producing. This is because fixed costs will exist anyway even if the firm closes down. Therefore if the firm is at least covering its variable costs then it is doing at least as well as if it produced nothing at all. If the firm's revenues did not cover variable cost then it would be making more of a loss by producing than if it ceased to produce altogether.

In the long run the firm must cover, with its revenues, both fixed and variable costs (called total costs) because the firm is not faced with fixed costs in the long run and can eliminate all costs of production if so desired by closing down the business. Therefore, in the long run the firm will only produce if it has covered all of its costs.

Total costs

As we have seen, this is the addition of fixed and variable costs and must be covered by the firm's revenues in the long run. Total costs will always rise as output rises because variable costs always rise as output rises. If the firm is not covering its total costs with revenues in the long run then it will be better to cease trading.

Average costs

Average costs are total costs divided by the number of units produced. As output increases average costs first fall and then rise. This is because of the law of diminishing returns and diseconomies of scale (see page 37). Up to a point there are increasing returns and economies of scale to be enjoyed. Where average costs are at their lowest is called *optimum output* because this is the most efficient or lowest cost level of output.

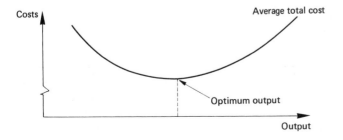

Marginal costs
These are the costs of producing one more unit and are found by dividing the change in total costs by the change in output. The shape of the curve is such that marginal costs diminish up to a level of output and then increase as the diminishing returns again set in.

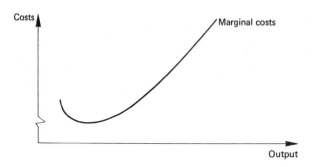

Marginal costs are important because where marginal costs are equal to marginal revenue (ie, the revenue or receipts gained from the last unit produced) then this will be the most *profitable* level of output. This is called the **equilibrium** or profit maximising level of output. If marginal cost was less than marginal revenue then the firm would produce extra units to increase profits. If marginal cost was greater than marginal revenue then the firm would reduce output because it is making a loss on these units. Profits are at a maximum where marginal costs equal marginal revenue.

Money costs and social costs
Money costs are the actual costs in terms of money of producing a good or service. They include fixed costs and variable costs. However, there are also social costs which are the external costs to society of the production process which may not be included in money costs. For instance, the money costs of producing coal may be fairly easily calculated to include the wages of the miners, the costs of equipment and machinery, interest on loans and so on. However, there are costs to society as a whole, in terms of the death of workers, pollution of the environment and unsightly coal tips. Thus social costs are the costs to society as a whole, of producing a particular good. Merit goods are those goods so called because they confer many benefits on society. De-merit goods confer adverse social effects on society. Alcohol and tobacco are examples of de-merit goods.

Sometimes when a decision needs to be made about whether production should or should not take place, a *cost benefit analysis* is undertaken. This calculates all the money costs and benefits and compares them with the social costs and social benefits of production. The problem with a cost benefit analysis is that it is very difficult to give a money value to a social cost or benefit. For instance, how does one calculate in money terms the fact that a bird sanctuary may be destroyed by a chemical works?

It is often a criticism of the price mechanism system that, when allocating scarce resources, the social costs and social benefits of any decision are ignored. A private entrepreneur is only concerned with the money costs and benefits – motivated only by profit.

Production possibility curves (transformation or opportunity cost curves)

These show how one commodity (commodity A) can be transformed into another commodity (commodity B) by reducing output of commodity A and transferring the resources released into the production of commodity B, or vice versa. They therefore show all those possible combinations of the two types of commodity and are drawn on the assumption that resources in the economy are fixed in total.

Consider the following diagram.

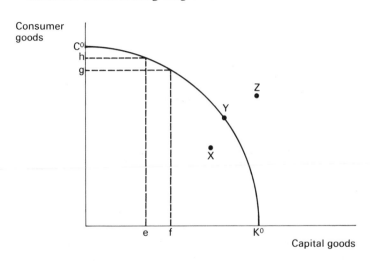

If all resources are devoted to the production of consumer goods then C^0 consumer goods will be produced but no capital goods. If all resources are devoted to the production of capital goods then K^0 capital goods will be produced but no consumer goods. Any combination of consumer and capital goods is possible along the production possibility curve C^0–K^0 eg point Y. Point X indicates a combination of capital and consumer goods where all resources are not employed. Point Z is not technically possible given present resources and technology.

The production possibility curve also illustrates opportunity costs because an increase in production of consumer goods implies less production of capital goods, ie, there is an alternative forgone. The shape of the production possibility curve illustrates diminishing returns because as more and more consumer goods are produced then small additions in consumer goods are gained at the cost of larger amounts of forgone capital goods. This indicates that the resources being transferred into consumer goods are not as efficient (productive) as early resources used. For example, to gain (hg) consumer goods implies a loss of (ef) capital goods.

A movement outwards of the production possibility curve may be due to

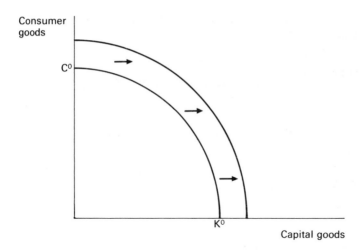

improvements in technology and/or improvements in the quality and quantity of resources. This is indicative of increased production and therefore economic growth (see page 140).

Types of economy

There are basically three types of economy in the world today:

(a) *A price or market economy* Based on the principles of competition, private enterprise, capitalism and 'laissez-faire' (no state intervention and the economy is unplanned). In its purest form this does not exist but perhaps it is at its nearest in the USA.

(b) *A planned or command economy* Here there is much government intervention in all spheres of the economy: on how factors of production should be allocated, what should be produced (and therefore consumed) and where. The government in fact 'plans' the economy. For example, the USSR plans its economy by using 5 year plans.

(c) *A mixed economy* This contains elements of both the price and planned economic system. In other words although there is much private enterprise there is also government intervention. The United Kingdom is an example because there is a public sector, organised and controlled by the government, and a private sector, owned and controlled by private entrepreneurs.

Why are there different types of economy?

Factors of production are scarce and thus economies must find a way to allocate (or distribute) these scarce resources efficiently. Resources are scarce relative to the desire for them. Consumers 'wants' then are greater than the resources to satisfy them. In such a situation, consumers must make a choice. In a free economy the choice is left to the consumer and this choice is reflected in prices (ie, high demand means high prices). In a planned economy the state makes the choice as to what goods the consumers will have and what is produced. Thus in the former, scarce resources are allocated by prices (which reflect consumer choice), and in the latter they are allocated by the state.

The price or market economy

In *private enterprise* wants are expressed through the price system. It is assumed that the amount consumers are ready to pay is an indication of the value they put on a good or service. Thus if consumers think good X is valuable then demand is high and prices are high and production will be greater to make a bigger profit. On the other hand, if consumers do not want a particular good, its price falls and producers make a loss and produce less. The price mechanism therefore indicates the wishes of consumers and allocates scarce resources.

Advantages of a price economy

(a) Consumers have freedom of choice. They are not confronted with goods and services which they have to purchase or go without. Consumers are said to be 'sovereign' because they decide what they want and producers respond by producing more of the good.
(b) Unlike a planned economy, there is no need for a bureaucracy or large civil service to be employed, at considerable expense, to make decisions.
(c) The price economy involves a profit motive to producers to work hard and make a profit. It gives producers an incentive to make the right decisions. If they do not, then they will make a loss and perhaps go out of business.
(d) In a price economy there will be many small producers who provide a variety of choice for consumers.
(e) There is less government interference in the everyday lives of people. They are able to make their own decisions.

Disadvantages of a price economy

(a) Consumers with a lot of money exercise great demand for luxuries and thus resources are allocated to the production of luxuries to the exclusion of the production of basic necessities for the rest.
(b) Certain essential goods and services, for example, defence, law and education, are not always provided adequately by private enterprise because there may be no profits available.
(c) The private entrepreneur ignores social costs. These are costs to the community as a whole of any decision made by the entrepreneur (see page 10). The entrepreneur is only concerned with making a profit and may produce de-merit goods.
(d) Monopolies may occur. A monopoly is a firm which dominates the industry and can set prices and output. Such a monopoly is in a position to exploit consumers with high prices.
(e) Unemployment of resources will exist in those industries which are declining due to a drop in demand and there will be a time lag before resources move into expanding industries. Indeed factors of production

(especially labour) are considered to be occupationally and geographically immobile (see page 278).

The planned or command economy

In a *planned economy*, the government makes the decisions about what shall be produced and directs the productive resources accordingly. For example, if the government thinks steel should be produced rather than wheat it may divert labour, capital, land and enterprise from the production of wheat to the production of steel. The government decides what shall be produced, where it shall be produced and in what quantities, and does not allow the amount of production to be determined by consumers' preferences as shown by prices. In the United Kingdom the economy becomes increasingly planned during war time because there are goods which have to be produced in enormous quantities, such as guns and planes.

The contrast between the United Kingdom and the USSR is largely one of degree. It is true that the United Kingdom leaves the greater part of its production to be determined by price movements but it has a big sector in which the state makes decisions without regard to prices.

Advantages of a planned economy

(a) Necessities can be produced by diverting factors of production away from the production of luxuries.
(b) Goods and services which may not be adequately provided by private enterprise because they are not very profitable, will be provided. This may include collective consumption goods (or public goods) such as education, health, roads, defence and libraries. These goods provide many social benefits for the community as a whole. The planned economy takes into account the social costs and benefits of any decision more than does the private entrepreneur in the price system.
(c) The government may aim to distribute income and wealth more equally rather than having a few rich people and a mass of poorer people. It is a feature of planned economies that the distribution of income and wealth is much more equal than is the case in a price economy.

Disadvantages of a planned economy

(a) It is almost impossible for the state to know how much of certain goods consumers require. Thus they overproduce in some goods and under-produce in others.
(b) Production may be less efficient without the profit motive. The USSR has introduced some private enterprise to make good such drawbacks, particularly in agriculture.
(c) Many planners are needed and are expensive. Also many may be frightened to make decisions because of fear of losing their jobs.
(d) Loss of individual freedom, not only economic but political, such as farmers

being forced to join collective farms. Has the government the right to tell people what to do and restrict choice?

(e) Some individuals, even under government rationing are disadvantaged: for instance, a consumer may receive the same amount of pork as everyone else but he or she may not like pork and prefer beef which is not being produced.

(f) The state decides what to produce and usually decides to produce necessities and transfer resources from luxuries. But should the government decide what is a luxury and what is a necessity?

(g) There may be more wastage of resources. Under free enterprise many producers make estimates of future demand, when these estimates are averaged out they may not be too incorrect. One planner is more likely to make a wrong estimate.

Type of economy	Advantages	Disadvantages
The price or market economy	1 Consumer choice exists 2 No bureaucracy 3 Profit motive exists 4 Many small firms producing a variety of goods 5 Less government interference	1 Too many luxuries produced for the rich 2 Essential goods/services, eg education may not be produced 3 Ignores social costs 4 Monopolies may exist 5 Unemployment in declining industries
The planned or command economy	1 Necessities are produced 2 Essential goods/services, eg education will be provided for all the community 3 More equal distribution of income and wealth	1 Large bureaucracy 2 Mistakes in amounts of goods/services produced 3 Little consumer choice 4 No profit motive 5 Little variety of goods/services 6 Loss of individual freedom
Mixed economy	Combines the advantages of the other systems	Combines the disadvantages of the other systems

The mixed economy

This is the middle way between the two systems which exists in the United Kingdom. For instance, the United Kingdom not only has a private sector but also a public sector (such as the nationalised industries). In the world economy today all economies are to some extent mixed and differ only in the degree of planned and price systems in their economies. We deal with private enterprise in Chapter 4 and public enterprise in Chapter 5.

The underdeveloped economy

Underdeveloped economies are called by several different names including developing economies, backward economies and the Third World.

What is an underdeveloped economy?

Underdeveloped economies have some of the following characteristics:

(a) *Low national income per head* This means that the average person living in these countries receives a very low income and therefore suffers a low standard of living. The concept of national income per head is dealt with in more detail on page 139.

(b) *Underdeveloped economies tend to be primary producers* A primary producing country produces mainly raw materials, minerals or has a very large agricultural sector. Such economies are often called *subsistence* economies because agriculture is so organised that workers can hardly produce enough for themselves, let alone produce surplus for export. Very often underdeveloped economies are *mono cultures* which means that they specialise in producing only one foodstuff or raw material. This can be a severe disadvantage if that sector suffers from a bad harvest or shortage.

(c) *Underdeveloped economies tend to have large populations* Agriculture is not efficient enough to provide for all of their needs. Such countries tend to have very high birth rates and death rates compared to developed economies. Moreover, life expectancy tends to be lower than in developed economies.

(d) *Scarcity of factors of production* Many underdeveloped economies suffer either from a lack of factors of production or a lack of good quality factors of production. For instance, a country may have a very large population but if the vast majority of these people are illiterate and unskilled then the economy will suffer. Also, such economies may have a large land area but if this land is mostly desert or forest then again the economy will suffer.

(e) *Customs and traditions* Very often underdeveloped economies follow a way of life which is not conducive to economic growth and increasing national income per head. Social and religious customs may prohibit certain activities. For example, some customs prevent particular groups of people from doing certain jobs, while others may prohibit people from travelling beyond the boundaries of their own village.

There is probably no one reason why any one country is underdeveloped. The causes are probably complex and varied.

How can the problem of underdeveloped economies be solved?

The underdeveloped economies must overcome their major problems such as overpopulation, over-reliance on agriculture, lack of an industrial or manufacturing sector and scarcity of good quality factors of production. This may involve the following:

(a) *A population control programme* This might involve birth control although this could clash with religious beliefs.

World population

Rapid-growth countries

Slow-growth countries

1986 population, m

GDP per person
Annual % change,
1973-85

00

Annual % change → 0.0

0.0

China 1050 +1.0 (9.7)

Soviet Union 280 +0.9 (na)

Japan 121 +0.7 (3.4)

Bangladesh 104 +2.7 (2.0)

Indonesia 168 +2.1 (4.0)

India 785 +2.3 (2.0)

Pakistan 102 +2.8 (3.1)

Iran 47 +2.9 (na)

Kenya 20 +4.2 (0.3)

Turkey 48 +2.5 (1.4)

Britain 56 +0.2 (1.1)

West Germany 61 −0.2 (2.1)

Nigeria 105 +3.0 (−2.5)

Egypt 46 +2.6 (5.4)

Ethiopia 42 +2.1 (−0.4)

United States 241 +0.7 (1.4)

Mexico 82 +2.6 (1.3)

Brazil 143 +2.3 (1.5)

(b) *An investment programme to build up industry* The funds to finance such investment will probably have to come from **foreign aid** from developed countries because these economies cannot initially generate enough funds themselves. However, there are problems in deciding where this foreign aid should be invested. The question is, should money be invested in a variety of different industries or just one or two industries?

(c) *Preferential treatment needs to be given to underdeveloped economies' exports* To allow such economies to expand, tariffs should not be imposed by developed economies on the exports of underdeveloped economies. However, this might not be easy if certain industries in the developed economy are directly suffering as a result of cheap imports from underdeveloped economies. For instance, the textile industry in the United Kingdom has suffered from cheap foreign imports.

(d) *Attempts to improve the quality of factors of production* These might be improved by building schools, hospitals, roads, dams, irrigation channels, and so on. However, again, such a programme will rely on foreign aid to a great extent.

Foreign aid
Many developed countries give foreign aid to underdeveloped economies. They do this for the following reasons:

(a) *The humanitarian reason* This is concern by citizens of rich developed countries for the situation of citizens in underdeveloped countries, especially during natural disasters and wars. Many charities, such as Oxfam and the Red Cross, are involved with such aid but a great deal comes from governments as well.

(b) *The economic reason* Developed countries hope that by giving aid to underdeveloped economies such economies will prosper and expand. In the long run this will benefit the developed country whose exports will be demanded and this will cause further economic expansion in the developed economy. Aid is being used to build up an export market.

(c) *The political reason* Western developed countries such as the USA, France and the United Kingdom are to a certain extent competing with the communist countries such as the USSR to gain the friendship of the underdeveloped countries.

The foreign aid may involve free gifts of foodstuffs and consumer goods, loans and grants to build up industry, technical advisers and engineers, teachers and money to build up educational facilities, preferential treatment for exports of underdeveloped economies. It is not only governments which provide such aid. The World Bank (see page 169), the IMF (International Monetary Fund, see page 167) and the United Nations also provide facilities for such aid to be given.

Checkpoints

1 The basic economic problem is that wants exceed resources leading to a scarcity of goods and services. Consumers have to make a choice about which

wants to satisfy and this involves an opportunity cost.

2 There are four factors of production: land, labour, capital and enterprise. Production depends on the quantity and quality of these factors of production.

3 Land is often used as the fixed factor of production to illustrate the law of diminishing returns.

4 Labour tends to be geographically and occupationally immobile.

5 The costs of production are the monetary expenditures on the use of factors of production. Economists also include opportunity costs in their definition of costs. There are different categories of costs. Especially significant is the distinction between fixed and variable costs.

6 There are three types of economy in the world today, all aimed at solving the basic economic problem: the market economy, the planned economy and the mixed economy. Each type of economy has advantages and disadvantages. The United Kingdom is a mixed economy.

7 The basic economic problem is most marked in the so-called underdeveloped economies. The better-off developed economies attempt to help in the form of foreign aid.

Multiple-choice questions – 1

1 In economics the real cost of resources used in the production of a commodity is 'the next best alternative which could have been produced'. The economic term for this concept is

    A average cost
    B factor cost
    C opportunity cost
    D marginal cost
    E fixed cost

2 The table below shows the relationship between the use of two factors of production, land and labour, and the harvesting of barley.

Units of land	Number of employees	Barley produced (kilograms)
1	1	1200
1	2	3400
1	3	4200
1	4	4700
1	5	5000

Diminishing marginal returns arise on the employment of the

    A 1st employee
    B 2nd employee
    C 3rd employee
    D 4th employee
    E 5th employee

3 The basic (central) economic problem can best be described as the

    A reduction of inflation
    B achievement of economic growth
    C unequal distribution of income and wealth
    D allocation of scarce resources to meet unlimited wants
    E prevention of unemployment

4 The following table represents the output of a small firm

Persons employed	Production (tonnes)
1	14
2	38
3	90
4	160
5	280

The marginal product when 3 persons are employed is

    A 30
    B 45
    C 52
    D 70
    E 74

5 All of the following are factors of production except the

    A teacher
    B company share
    C tractor
    D fishing grounds
    E factory manager

6 In a fully planned economy who decides what will be produced?

    A the government only
    B private entrepreneurs only
    C consumers only
    D the government in public enterprise and private entrepreneurs in private enterprise
    E the public in public enterprise and consumers in private enterprise

7 Which of the following is *not* true of a planned economy?

    A resources are allocated by government commands
    B there is a more equal distribution of income and wealth than in a market economy
    C private monopolies do not exist
    D workers and managers are motivated by profits
    E a black market may develop in those commodities in short supply

8 In a market economy, the entrepreneur decides upon the

    A price of the commodity
    B combinations of factors of production used
    C demand for the commodity
    D level of profits
    E costs of production

9 Increased environmental pollution resulting from the building of a chemical factory is an example of

    A marginal costs
    B opportunity costs
    C variable costs
    D fixed costs
    E social costs

10   Which of the following is *not* a characteristic of a mixed economy?

    A   subsidies for some industries
    B   profits play an important role in allocation of resources
    C   government control of some industries
    D   all property is privately-owned
    E   collective bargaining in wage negotiations

Answers on page 328.

Data response question 1

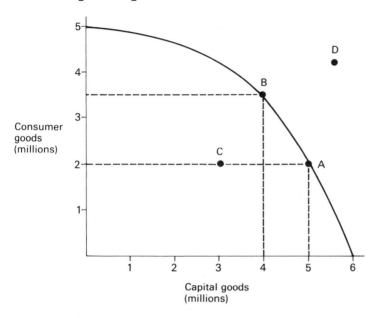

The diagram above shows the production possibility curve available to a country. Given its present quantity of resources the country can produce all consumer goods or all capital goods or some combination of the two.

(a) Distinguish between the terms consumer goods and capital goods. Give two examples of each.
(b) What combination of consumer goods and capital goods is indicated at point A?
(c) What is the maximum amount of capital goods which can be produced?
(d) Explain the meaning of the term *opportunity cost*.
(e) What is the opportunity cost for the country of producing at A instead of B?
(f) Which point, A or B, indicates a higher standard of living for the citizens of the country (i) now and (ii) in the future? Explain your answer.
(g) What problems might the country face if it was producing at point C?
(h) Explain how the economy might achieve the level of production indicated at point D.
(i) What problems might result if the country did manage to achieve the level of production indicated at point D?

2 How to produce

Specialisation or division of labour

In a developed economy people specialise in doing certain jobs – some are teachers, some are members of the police force, some car workers, some textile workers and so on. This is called the *division of labour* and is *specialisation by the individual* in a particular process. Division of labour occurs where the production process is broken up and one person undertakes only a small part of the total work and each individual specialises in a single process.

Division of labour was first advocated by the economist Adam Smith, who wrote a book entitled *The Wealth of Nations* in 1776. Smith wrote this book at the beginning of what is now called the Industrial Revolution. This was when the United Kingdom, in a short period of time at the end of the eighteenth century and beginning of the nineteenth century, changed from a mainly agricultural economy into an industrial economy. Adam Smith gave some thought to the best way for the new factories to produce their goods. He studied the manufacture of pins in a pin factory and noticed that if one person carried out all the processes involved in pin production then not many pins were produced. On the other hand, if one worker drew out the wire, another straightened it, another cut the wire, another pointed it and another made the head then the production of pins increased dramatically.

Of course there are many more up-to-date examples of division of labour to be seen, for example, in the manufacture of motor cars or textiles. Indeed, the economy of the United Kingdom, like other developed economies, is based on division of labour. This is in contrast to the economies of the underdeveloped countries which are mainly agricultural, and people in these countries attempt to do almost everything for themselves. Such economies are often referred to as subsistence economies as they barely produce enough to guarantee their own survival.

Advantages of division of labour

The main advantage of division of labour is that production is increased and there are lower costs per unit of output produced. This is because of the following factors:

(a) *Specialists can be employed* No individual is good at everything. For instance, some people are good at doing electrical work, some are good at plumbing, and some are good teachers. Division of labour allows people to specialise in doing a job at which they can become both proficient and efficient.

(b) *Leads to greater skill among workers* By doing the same task day after day an individual becomes efficient at performing that task. This is a development of the idea that 'practice makes perfect'. However, repetition of certain jobs might make the job tedious and boring. We deal with this point when discussing the disadvantages of division of labour.

(c) *Saves time* Individuals need only train for one job and this obviously saves time and effort in training people. Individuals can learn a single skill very quickly.

(d) *Economy in the use of skills/tools* If a person has trained to do only one specific job, then they only need to possess the tools to do that particular job. These tools will be in constant use.

(e) *Allows the use of specialist machinery* Machinery can be quite easily developed to perform a specific task in the production process. It would be very difficult, for example, to construct a machine to manufacture a whole car. On the other hand, a machine could be developed to perform a specialised task, such as welding.

The advantages of division of labour are accepted by most producers in developed economies. However, division of labour does have its disadvantages.

Disadvantages of division of labour

(a) *Boredom and monotony* People can become bored by doing the same job day after day and this may, among other things, have a bad effect on the quality of the product. It may lead also to other problems such as alienation, industrial unrest and absenteeism.

(b) *Decline in craftswork* Workers lose their skills and crafts in doing the same job everyday. Indeed, many workers become little more than extensions of the machines, simply pressing a button or pulling a lever.

(c) *Interdependence* For the good to be produced, workers are dependent on other workers to do their job efficiently. If this does not happen at every stage of the production process, then the production chain will break down. For instance, the paint sprayer in a car factory is dependent on the body builder having produced the car body. Indeed, whole firms might be dependent on other firms to produce their particular item for the production of the finished good.

(d) *Alienation* Workers sometimes feel alienated from fellow workers and the management. They see themselves as being regarded as little more than machines and have little contact with the people making the decisions. This feeling of alienation may develop into a high level of industrial unrest (strikes) or absenteeism.

(e) *A greater risk of unemployment* Workers specialise in performing a particular task as part of the production of a particular good. However, if demand for that good declines some workers might have difficulty finding other jobs because they have only been trained to perform one specific task.

(f) *Standardised products and a lack of variety* Due to division of labour, the finished products will be indistinguishable one from another. Consumers will be faced with a lack of variety or choice because each product has passed through exactly the same process.

(g) *Occupational diseases* Certain jobs are dangerous and workers doing these jobs run the risk of disease or accident. For example, asbestos workers run the risk of cancer, paint workers may get lead poisoning, or fishermen might drown.

These disadvantages have led certain firms to break away from traditional division of labour techniques. For instance, the Volvo Motor Company allows its workers to change jobs or work in groups to produce the final product.

Division of labour is when the production process is divided into smaller parts and individuals specialise in only a small part of the total production process.

Advantages
1 Specialists can be employed
2 Practice makes perfect
3 Time is saved
4 Economy in the use of skills/tools
5 Machinery can be easily introduced

Disadvantages
1 Boredom and monotony
2 Decline in craftswork
3 Interdependence between workers
4 Alienating some workers
5 Risk of unemployment
6 Lack of variety of goods/services
7 Occupational diseases

Division of labour requires exchange
If division of labour is going to be successful in an economy then there must also be the means of exchange. If exchange did not occur, then the baker would have plenty of bread but no clothes. The tailor would have clothes but no bread. The exchange of goods and services must take place and is facilitated, in a developed economy, by a good transport system and a sophisticated system of money and banking. Indeed, money is characterised by being a medium of exchange (see page 183). Thus, the provision of road, rail, sea and air links allows the goods to be distributed from producers to consumers very efficiently. The provision of

money and banking facilities allows the exchange to take place smoothly and in a manner acceptable to producers and consumers.

Division of labour is limited by the size of the market

In this context the term market means demand. If there is a large demand for a product then it is worthwhile producing as many units of the good as is necessary to satisfy the large demand. In such a situation division of labour would be worth introducing. However, if demand for the good being produced is small it would not be advisable to introduce division of labour because there would be no point in expanding production.

There are other limitations to whether division of labour can be successfully introduced. For instance, there are certain jobs which cannot normally be divided up, such as writing a book. Also, division of labour is limited by how many workers are available in the economy. If there is a shortage of labour then specialisation will be restricted and some people will have to do more than one job.

Technological change

Mass production

Since Adam Smith first argued in favour of division of labour his idea has been extended and developed. In America, Henry Ford, when making 'Model T' Ford motor cars, introduced the technique of mass production. This is a system aimed at producing the **greatest output** with the **fewest workers**, by means of **standardisation** and **simplification** of the product. Mass production is usually associated with assembly line techniques where the work flows endlessly through the factory with operators performing their tasks as each unit passes by.

Automation

Automation is mass production performed by electronically-controlled (robot) machines. The term automation is usually applied to a situation where there is a large number of machines and a small number of workers. Automation has been developing over many years. For instance, during the Industrial Revolution workers were unhappy about machines taking over their jobs, and some workers, who became known as the 'Luddites', went so far as to raise riots for the destruction of machinery. A recent example of automation in British industry is the robot welding machines used to produce Austin Rover Metro cars at their Longbridge plant in Birmingham. Automative processes are used throughout the economy of the United Kingdom and would include the increasing use of **computers** and **microchips**.

Advantages of automation

(a) Machines can be very efficient and produce a great many more goods with fewer mistakes than human beings. Thus there is a greater output of a more perfect product which improves consumers' standards of living. Also, it may mean that goods become cheaper as costs per unit of output diminish.

(b). Automation means that boring and monotonous jobs can be done by machines. Humans can specialise in doing more interesting tasks.

(c) There may be more leisure time as machines increasingly replace humans. The quality of people's lives may improve as they spend less time at work.

(d) Medicine, space travel, the defence services, social services and under-developed countries can all be greatly helped and improved by the results of automation and computers. For instance, in medicine, many important life-saving functions are performed by machines.

(e) There will be more jobs in the service industries (tertiary production), which will have to grow to meet the increasing needs of an expanding and more efficient manufacturing (or secondary) sector and to cater for the improved standards of living of consumers.

Disadvantages of automation

(a) Workers are afraid that they will become unemployed when machines are introduced. There is, and always has been, a natural distrust by people of machines. Trade unions tend not to be in favour of the introduction of machinery if it means unemployment among their members.

(b) It is not evident that the government is producing more leisure facilities for people to use when they are working less. This might mean people become bored and restless and may lead to undesirable social consequences such as hooliganism.

(c) Old traditional skills which have been handed down over the years may be lost as ways are found for these jobs to be done by machines.

(d) Automative processes are increasingly being used by countries to make their armed forces more and more sophisticated. Automation has made the 'war game' increasingly perilous to all inhabitants of the world.

(e) Automation tends to affect either those occupations which have become very specialised, or those occupations demanding a very low level of skill. People made unemployed by automation therefore find it very difficult to get alternative work. Indeed, they may become permanently unemployed.

Microelectronics (microchips)

The term *microelectronics* is applied to electronic components or circuits of extremely small dimensions. These are called microprocessors or micro (electronic) chips which can be regarded as a mass of miniature transistors. This device can be used to replace and improve mechanical and electronic control systems in a vast range of existing goods and processes. Microelectronics is being increasingly used in manufacturing industry, for example, the motor car industry. It is evident that the continued development of microchips will have wide-ranging economic and social effects throughout the world.

The expected effects of microchips are very similar to the effects of automation and these should be re-read with the microchip in mind. Pessimists argue that the increasing use of microchips will cause higher unemployment as industry becomes yet more capital intensive. Optimists argue that it will enable workers to move to new and more pleasant jobs in service industries and, indeed, in the new microelectronic and associated industries. Moreover, productivity (output per worker) will be increased which will mean a higher standard of living for all. The microchip may also improve the quality of life with potentially more leisure time and less time at work doing mundane and boring tasks. The microchip will also bring with it new products and new processes which will revolutionise industry, medicine and society.

Types of production

We have already discussed division of labour by individuals. Division of labour or specialisation can also be applied to industries. For example, the coal mining industry specialises in mining coal and the railways industry specialises in providing a railway service. Industries are categorised into one of the three main types of production: primary production, secondary production and tertiary production.

Primary, secondary and tertiary production
Primary production
This includes all those industries involved in the first stage of the production process – they are at the primary stage of production. It includes the extractive industries such as coal mining, iron ore mining, agriculture and fishing. These industries provide the raw materials which are made into finished goods by manufacturing industries.

Secondary production
This includes all those industries involved in manufacturing the finished goods from the raw materials provided by primary producers. It includes textile manufacturers, the motor car industry, the steel industry and the consumer goods industry in general.

Tertiary production
These industries do not produce goods but instead provide services which enable the production of goods by primary and secondary producers to take place more efficiently. Tertiary production consists of two parts: commercial services and direct (personal) services.

(a) *Commercial services* Usually called *commerce*, these include all those industries engaged in the movement of commodities so that they reach the final consumer on time, in good condition and in the correct quantity. There are six divisions of commerce: trade (home trade including wholesaling and retailing, and foreign trade including exporting and importing), transport, warehousing, banking, insurance and advertising.

(b) *Direct (personal) services* These are services not rendered to material goods, as in commerce, but to persons by, for example, doctors and teachers. They are very important to the production process because they increase efficiency, in this case by providing a healthy and educated work-force.

The importance of tertiary production in the modern economy

Prior to the Industrial Revolution in the United Kingdom, tertiary production was not an important sector in the economy. This is true of many developing economies today, where most of the working population is involved in primary industries, particularly agriculture. However, as an economy becomes more industrialised the percentage of workers in secondary industries increases. When the economy is advanced and heavily industrialised, as it is in the United Kingdom today, secondary industries need more services and thus tertiary production becomes extremely important.

In most advanced economies, at present, tertiary production is the most important sector in terms of the number of workers it employs and as a percentage of gross domestic product.

Shares of UK's GDP (total domestic output) by sector (%)

	1975	1980	1985
Primary industry	7.8	11.8	13.4
Secondary industry	35.9	32.9	30.1
Tertiary industry	56.3	55.3	56.5

Note: for a definition of GDP see page 136.

Primary production employs fewer people because more machinery has been introduced displacing some workers involved in agriculture and mining. Also, as people become wealthier they tend to demand proportionately more manufactured goods and services. Between 1945 and the mid-1970s primary industry accounted for a declining proportion of the United Kingdom's gross domestic product. Since the end of the 1970s, however, the growth of North Sea oil extraction has led to primary production accounting for an increasing proportion of GDP, although the proportion of employees accounted for by primary production has continued to decline.

Secondary production has increased its share of employment since the Industrial Revolution, because if a country is to produce more goods it usually needs more workers involved in secondary industries. There is, for example, a large demand for industrial manufactures, reflecting a high standard of living. Between 1945 and 1980 secondary industries accounted for approximately the same numbers of employees but a declining proportion of the United Kingdom's gross domestic product. Since 1980, the number of employees in secondary industries has fallen, due to a decline in manufacturing employment, and secondary production continues to account for a declining proportion of GDP.

Tertiary production is now the largest sector in the economy and has become so for the following reasons.

1 Secondary industries have increased their output and therefore need further banking and transport facilities (commercial services). The growth of financial and banking services provided by the 'City of London' is especially significant.

The changing
occupational balance

Expanding
occupations

Contracting
occupations

Engineers, Scientists and
Technologists
Technicians
Multiple-skilled Craftsmen

Production
industries

Single-skilled Craftsmen
Operatives
Support services (e.g.
clerical)
Personal services

All professions
Support services (part-time)
Personal services (part-time)

Services
industries

Managers and administrators
Technicians, Craftsmen
Operatives
Support services (full-time)
Personal services (full-time)

Sectoral change
UK workforce 1985-90

'000

400

200

0

200

400

Agriculture

Energy

Process industries

Engineering-related

Light
industries

Construction

Distribution,
Finance,
Business
services

Transport and communication

Leisure; Other services

Public services

Production

Services

2   The living standards of most of the population have improved and people spend money on holidays and leisure pursuits (personal services).
3   The government has become increasingly involved in the economy to extend and improve the provision of education and health services – more doctors, teachers, and Civil Servants are required (direct services). However, since 1980, employment in the public sector has declined (see the statistics on page 87). Tertiary industries account for the largest percentage of employees and an increasing proportion of the United Kingdom's gross domestic product.

Read page 267 on occupational distribution of population which closely complements this section and also page 320 which discusses the decline in manufacturing industry.

We have so far discussed specialisation by individuals and specialisation by industries. There is also *specialisation by regions* in particular industries (see page 52) and *specialisation by countries* in the production of certain goods and services. This last type of specialisation is discussed in Chapter 8.

The size of firms

Some businesspeople, politicians and economists, when referring to the size of firms, suggest that 'big is best' whereas others say that 'small is beautiful' and that 'big is bad'. In this section we shall discuss the advantages and disadvantages of large firms as against small firms. There is, however, no simple answer to the question about which is the most efficient (optimum) size of firm. The most efficient size of firm depends upon what industry the firm is in. What might be appropriate for the steel industry may well not apply to the fashion industry, for example.

Production is carried on by many firms varying in size from sole traders to huge joint-stock companies with thousands of shareholders. The trend has been for firms to become bigger and bigger. Some firms are taken over by others, other firms expand. It is not unusual for entire industries to be dominated by a few large firms which may monopolise a particular sector of production. For example,

Banking: Barclays, Lloyds, Midland, National Westminster, and the TSB.
Motor cars: Austin Rover, Ford, General Motors (Vauxhall) and Peugeot Talbot.

Both in private enterprise (see Chapter 4) and public enterprise (see Chapter 5) the main reason for this trend towards increasing size has been the economies of large-scale production. The term *economies of large-scale production* (or economies of scale) means the advantages in production for a large firm which, as the firm becomes bigger, can greatly increase production and, therefore, benefit as the average costs per unit of production fall. There are two types of economy of scale: *internal* economies of scale and *external* economies of scale.

Internal economies of scale
These economies arise from within the firm itself as a result of its own decision to become big. As a result of becoming bigger the firm which experiences internal economies of scale enjoys a situation where average costs per unit of production are falling as output is rising. Therefore the firm is becoming more efficient.

The British workforce

Aggregate forecasts of workforce 1985–90

Sector	Employment 1985			Employment 1990			Av annual % change
	Full	Self	Total	Full	Self	Total	
Primary Industries							
Agriculture/Forest/Fishing	364	291	655	328	270	598	− 1.9
Energy/Water supply	596	—	596	526	—	526	− 2.6
Manufacturing							
Process	779	—	728	728	—	728	− 1.5
Engineering + related	2549	—	2549	2305	—	2305	− 2.2
Light production	2042	—	2042	1871	—	1871	− 2.0
Construction							
Construction	933	467	1400	840	510	1350	− 0.8
Services							
Distrib/Finance/Business	5049	1055	6104	5260	1225	6485	+ 1.4
Transport/Communication	1266	103	1369	1180	113	1293	− 1.2
Leisure + other	2196	467	2663	2397	560	2957	+ 2.4
Public	5010	—	5010	4950	—	4950	− 0.2
Total Great Britain	20784	2383	23167	20385	2678	23063	—

There are six main categories of internal economies: technical economies, financial economies, marketing economies, managerial economies, risk-bearing economies and welfare economies.

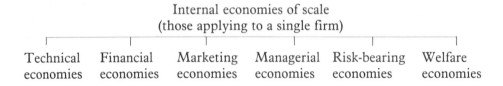

Internal economies of scale
(those applying to a single firm)

| Technical economies | Financial economies | Marketing economies | Managerial economies | Risk-bearing economies | Welfare economies |

Technical economies
These involve several advantages such as:

(a) The large firm can introduce *more division of labour* and specialisation as it increases in size. Small firms employing only a few staff have less scope for division of labour. We have already discussed the advantages of division of labour on page 24.

(b) The large firm can afford to employ large and specialised machinery. Moreover, the firm has the output to fully occupy the machine over a long period of time and therefore it can be operated efficiently. Indeed, some machines are *indivisible* in that they are only efficient if they are large in size, such as blast furnaces. Small firms cannot afford to purchase these large and indivisible machines and have not the output to keep them fully occupied over a long period.

(c) Larger machines sometimes cut costs per unit of output. This is because a large machine can cater for a much larger output but this may involve only a slightly greater cost. For instance, a double-decker bus can carry twice the amount of passengers as a single-decker yet only the same labour is required. A large oil tanker may carry twice as much oil as a small tanker but needs only a few more workers to operate it. This is called the *economy of increased dimensions*.

(d) Large firms can afford to link certain processes which reduce costs per unit of output. For instance, a large steel firm can afford to have a rolling mill next to a steel mill, thus the steel is immediately rolled flat while still hot thus avoiding the need to reheat the sheet steel. This is called the *economy of linked processes*.

(e) A related advantage to linked processes is the *principle of multiples*. This means that a large firm can afford to make use of a variety of different machines each having a different capacity. If machine X produces 20 units per hour and machine Y produces 5 units per hour then for every one machine X the firm needs four Y machines to operate efficiently and at full capacity. The large firm can afford to purchase a wide variety of machines and in such numbers that each machine is working to full capacity.

(f) The large firm can afford to organise a research laboratory and employ scientists to develop new and better techniques of producing the good.

Financial economies

(a) The large firm finds it easier to get large bank loans. This is because large firms are considered less of a risk and can offer more security for the loan than could a small firm. They may also be able to negotiate lower rates of interest for these loans because the bank has confidence in their ability to repay.

(b) Large firms can issue shares and debentures on the Stock Exchange. Again, investors are more likely to have confidence in buying securities in a large company than in a small company.

Marketing economies

(a) The large firm can afford to advertise on television and in newspapers and magazines. Indeed, the firm may produce so many related products that the brand name helps to advertise all of these different products. The large firm can afford to buy in bulk. When buying its raw materials the large firm probably places large orders and could demand lower prices and special privileges from the supplier. The large firm is in a position to achieve special consideration because it will be a valued customer of the supplier.

(b) On the selling side the large firm has many advantages. For instance, the large firm can afford to employ specialist sellers (and buyers) which gives them great advantages over their smaller competitors. Moreover, packing and distribution costs are likely to be lower per unit of output, as will transport, clerical and administration costs. It is probably cheaper per unit of output to package and distribute 1000 units than 100 units.

Managerial economies

Specialists can be employed in every department of the large firm. Specialist buyers and sellers can be employed. There will be specialists on transport, personnel and administration. This is really applying division of labour to management. Managers can specialise in their own departments rather than attempting to perform several different roles.

Risk-bearing economies

Businesses are faced with many risks, not least changes in consumer demand. Large firms are better able to bear such a risk of decline in demand for a particular product because they will probably have diversified their output. They will produce a wide variety of different goods and can therefore 'weather the storm' if demand for a particular good declines. The large firm is also better able to sell products in different regions of the United Kingdom and even to export to other countries. Thus again they are able to spread their risks. The small firm, on the other hand, will suffer from the problem of having 'all its eggs in one basket'. Therefore if demand for the good declines then the small firm is much more vulnerable.

Welfare economies

Large firms, more than small firms, can afford to spend money on providing good working conditions, canteens, social and leisure facilities for employees. This is an important factor in helping to attract the best staff and keep workers happy and therefore more productive.

External economies of large-scale production

These are the economies which apply to the industry in which the firm is operating and each particular firm can enjoy these economies as the industry expands. These external economies are especially evident where the industry has concentrated in a particular area, for example, textiles in Lancashire and Yorkshire, motor cars in the West Midlands and cutlery in Sheffield. Since external economies of scale are often associated with industries concentrated in particular areas they are sometimes referred to as the *economies of concentration*.

Advantages

(a) *Regional specialisation of labour* Labour in a particular area may become skilled at a specific occupation. A firm in the area should have less of a problem in finding supplies of labour with the skills required. Such skills are handed down 'from generation to generation' and the expectation is that the child will follow the parent into a particular trade. In the West Midlands, for instance, a high percentage of the labour force is involved in engineering.

(b) *Education* The type of education offered reinforces the industry which dominates the region. Schools, technical colleges, polytechnics and universities will reflect the region's industries. For instance, the importance of engineering in the West Midlands is reflected in the type of educational facilities provided, and the University of Aston in Birmingham is noted for its engineering department.

(c) *Specialised services* Specialised banking, marketing, and insurance services will have grown up in the area to deal with the particular requirements of the industry.

(d) *Ancillary firms will have developed* Ancillary firms provide components and parts for other firms. Such ancillary (or subsidiary) firms will exist and cater for the needs of the industry of the region. For instance, in the West Midlands there are many firms providing components for the motor car industry, such as Dunlop at Fort Dunlop (Birmingham) and Lucas Electrics in Birmingham.

(e) *Transport* A good system of road, rail, air and sea links will be important to all firms in the area and they all share the advantages of the adequate provision of these links. For instance, Birmingham has an airport, and is very well served by motorways and rail links.

(f) *Information* The firms in the region may co-operate and take advantage of research centres in the area. Also, firms may come together and form trade associations to represent the interests of the industry to the government and community as a whole.

We have now discussed the advantages of large firms. However, large firms do have disadvantages and these are termed the diseconomies of large-scale production (or simply the *diseconomies of scale*).

The diseconomies of scale

(a) *Loss of personal contact with both employees and customers*
   (i) Workers may not feel as though they are a part of a large firm. There may be a 'them and us' attitude among both workers and managers. Workers may regard themselves as just numbers in a large firm and feel that they are not appreciated as individuals. This may lead to industrial unrest and lack of productivity.
   (ii) Customers may not be dealt with as quickly and as politely as in a small firm. The large firm has a large bureaucratic set-up and a great deal of 'red tape' may have to be gone through to register a complaint or put forward an idea.

(b) *The disadvantages of division of labour*
   Since division of labour is introduced on a wide scale in large firms, they will suffer from its disadvantages.

(c) *Decision-making is made more difficult and there may be a slow response to changes in market conditions*
   Large firms have a large bureaucracy and there is a lot of red tape to overcome when making a decision. Specialist managers have to be consulted, meetings have to take place, records have to be kept and filed, decisions have to be communicated downwards to the shop floor. Thus decision-making is very sluggish and a great many administrative problems have to be overcome.

(d) *A lack of self-interest and profit motive*
   Workers and managers, as has been suggested, may regard themselves as only small cogs in a big machine. Therefore, there is little incentive to work hard and efficiently. The feeling is that their efforts will not be sufficiently rewarded.

(e) *Diminishing returns set in*
   As a firm becomes bigger it employs more and more units of labour and there will come a point where returns will eventually begin to diminish.

The economies of small-scale production
Reasons why small firms still exist
Small firms, although they are declining, still predominate in the United Kingdom's economy. This is the case despite the economies of scale which large firms can enjoy. What, then, are the reasons why small firms still exist?
   Small firms have certain advantages over big firms.

(a) *Personal service is provided for both employees and customers*
   Small firms are small enough to deal quickly and efficiently with customer enquiries. A personal interest can also be taken in the welfare of individual workers.

(b)   *Workers and managers have a self-interest and profit motive*
Workers and managers will probably all know each other and feel part of a team. They will feel that they are directly benefiting from the success of the firm and that their efforts will be recognised and rewarded.

(c)   *Decisions can be made quickly and effectively in response to any change in market conditions*
Decisions are probably made by one person or only a few people. Thus decisions can be made quickly to effect any change in output.

These economies of small-scale production are basically the diseconomies of large-scale production. What might be a disadvantage for a large firm can be interpreted as an advantage for a small firm. This applies in the other direction. What might be an advantage for a large firm can be interpreted as a disadvantage for a small firm. Therefore, for the *diseconomies of small-scale production* refer to the economies of large-scale production and note that the small firm does not enjoy such advantages.

Other reasons why small firms still exist

(a)   The small entrepreneur may prefer continued independence to expansion and perhaps losing some control over decision-making.

(b)   A small firm may not be able to finance an expansion programme even if they wished to become bigger, since a bank may regard a loan to a small firm as too risky.

(c)   The demand for the firm's product may be so small as not to warrant expansion. This applies especially to luxury or prestige items like high quality jewellery and furs. Related to this is the problem of a firm being limited by geographical considerations. Sometimes a firm has to remain small because it is restricted by its local market. For example, small village shops will not find it worthwhile to expand because of lack of demand.

(d)   In some industries consumers demand a variety and choice of product. Thus firms remain small so as to be flexible and willing to adapt to any changes in demand. This particularly applies to the fashion industry.

(e)   In some industries, consumers demand a personal service. This applies to solicitors, doctors, accountants, and hairdressers. Consumers require a personal touch which large firms could not provide.

(f)   Flexibility and quick decision-making is required in certain industries. For instance, many firms remain small because of the vagaries of climate and the need to adapt quickly to any change in conditions.

(g)   The formation of chains and co-operatives has allowed many small firms to remain small but still imitate the large firms. For instance, in retailing, voluntary chain stores consist of small independent stores which combine with a wholesaler to take advantage of the economies of scale. Also, in farming, farmers may form co-operatives to finance the purchase of expensive machines for their common use and benefit.

(h)   The government may encourage small firms with subsidies and tax allowances (especially in the assisted areas of the country) because they provide jobs, are the source of many new ideas and inventions, and contribute to the economy's national output and level of exports.

What is the best size of firm?

The best size of firm is often called the *optimum size* which is the size where the firm is most efficient and where average costs are at their lowest. At any level of output below the optimum size average costs are falling and economies of scale are still to be exploited. At any level of output above the optimum size average costs are rising and diseconomies of scale have set in.

The optimum size of firm varies from industry to industry. For instance, small firms are best in those industries where quick decisions have to be made, such as in advertising, or where a variety of goods produced is required, as in fashion, or where a personal service is needed, as in small retail shops. On the other hand, large firms are best in those industries where much capital is needed, where there is a large demand and where the economies of scale are to be found, as in the steel industry or the motor car industry. Thus there is no single best size of firm.

How and why firms become bigger: integration

How firms become bigger

Firms can become bigger by expanding from within. This means that they produce more of a particular good and probably increase the range and variety of the goods that they produce. They need not amalgamate with any other firm but achieve the economies of large-scale production by internal expansion.

Some firms may form a *cartel*. This arises when a group of firms maintain their own separate identity and independence but meet (formally or informally) to set prices and output of the good or service which they are all producing. By doing so they are imitating a *monopolist* because they are able to fix prices and output and prevent newcomers from entering the industry. Monopolies are discussed in greater detail on page 42.

Another way in which firms can expand is by *amalgamation* with another firm or firms by means of a *merger*. A merger normally means that the firms have joined together to become a single firm. A merger may involve two previously independent firms of roughly equal size joining together or it may involve a larger firm completely absorbing a smaller firm which may lose its name and identity completely. The latter type of merger may be described as a *take-over* which is usually achieved by holding companies. A *holding company* is formed with the purpose of taking over other companies which are known as subsidiary companies. This can be achieved by purchasing more than 50% of the ordinary shareholding in the subsidiary. Holding companies are discussed in detail on page 77.

Types of integration

Yet another term for amalgamation or merger is *integration*. There are several types of integration.

Horizontal integration

Firms may become bigger by amalgamating with other firms which are at the same stage of the same production process. For instance, the National Provincial Bank and the Westminster Bank amalgamated to become the National Westminster Bank, the Rowntree and Mackintosh sweet companies amalgamated to become Rowntree Mackintosh, and Austin Rover consists of many previously independent car firms, such as Morris, Triumph and Rover.

Vertical integration

Firms may become bigger by amalgamating with other firms which are at different stages of the same production process. For instance, a brewery may own the hop fields and the public houses, or a manufacturer of chocolate may own a cocoa plantation. There are two types of vertical integration:

(i) *Backward integration* This is when a firm amalgamates with the suppliers of its materials or component parts.
(ii) *Forward integration* This is when a firm amalgamates with firms which sell and market its products.

Lateral integration

A merger between firms where they have a common source of raw materials or market outlets or have similar products, for example Cadbury Schweppes.

Conglomerates

A conglomerate merger is one in which a firm integrates with firms with which, very often, it has no conceivable direct link. For instance, Hanson Trust owns the Imperial Group which includes Imperial Tobacco and Ross Frozen Foods.

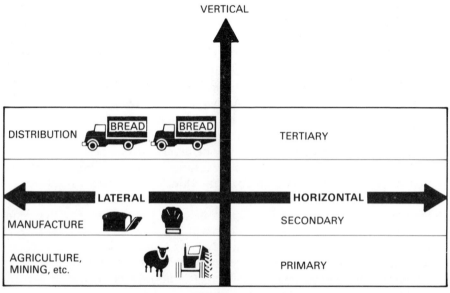

INTEGRATION

Reasons (motives) for integration
There are three main motives which apply to each type of integration:

- to be able to achieve the economies of large-scale production
- to achieve a greater share of the market and, if possible, a monopoly position to reduce competition
- to achieve greater security in the market by offering a larger range and variety of products within a single market.

However, there are advantages and disadvantages which may be peculiar to each type of integration.

Advantages of horizontal integration

(a) Economies of scale, increased market share and security (see the three motives for integration, above).
(b) To achieve rationalisation which is the concentration on the profit-making aspects of the industry and the elimination of the loss-making aspects. This may involve closing down certain firms and expanding other firms.

Disadvantages of horizontal integration

(a) The diseconomies of scale.
(b) The formation of monopolies may not be in the interests of the consumer.
(c) The problems of managing and welding together previously separate firms into the one large firm.
(d) The new firm would assume more risks of production.

Advantages of vertical integration

(a) Vertical integration backwards will ensure that the firm gets its raw materials at the right time and place, at the right quality and in the right quantity.
(b) Vertical integration forwards will ensure that the firm can sell its goods at the right time, in the right place, at the right quality and in the right quantity. Moreover, integration with suppliers and with the sellers of the good prevents them from adding their profit margins on to the final price of the good.

Disadvantages of vertical integration

(a) As for horizontal integration.
(b) Each section of the firm needs to be co-operating closely with the other sections. For instance, it would be uneconomic to have one plant increasing production of the raw material if the manufacturing firm in the group has not got the capacity to handle a large input of raw materials. Problems like these need to be resolved at each stage of production.
(c) The firm which now controls the raw materials and market outlets assumes all of the risks and uncertainties involved at these stages of production and will have to absorb any losses made at these stages due to changes in market conditions.

Advantages of conglomerates

(a) As for horizontal integration.
(b) It means that the firm can *diversify* its products and not rely on one specific good. This applies particularly to firms which have already absorbed a vast proportion of the market for the good which they already produce or when a firm already dominates the home market.

Disadvantages of conglomerates
As for horizontal integration.

Monopoly versus competition

In the United Kingdom there are certain industries, such as retailing and farming, where there are a great many small firms competing against each other. On the other hand, there are industries which are either dominated by a single firm or by a few very large firms such as in banking and the motor car industry. There are also industries dominated by large public corporations (see page 85), such as British Rail and the Post Office. In this section we shall examine what is meant by the terms competition and monopoly, we shall discuss their respective advantages and disadvantages and, finally, examine government attitudes towards competition and monopolies.

Competition
What is meant by competition?
Competition is an important characteristic of a private enterprise or price economy. Competition is a situation where production is organised by a large number of small firms and they are faced with a large number of consumers. There is a variety of goods and services produced by the many small firms. Market prices are determined by the interaction of demand and supply and provide a signal to producers about which goods to produce. If prices are high then more of the good will be supplied. On the other hand if prices are low then less of the good will be supplied. Demand is determined by the totality of consumer wants and, in competition, the consumer is said to be sovereign (or king) because consumer wants will determine which goods are produced through price signals. The only aim of suppliers is to make a profit. Another very important characteristic of competition is that there is no government interference with firms. This policy is called 'laissez-faire' (leave well alone). Competition is based on the ideas of perfect competition and the price economy.

Advantages of competition

(a) There are a large number of producers and, therefore, there is a wide variety and choice of similar goods.
(b) The consumer is king, and, therefore, what consumers want will be supplied by suppliers. There is freedom of choice.
(c) Competition is efficient because there are many firms which are in the

industry and their sole reason for producing is to make a profit. There is a profit motive in competition which provides firms with an incentive to do well.

(d) Through competition, many new products and ideas evolve as firms attempt to be better than their competitors.

(e) Competition is believed to mean lower prices and a greater output than is achieved in a monopoly. We shall come back to this point later.

(f) Small firms enjoy the economies of small-scale production (see page 37).

Disadvantages of competition

(a) There are wastages involved in competition. Small firms competing against each other tend to duplicate each others' goods and services. These might be more efficiently provided by one large firm. Also, a great deal of money will be spent on advertising.

(b) Small competitive firms may not have the necessary capital to invest in new ideas and developments, whereas large monopolistic firms may have such capital to invest. Therefore competition could lead to technological stagnation in the industry.

(c) Small competitive firms do not enjoy the economies of scale which large firms, like monopolies, will enjoy. Thus some economists argue that competition need not necessarily mean lower prices and greater output than a monopoly situation.

Monopoly

What is meant by monopoly?

In economic theory a monopoly is when a single firm produces the entire output of the industry. There is no competition, ie, no substitute good available, and the monopolist firm is in a position to fix whatever price and output that it wishes. This is not a very realistic definition because it is almost impossible to find industries completely dominated by a single firm, but perhaps some of the nationalised industries are the best examples. Therefore, a monopoly is legally defined as a situation where one firm controls at least 25% of the industry's output. According to this definition it would be possible to have more than one monopolist in a particular industry. Monopolists are characterised as having a dominant market position and there will be a lack of close substitutes for the good. They also present barriers to entry to newcomers so that they cannot enter the industry.

Presenting barriers to entry to newcomers

There are many barriers to entry which will stop new firms joining the industry and thereby these barriers perpetuate the monopolist's position. These may include the existence of a patent to prevent firms copying the good or service, restrictive agreements with suppliers or marketing outlets, or the formation of cartels or price rings with existing firms all of which would present barriers to new firms.

Heavy expenditure on advertising is undertaken which new firms could not afford. Massive economies of scale can be achieved which new firms would probably not be big enough to attain. Finally, price cutting in the region of the industry where newcomers *have* arrived will restrict the development of the newcomer. All of these factors will prevent new firms from successfully entering the industry.

Types of monopoly
Local monopolies
When the monopoly is only local in character. For instance the local fish and chip shop may have a monopoly in the local neighbourhood.

Statutory monopolies
These are monopolies which are based on Acts of Parliament, for example, the nationalised industries. Also, patents may have been granted to a particular firm which will mean that no other firm can copy a particular process for a specified period of time. This will give the firm a monopoly in producing the good.

Natural monopolies
These are monopolies which are in industries where the economies of scale are to be achieved. Thus the optimum size of firm will be large and monopolies may develop, such as those in the motor car and chemical industries.

Advantages of monopoly

(a) Monopolies tend to be large firms and can therefore enjoy the economies of scale and reduce costs.
(b) Since monopolists enjoy the economies of scale, these lower costs may be passed on to the consumer in the form of lower prices and a high output.
(c) A monopoly can afford to research and develop new technology. Monopolists will ensure that they keep ahead in terms of technology to maintain their position. Moreover, they have the required capital needed to invest in research.
(d) Monopolies avoid the wastes of competition such as unnecessary duplication of services.
(e) Monopolies can sometimes offer more variety and choice to consumers. For instance, compare BBC radio services with commercial radio services. The BBC offers a much greater variety than commercial radio.

Disadvantages of monopoly

(a) Monopolies are often criticised for charging higher prices for a lower output either because of inefficiency (the diseconomies of scale) or because any savings in costs due to the economies of scale are absorbed in the higher profit margins of monopolies.

(b) Monopolists operate restrictive practices to prevent newcomers entering the industry (barriers to entry).

(c) Monopolists have no incentive to innovate and research because they know that their dominant position can be safeguarded by barriers to entry. Monopolists often become lazy and inefficient.

(d) Monopolists, by restricting output, reduce the variety and choice of goods to consumers.

(e) Monopolists can sometimes have political ambitions. Monopolists are so powerful in the economy that they might wish to dominate the government and threaten democracy.

(f) The monopoly may suffer from the diseconomies of scale and is therefore inefficient.

Monopolies probe into Access and Barclaycard

THE Monopolies Commission is to investigate the Access and Barclaycard credit empires.

Office of Fair Trading Director-General Sir Gordon Borrie said yesterday he had ordered the probe because of evidence that 'monopoly profits are being made'.

He was concerned that the banks involved were making profits on capital estimated at between 45 and 50 per cent.

Sir Gordon said the monopoly position of Access and Barclaycard appeared to be unchallenged, while the number of cardholders had increased to 8.5 million for each company.

The only real competitor to enter the market was Trustee Savings Bank Trustcard, which now has 2.5 million cardholders.

'There is a prima facie case that there are monopoly profits being made here and that it is difficult for other companies to enter into this market when such a big slice of the population have credit cards already', said Sir Gordon.

He said his office had been monitoring the growth of credit card companies since 1980, when they were last investigated by the Monopolies and Mergers Commission.

The commission reported then that monopoly conditions did exist in relation to Barclaycard and Access, but ruled that these did not operate against the public interest.

The inquiry, however, only investigated the relationship between credit card companies and retailers. The commission will now investigate the companies' relationship with credit card customers. It will report in two years.

Peter Ellwood, chief executive of Barclaycard, said: 'We are ready to co-operate with the Monopolies and Mergers Commission and we believe they will find that Barclaycard is a service giving good value to customers and retailers alike'.

An Access spokesman said: 'It is premature to respond fully as the terms of referral have only just been notified to us.

'However, the participant banks in the Access scheme (Midland, Lloyds, NatWest and the Royal Bank of Scotland) will of course assist fully in the inquiry.'

On the day the investigation was announced Barclays Bank backed down in a battle with retailers over their new Connect card.

The new card system, due to start on June 3, transfers money automatically from the customers' account.

Barclays had wanted to charge retailers 2-2½ per cent for the service but is now prepared to make a handling charge closer to the 13p charged for cheques.

Retailers, who feared the cost would have to be passed on to customers in price rises, hailed the climbdown as 'a victory for common sense.'

Many of these advantages and disadvantages may seem contradictory and confusing. For instance we have said that an advantage of a monopoly is that it leads to lower prices and higher output. However, we have also said that a disadvantage of monopoly is that it leads to higher prices and lower output. There is no simple answer to whether a particular monopoly is good or bad – some are good and some are bad.

Government legislation on monopoly

On the whole governments have preferred to believe that monopolies are more bad than good and have therefore passed much anti-monopoly legislation. Let us examine some of the more important legislation.

Monopolies and Restrictive Practices Act 1948

This set up the *Monopolies Commission* which had the power to investigate certain types of monopoly, such as if one third of an industry's output was in the hands of a single firm. The Commission could only report and could not enforce its findings. Moreover, it was often criticised for being slow.

The Restrictive Trade Practices Act 1956

This set up a Restrictive Practices Court with which restrictive trade practices had to be registered (such as *resale price maintenance*, where a retailer is forced to sell the good at the price forced by the monopolist). The court would only allow restrictive trade practices to exist if they were in the public interest.

Resale Prices Act 1964

This declared resale price maintenance to be illegal and if a firm wanted it to continue it had to prove to the Restrictive Practices Court that the removal of resale price maintenance would harm the consumer according to different criteria, for example the consumer's health would be adversely affected.

Monopolies and Mergers Act 1965

This extended the power of the Monopolies Commission which could investigate mergers or proposed mergers that would lead to a monopoly or increase the power of an established monopoly. On the strength of the report the Board of Trade, as it was then, was allowed to prevent the merger and even unscramble past mergers. These powers were greatly increased. For instance, the proposed merger between Boots and Glaxo was disallowed after an adverse report by the Monopolies Commission.

Fair Trading Act 1973

This created a Director General of Fair Trading whose function was to keep the register of restrictive practices made with the Restrictive Practices Court. Preliminary investigations on monopolies could be carried out and referred to the newly named Monopolies and Mergers Commission. This Commission, previously the Monopolies Commission, could now investigate local as well as national monopolies and nationalised industries and restrictive practices in the labour market. Moreover a monopoly was now defined as having a 25% (not 33%) market share.

Restrictive Trade Practices Act 1976
The Director General of Fair Trading was made responsible for bringing cases before the Restrictive Practices Court.

The Competition Act 1980
The Monopolies and Mergers Commission was given the power to look into the efficiency of the nationalised industries. Also the Director General of Fair Trading could deal directly with firms regarding restrictive practices, especially those aimed to restrict competition from small firms.

Checkpoints

1 Division of labour is specialisation. Developed economies are characterised by division of labour. Division of labour has advantages and disadvantages. It requires exchange and is limited by the size of the market. Division of labour applies to individuals, regions and countries.
2 Technological change involves developing mass production, automation and micro-technology.
3 There are three main types of industry: primary, secondary and tertiary production. Tertiary production is the biggest category of industry within the United Kingdom economy.
4 Firms are expanding in size because of the internal and external economies of large-scale production. There are various types of internal economy of scale, such as technological and financial economies. However, large firms do suffer from diseconomies of scale and small firms enjoy the economies of small-scale production. Small firms continue to exist for a variety of different reasons.
5 Firms may become bigger by merging with other firms. The main forms of integration are horizontal, vertical and lateral integration and conglomerate mergers. There are several motives for the different types of merger.
6 Both competition and monopoly, as market forms, have advantages and disadvantages. However, recent governments have passed some anti-monopoly legislation and, in general, tend to frown on monopoly firms.

Multiple-choice questions – 2

1   If a firm is producing at its optimum size output, a further increase in output will

    A   increase average cost per unit
    B   decrease average cost per unit
    C   decrease the marginal cost per unit
    D   reduce variable costs
    E   have no effect on total costs

2   Economies of scale occur where a firm

    A   increases output with a less than proportionate increase in costs
    B   increases costs with a less than proportionate increase in output
    C   increases its sales despite a fall in output
    D   raises prices despite a rise in output
    E   reduces both output and costs

3   The establishment of a new industry makes it economic for a local polytechnic to run suitable courses for all firms in the area. This is an example of

    A   an internal economy of scale
    B   increasing productivity
    C   increasing returns to scale
    D   regional policy
    E   an external economy of scale

4   Which of the following combinations is correctly classified?

	Primary	Secondary	Tertiary
A	mining	farming	banking
B	forestry	steel production	teaching
C	electricity generating	car manufacturing	house construction
D	retailing	brick manufacture	catering
E	oil extraction	insurance	dentistry

5   An example of horizontal integration would be a merger between

    A   a car manufacturer and a steel producer
    B   a bank and an insurance company
    C   a public house and a brewery
    D   a soft drinks manufacturer and another soft drinks manufacturer
    E   a builder and a building supplies merchant

6   Which of the following is *not* an advantage of division of labour?

    A   workers are trained more easily

    B workers spend less time moving from job to job
    C workers become dependent on other workers
    D workers become more efficient at performing repeated tasks
    E machinery is more easily introduced to perform simple tasks

7   As the division of labour increases in an economy

    A interdependence between people and firms diminishes
    B the standard of living of workers falls
    C the proportion of specialists in the labour force declines
    D a greater proportion of workers are employed in tertiary production
    E the value of output diminishes

8   In which of the following would a small firm be suitable?

    A where a personal service is required
    B where mass production techniques are possible
    C where large amounts of capital are required
    D where there is a large demand
    E where standardised commodities are wanted

9   A market situation where there are only a few large firms in existence is known as

    A a monopoly
    B competition
    C a cartel
    D a multinational
    E an oligopoly

10 Organisations which employ mass-production techniques need

    A to produce a wide variety of commodities
    B to employ highly-skilled workers
    C a large market for their products
    D to sell their products throughout the world
    E to form a cartel

Answers on page 328.

Data response question 2

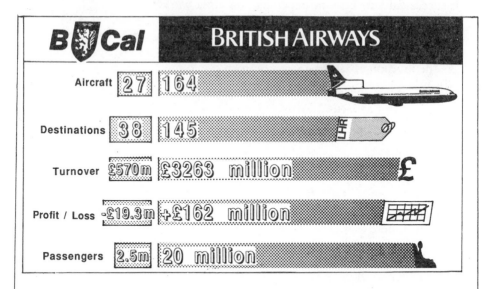

	BCal	BRITISH AIRWAYS
Aircraft	27	164
Destinations	38	145
Turnover	£570m	£3263 million
Profit / Loss	-£19.3m	+£162 million
Passengers	2.5m	20 million

The MMC is too often looked upon as a hanging judge: reference is treated tantamount to prevention. It is nothing of the kind. Lord King would argue that airlines are an international business; that he is as keen as anyone to call quits to the European cartel; but that survival of a second UK carrier to which his routes are handed on a plate does nothing for consumer choice. Questions would also be raised about the ability of BCal to survive in independence — but also about the alternative, of transfer of its routes to the other UK independents. These are all matters upon which the MMC exists to ajudicate. Clearance of this merger without MMC scrutiny, following as it would the clearance of the Murdoch acquisition of "Today" (albeit a vastly different proposition), would leave competition policy in tatters. This is one case where the immediate convenience of the respective owners has to take a second place.

£237m takeover plan for BCal brings fears of airline monopoly

BA in bid for rival to fight US giants

By Michael Smith, Industrial Editor

British Airways is trying to establish a formidable position in the world airline industry by launching a controversial but agreed £237 million take-over bid for rivals, British Caledonian.

The deal, if approved, would create a giant British airline business, carrying almost 23 million passengers a year on nearly 200 aircraft to about 170 destinations in every corner of the globe.

The take-over would give BA a 92 per cent share of the UK-based airline market against its present 77 per cent share and has aroused fierce controversy over abuse of monopoly power.

(a) Assuming that the merger between British Airways and British Caledonian is successful
    (i) how many aircraft would the new company have?
    (ii) how many passengers would the new company carry?
    (iii) what proportion of the United Kingdom based airline market would *not* be in the hands of the new company?

(b)   (i) What is the economist's term for the type of integration proposed between British Airways and British Caledonian?
    (ii) What other types of integration exist?

(c) What might the 'European cartel' be which is referred to, and how might it be working against consumer interests?

(d) Give three possible motives British Airways may have in 'taking-over' British Caledonian.

(e) How might the merger affect
    (i) shareholders?
    (ii) consumers?
    (iii) workers?
    (iv) independent airlines?

(f)   (i) Explain the role of the Monopolies and Mergers Commission.
    (ii) What role is advocated for it in this proposed merger?

3 The location of industry and regional policy

Certain industries are concentrated in specific regions of the country. This does not mean that these industries cannot be found in any other regions, but that they are most heavily concentrated in certain locations. Here are some examples:

The car industry is concentrated in the West Midlands of England;
The cotton industry is concentrated in Lancashire;
The pottery industry is concentrated around Stoke-on-Trent (known as The Potteries);
The cutlery industry is concentrated around Sheffield.

This is another example of specialisation which we discussed in Chapter 2. The location of industry illustrates *regional specialisation* (ie, certain regions specialise in particular industries).

Factors which influence the location of industry

Industries wish to locate in regions where their costs are at a minimum and where they will be most profitable. There are several influences which each industry will take into account.

It is unlikely that any one area will have all of the advantages required by a certain industry. Consequently, the industry chooses to situate in the region which has more of these important factors than other regions. Let us examine some of these factors.

Nearness to raw materials
The firms in the industry do not want to be situated too far away from the required raw materials because these may be expensive to transport. There are certain industries, such as the extractive industries, where the location decision is made very simple. For instance, coal can only be mined where there are supplies of coal, and iron ore can only be mined where there are supplies of iron ore.

Nearness to markets
The firms in the industry do not want to be situated too far away from the market (where the demand for the product is) because it may be expensive to transport the finished good to the market. There are certain firms, such as those in the service industries (for example, retailers and hairdressers), where the location decision is again very simple. Such firms have to be located where there is a demand for their services. It would be worthless having a retail shop in the middle of nowhere.

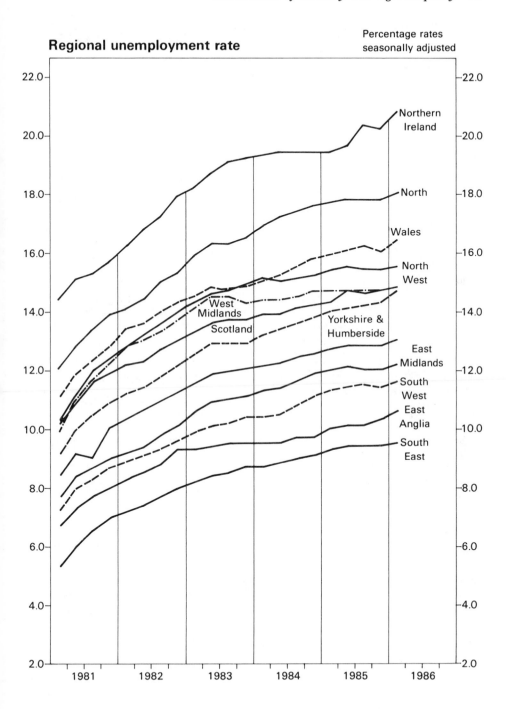

Regional unemployment rate

Percentage rates
seasonally adjusted

Northern
Ireland

North

Wales

North
West

West
Midlands

Scotland

Yorkshire &
Humberside

East
Midlands

South
West

East
Anglia

South
East

1981   1982   1983   1984   1985   1986

Transport costs

Transport costs are a major consideration when deciding where to locate the industry. The problem is especially evident when raw materials for the industry are situated in one part of the country and the market is in another part of the country.

(a) *Material orientated industries* If the raw materials used are bulky and expensive to transport compared to the transportation of the finished good, then the industry will be located near the raw material, as in the steel industry and saw milling.

(b) *Market orientated industries* If the finished good is bulky and expensive to transport compared to transportation of the raw material then the industry will be located near the market, as in the car industry, brewing and bakeries.

However, many industries are said to be *footloose*. This means that transport costs are not a major factor influencing location. Such industries are neither material- nor market-orientated, probably because the raw materials and finished goods are equally easy and cheap to transport. Also, developments in transport and technology have meant that firms need not be material- or market-orientated.

Nearness to power supplies

Industries require power to drive the machines and to provide heating and lighting. Before the Industrial Revolution power was based mainly on water and, therefore, factories had to be located near fast flowing streams or rivers. However, at the beginning of the Industrial Revolution steam power was developed, by James Watt, and to provide steam power industries needed coal. Therefore, throughout the Industrial Revolution industries were located near the coal fields of South Wales, Northern England and Central Scotland. In the modern economy electricity is generally available on the national grid and consequently industries have power at their disposal wherever they are located in the United Kingdom. The nearness to coal has declined as a major location influence.

The availability of factors of production

Industries need to be situated near to the quantity and quality of land, labour, capital and enterprise which is required. Some industries may require a great deal of cheap, flat land. Some industries may require supplies of skilled labour. Some industries will need supplies of cheap capital.

The external economies of scale

The external economies of scale are discussed in great detail on page 36. Firms will locate wherever these external economies are available to all firms in the industry. Firms will locate themselves in an area where they can find supplies of skilled labour, where ancillary component firms are situated, where transport links are of a good standard, where education and local services are orientated towards the particular industry. These external economies of scale are acquired over a period of time and are not the natural or original reasons for location.

Inertia
Inertia is when firms still locate themselves in particular areas even though the original reasons for location may have disappeared. If there is a strong tradition that a particular region is known to be the home of a certain industry then it will be very difficult for new firms to break away from this tradition. For instance, pottery firms still locate themselves around Stoke-on-Trent mainly for reasons of tradition or inertia.

Special factors
There are various special factors which might influence location decisions within certain industries.

Facilities for waste disposal
The chemical industry needs to dispose of a great deal of waste and in consequence tends to be located near rivers or near the sea. However, governments are now beginning to take action against industries which cause pollution.

Climate and geography
Certain industries may require a special type of climate. For instance, one of the original reasons why cotton was manufactured in Lancashire was because of the damp and humid climate. Burton-on-Trent is a centre for brewing because of the qualities of its water and climate. In agriculture, certain types of crop may require certain climates, for example, for market gardening in the Vale of Evesham or hop growing in Kent.

Cheap, flat land
The oil refining industry is situated in areas where there is a lot of cheap and flat land as in Fawley, near Southampton because oil refineries take up a great deal of space.

Away from areas of population
Certain industries are considered to be too dangerous to be carried on near large areas of population in case of any accidents, and these, such as nuclear power stations, are located away from large towns.

Personal factors
There are examples of the entrepreneur's personal preference for a location being a decisive influence. For instance William Morris, later Lord Nuffield, built his Morris cars in Cowley, Oxford because he was born in Oxford. For similar reasons the Pilkington glass works is at St Helens (Lancashire) and Cadbury's chocolates at Bournville (Birmingham). However, this personal preference for a location would probably only be decisive if there were no outstanding economic reasons why the firm should go to another location.

Government regional policy
The government provides many financial incentives in an effort to persuade

firms to go to certain assisted areas of the country. We shall discuss this on pages 60–4.

The difference between the original (natural) factors and the acquired factors influencing location of industry

Certain industries still continue to be located in particular regions of the country even though the original factors for explaining their location may have disappeared. For instance, pottery is still manufactured mainly in 'The Potteries' even though the original reasons for its location (ie, deposits of kaolin) have long since been worked out. Cottons are still manufactured in Lancashire although its previously special advantages, such as a humid climate and available sources of power, can be simulated elsewhere. The main reasons why industries continue to be located in regions where there are no longer any natural advantages are:

(a) *inertia*
(b) *the external economies of scale* These are the acquired advantages or the economies of concentration (see pages 36–7), which have grown up over time although they did not exist originally when the industry was first set up. They now form a very important location factor to be considered.

Changes in the importance of location influences

Improvements in transport and new inventions have meant that the pull of raw materials is now less of an important influence. Both raw materials and finished goods can be quickly and effectively transported by modern transport links. Industries no longer have to be congregated around the coal fields.

Coal is no longer a major source of power. The national grid provides firms all over the United Kingdom with electrical power. Consequently, industries need no longer go to South Wales or the North of England for power supplies.

New technology allows certain conditions, previously only found in certain regions of the country, to be produced. For instance, humidifiers can produce a damp atmosphere and there are water softeners to produce a certain quality of water.

Certain raw materials, such as iron ore and copper, have now been worked out, which means that the pull of raw materials is less important. Indeed, the steel industry, once located inland near the iron ore deposits of South Wales and Northern England, is now situated on the coast to allow easy import of foreign ores (eg Port Talbot, South Wales).

Many industries today are more capital intensive and therefore labour has become less important as a factor to be considered. Basically many industries require no more than machine operators and look for supplies of cheap labour.

Owing to these changes in locational influences, many firms have a great deal of freedom to choose where they will be located. They no longer have to go to the coalfields, or to where the climate is especially suitable, or where raw materials are to be found. There has in fact been a drift south to the Southern and Midland areas of England. This has been due to the fact that these are the areas where there are large urban populations which provide a large market. Moreover, since joining the Common Market in 1973, these regions of the country had the attraction of being near to the United Kingdom's main export markets in Western Europe.

This drift south has led to the emergence of an increasingly important influence on location decisions – government regional policy. This is an attempt by governments to encourage firms and industries to move out of the South and Midlands of England into the assisted areas of Wales, the North of England, Scotland and Northern Ireland where unemployment is now a characteristic feature.

The disadvantages of the location of industry

If a region is dominated by a particular industry then it may suffer the disadvantages of specialisation. This is because if that industry declines there may be no alternative source of employment and in consequence the whole region may become depressed and suffer large-scale unemployment. This is exactly what has happened to the assisted areas of Wales, Scotland, Northern England and Northern Ireland. For instance, South Wales specialised in coal mining and steel production. Both of these industries have declined due to foreign competition and the development of new products. Coal has been adversely affected by oil and gas development, steel has been adversely affected by the development of synthetic products such as plastics. The decline of coal and steel has meant that the South Wales region has become depressed and suffers high unemployment and other related problems. The main industries which have declined are known as the traditional (staple) industries and these are coal, textiles, shipbuilding and steel. These industries have concentrated in the now assisted areas of Scotland, Wales, the North of England and Northern Ireland.

Assisted areas tend to have the following characteristics:

(a) *Unemployment is above the national average.* This unemployment is called structural unemployment or regional unemployment (see page 279).
(b) *Levels of income tend to be below the national average.*
(c) *Educational achievement is lower among young people.*
(d) *There is net emigration* especially among young people leaving an 'ageing population'.
(e) *There is a poor regional and social infrastructure.* Roads, hospitals, schools, houses are all in poor condition.
(f) *Low level of service provision,* such as shops, cinemas and recreational activities.

Even those areas where industry is expanding (ie, growth areas) have problems. These are mainly social problems such as overcrowding, lack of housing, overcrowded schools, pollution, heavy traffic congestion and a great strain on medical and health facilities. There will also be economic problems for firms in these areas such as a lack of skilled labour relative to the demand for skilled labour, wages will have to be higher, traffic congestion may make transport less

Job losses and gains

A regional breakdown of employment changes
between 1979-1986

efficient, house prices will be high and there will be shortages of space for
expansion and development.

A problem which may be common to big cities in both the depressed and
growth areas is the *inner-city problem*. The inner-city areas are those in the centre
of large cities such as London, Liverpool, Birmingham, Leeds, Bristol and
Glasgow. These were once prosperous areas but are now in a state of deprivation
and degradation. There are large-scale social problems to be solved in these areas,
such as unemployment, bad housing, overcrowding, pollution and lack of
services and facilities. It is no accident that riots and vandalism have broken out in
these areas in recent years and it is a major problem to be solved.

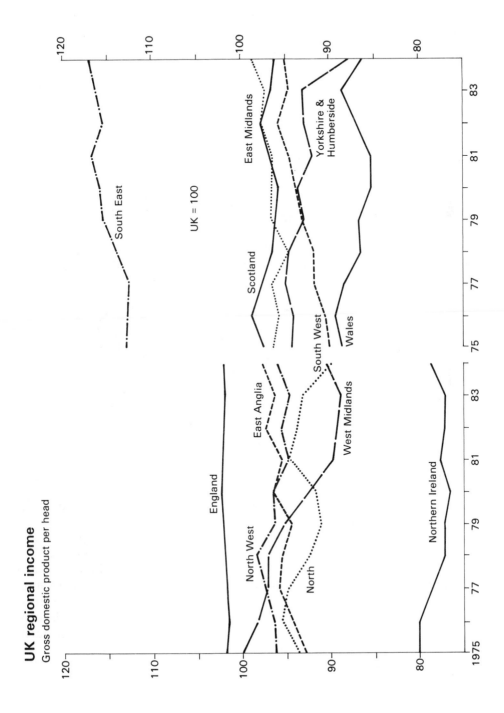

UK regional income
Gross domestic product per head

Regional policy

What is the regional problem?
The regional problem is the problem of unemployment and related problems such as low levels of income and the poor regional infrastructure which characterises the depressed areas. The areas which need government help are called assisted areas. Regions are classified into one of three types.

Growth areas
Much of the South East of England is a growth area. The area needs no government help and indeed the aim is that industry is to be attracted away from the region.

Intermediate areas
These show some need of government aid but do not receive the same amount of aid as other depressed areas. These areas include Humberside, and the Plymouth area in the South West of England.

Development areas
These areas show more need of government aid but again they do not merit all of the aid which is available. Examples include much of the South West of England, North and Mid-Wales, much of Scotland and Northern England.

Why is the government concerned about the regional problem?

(a) Unemployment means that there are productive resources which are being wasted with land, labour, capital and enterprise lying idle and making no contribution to the United Kingdom's national income.
(b) There are social problems involved with the unemployment of labour. Unemployment can be considered to be a social and moral problem causing associated difficulties such' as poor health, violence, hooliganism and a feeling of despair. It is not only the unemployed person who is affected but also other members of the family.
(c) The cost of unemployment in terms of social security and unemployment benefits. There is a considerable cost to the taxpayer of a large pool of unemployed.
(d) An unbalanced economy with growth areas and assisted areas causes social and economic problems in both types of region.

The government is concerned with the regional problem for a mixture of social and economic reasons. Thus governments have adopted a regional policy in an attempt to overcome the regional problem.

Regional policy: 'Taking the work to the workers'
Regional policy is based on the idea of 'taking the work to the workers'. This policy is preferred to the alternative policy of taking the workers to the work because labour on the whole has proved to be both geographically and

Great Britain Assisted Areas

as defined by
The Department of Trade and Industry
as from 29.11.84

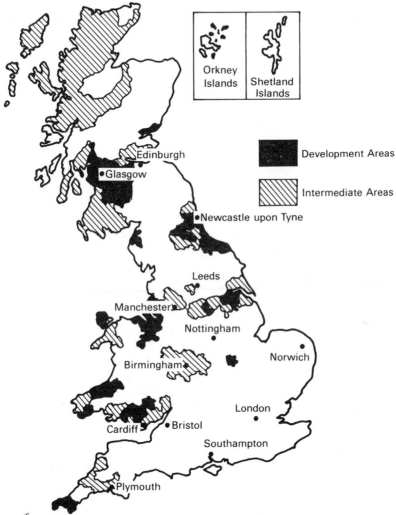

Orkney
Islands

Shetland
Islands

■ Development Areas

▨ Intermediate Areas

Edinburgh
•Glasgow

•Newcastle upon Tyne

Leeds

Manchester

Nottingham

Norwich

Birmingham

London

Cardiff • Bristol

Southampton

Plymouth

Isles of Scilly (The Isles of Scilly are a development area)

occupationally immobile. Immobility of labour and its causes is discussed on pages 278–9 and this should be understood before proceeding further.

Much of the present regional policy is based on the Industrial Development Act 1984 which classified two main types of area which needed help: intermediate areas and development areas. However, regional policy has existed since the 1930s when the early industrial estates were set up in what were called the 'special areas'.

Aspects of regional policy

Regional policy is sometimes referred to as a 'carrot and stick policy' because on the one hand it is attempting to induce new firms into the assisted areas and on the other hand it attempts to force firms out of the growth areas.

Inducements offered to firms going to assisted areas

(a) *Regional development grants* These are grants available for projects resulting in improvements and modernisation. They are intended to encourage investment in new factories and buildings in the depressed areas. This is the main form of assistance and is available only to firms operating within development areas.

(b) *Removal grants* These are available for firms moving into the assisted areas. They are subsidies to cover removal expenses.

(c) *Retraining grants* The government gives grants to firms to help them finance the retraining of workers. The government itself also sets up *Government Retraining Centres* which should improve the occupational mobility of labour.

(d) *Advance factories* are built which are vacant and awaiting new firms to utilise their facilities. Also, factories can be used rent free for a period of time.

(e) *Loans* are available at low rates of interest.

(f) *Financial aid* is available to attract key workers to work for the firm.

(g) *Preference* may be given to firms in these assisted areas by the government when it allocates its own contracts.

(h) The government finances *industrial estates* which exist throughout the United Kingdom. It also finances organisations such as the Welsh Development Agency, whose role is to advertise the advantages of the region and attract new firms.

(i) The government has attempted to improve the *regional social infrastructure* of the assisted areas by building new roads, hospitals, schools and leisure centres.

Industrial development certificates (IDCs)

When building or extending a factory in a growth area, the firm has to get planning permission from local authorities. If the floor space is over a certain amount, an Industrial Development Certificate may be required from the Department of Trade and Industry. These IDCs are extremely difficult to get unless the government is sympathetic to the firm setting up in a growth area. Very often an IDC will be refused in an effort to force the firm to build its factory in an assisted area. IDCs are more readily available for firms going to assisted areas.

The government sets an example

The government has dispersed some important controlled offices and factories into the assisted areas to set an example to private industry. Examples include the Driver and Vehicle Licensing Centre at Swansea, the Royal Mint in Llantrisant,

South Wales, the Department of Health and Social Security in Newcastle and National Giro in Bootle, Liverpool.

New towns
New towns have been created mainly to attract people out of the inner-city areas and reduce congestion and overcrowding in large urban areas. Examples include Welwyn Garden City, Crawley Newtown, Telford in the West Midlands, Newton Aycliffe in the North East and Skelmersdale near Liverpool.

Enterprise zones
Since July 1982 there have been *enterprise zones*. The zones are a response to the needs of derelict, especially inner-city, areas lacking in industrial development. Some of these zones are not in assisted areas. Firms in these zones receive financial assistance, such as rates exemption for 10 years and allowances for commercial and industrial buildings. They can also take advantage of simplified planning procedures. The policy is designed to create jobs in areas of deprivation. Enterprise zones, are located mainly in inner-city areas or where there is derelict land, not necessarily in an assisted area. Examples include Swansea, Clydebank, Middlesborough and the Isle of Dogs (London).

It is difficult to be precise about exactly what constitutes regional policy. This is because regional policy is constantly being reappraised by governments and is always in a state of change. Moreover, it must not be forgotten that, since joining the Common Market, the United Kingdom has taken advantage of grants and cash handouts from the European Community *regional fund*. However, it must be said that the EC spends a great deal more on aid to agriculture than on aid to industry.

An assessment of regional policy
It is apparent that although regional policy has been in existence for over fifty years, the regional problem still exists (ie, there are still assisted areas). Moreover, the assisted areas are especially badly hit by recessions and slumps in the economy (such as those experienced since 1979 and in the early 1980s). However, supporters of the policy say that without such a policy the assisted regions would be even more depressed, and that there have been some considerable successes such as the Ford Motor Company plant at Bridgend, built in the late 1970s, and the Nissan factory in Sunderland, built in 1986.

Criticisms
The effectiveness of the regional policy has been criticised on the following grounds:

(a) *The policy itself is the wrong one* Some economists suggest that there should be no policy to help the assisted areas and that the laws of supply and demand should not be interfered with. Other economists suggest that the policy should be one of 'taking the workers to the work' which would save the government a great deal of money in regional aid and also firms would be situated in areas where they are most efficiently located. This brings us to the main criticism of the present policy of 'taking the work to the workers' – *it forces firms to go to areas where they are less efficient* and where fewer advantages are available. Critics of the present policy also point to the fact that regional aid is very expensive to the taxpayer and it has not been very successful.

However, the policy of 'taking the work to the workers' can be defended on the grounds that to do nothing would be socially and economically disastrous as far as unemployment is concerned. Also, the policy of moving the 'workers to the work' will be frustrated by geographical and occupational immobility of labour. It would lead to an unbalanced economy of depressed and growth areas.

(b) *Much of the aid has encouraged firms to be more capital intensive* Only regional Employment Premiums (now withdrawn) encouraged firms to employ more labour. Most of the aid has been used to install more machinery. It has encouraged the employment of capital and not labour.

(c) *Some firms do not invest at all* If a firm is faced with not receiving an Industrial Development Certificate in a growth area, then it may decide not to build the new factory at all. Thus no region benefits because the investment will be lost completely.

(d) *Government policies are always changing* Successive governments have differences in emphasis in their regional policies. Thus entrepreneurs are reluctant to go to an assisted area in case the aid they require is limited or withdrawn by a new government. Regional aid has proved to be uncertain.

(e) *Regional policy is only one location influence to be considered* Regional policy is only one of a whole number of factors which determine the location of an industry. If all of the other advantages are not available to the industry in an assisted area then it is unlikely that regional aid by itself will persuade the firm to move to the depressed area.

(f) *Regional policy has provided jobs for the wrong sections of the labour force* This means that in many cases the types of jobs provided by new firms have been for part-time unskilled and mainly female labour, this in areas where the unemployment problem is one of unemployed steel workers or shipyard workers. There are jobs being provided for their wives and daughters, but not for them.

Checkpoints

1 Industries are located in those regions where their costs of production are at a minimum. There are several factors which influence the location of industry, such as nearness to raw materials or markets and government regional policy.

2 The factors which influence the location of industry change over time and some factors, such as nearness to coal deposits, are no longer significant.

3 Some regions of the United Kingdom have specialised too much in certain

industries. These industries have declined leaving the region with problems such as high unemployment. This is the so-called regional problem.

4 The government has adopted a regional policy aimed at helping these depressed regions with the objective of attracting work to the assisted areas. This regional policy offers a range of financial inducements to attract firms into the assisted areas, such as regional development grants. Enterprise zones have also been created in certain city areas.

5 Regional policy has been subject to much criticism.

6 The major industries of the United Kingdom (energy, iron and steel, motor vehicles, textiles and chemicals), are located in different regions of the United Kingdom for a number of reasons.

Multiple-choice questions – 3

1 A bulk reducing industry will tend to locate near to

    A coal deposits
    B cheap land
    C markets
    D raw materials
    E skilled labour

2 Many people now purchase clothing made from synthetic materials rather than cottons or woollens. This has led to unemployment in both the cotton and woollen industries. Such unemployment is termed

    A structural
    B frictional
    C mass
    D seasonal
    E residual

3 Which of the following characteristics is common to all development areas?

    A Low levels of population
    B Levels of unemployment above the national average
    C Poor transport facilities
    D Too much dependence on textiles
    E Too much dependence on primary industries

4 Which of these factors is most likely to result in the concentration of an industry in one particular area of the United Kingdom?

    A The finished product is mainly exported
    B The industry requires large amounts of capital investment
    C A high proportion of the labour force is unskilled
    D Internal economies of scale exist
    E External economies of scale exist

5 Which of the following is *not* an example of external economies of scale?

    A The cutlery industry in Sheffield assisted by a bias in that city's university and polytechnic towards metallurgical subjects
    B Birmingham benefits from good motorway links
    C The West Midlands motor industry benefits from the existence of specialist component suppliers
    D Pottery manufacture in the Stoke-on-Trent area benefits from skilled workers
    E Bulk purchases of components at favourable terms by a large car manufacturer

6   Acquired advantages for the location of an industry are

    A   those which are of marginal importance
    B   those which originally led the industry to be located in the area
    C   those provided in neighbouring regions
    D   those which develop as the industry becomes more established in
       the area
    E   those which are provided by the local authority

7   Which of the following areas receives no regional aid assistance from the
   government?

    A   South Wales
    B   South-eastern England
    C   Tyneside
    D   Merseyside
    E   Clydeside

8   Government regional aid policy attempts to persuade firms to move into
   areas where (perhaps) they have relatively higher costs of production. This
   does *not* conform with which of the following concepts?

    A   Eventually diminishing returns
    B   Diminishing marginal utility
    C   Comparative costs
    D   Diminishing marginal productivity
    E   The multiplier

9   Which region in the United Kingdom has the highest level of regional
   unemployment?

    A   Northern Ireland
    B   Northern England
    C   Southern England
    D   Central Scotland
    E   South Wales

10   Which of the following is *not* an enterprise zone?

    A   Swansea
    B   Isle of Dogs (London)
    C   Corby
    D   Southampton
    E   Belfast

Answers on page 328.

Data response question 3

Development areas: nowhere else comes within miles of Corby

If you're planning to develop your business you need look no further than Corby.

Corby is a **Development Area** so your business gets the help of Development Area benefits. For most companies this means the better deal for them of either 15% grants on plant, machinery and equipment or £3000 per job created. There is also selective assistance for some job creating projects.

Corby is also a **Steel Opportunity Area,** and this means even more incentives.

Corby is **England's first Enterprise Zone.** There are factories off the peg, from 500 sq.ft. to 50,000 sq.ft., some of which are rates free until 1991. You can also choose from offices, warehouses, and high tech buildings.

Corby has **EEC aid for small businesses.** £1m is now available to aid efficiency.

Above all, Corby is right in the heart of England. Within 80 miles of London. 50 miles from Birmingham. Strategically placed for any business that needs fast, inexpensive, easy access to the big South East and Midland population centres.

However far you look, you will find that, as a total package for the success of your business, nowhere else comes within miles of Corby.

Development Areas

as defined by
The Department of
Trade and Industry
to take effect from 29.11.84

Manchester

Nottingham

Birmingham

CORBY

London

Name: ....
Company: ....
Position: ....
Address: ....
....

For more information, send to Roy Jackson.
Director of Industry, Corby Industrial Development Centre,
Douglas House, Queens Square, Corby, Northamptonshire
Telephone Corby (0536) 62571 Telex 341543
Prestel Key ✱ 20079 #

E14/3

CORBY WORKS

(a) (i) Name three other development areas (apart from Corby) illustrated by the map of the United Kingdom in the advertisement.

     (ii) Apart from enterprise zones and development areas, what is the other category of assisted area?

(b) According to the advertisement, what regional aid does Corby receive because it is designated

     (i) a development area?

     (ii) an enterprise zone?

(c) Apart from those mentioned in the advertisement, give three other types of regional aid available to a development area.

(d) What economic problems would you expect to find in an area designated as a development area?

(e) Why does the advertisement attach such importance to Corby being near to London and Birmingham?

(f) Outline three ways in which a development area might benefit from attracting new industries.

(g) What problems might develop in Corby if the advertisement is successful in attracting new industries?

(h) (i) How much EC aid is available for small businesses in Corby?

     (ii) Why is the United Kingdom government (and the EC) encouraging the development of small businesses?

4 Private enterprise

In the first chapter we discussed the fact that the United Kingdom is a *mixed economy*. This means that the United Kingdom economy includes industries owned by the government (nationalised industries or public corporations, see Chapter 5) and industries owned by private entrepreneurs. In this chapter we are going to discuss the activities of those firms owned by private entrepreneurs (ie, private enterprise or the private sector).

There are five types of firm to be discussed in the private enterprise sector:

Sole traders or *sole proprietors*
Partnerships
Joint stock companies (two types: public joint stock companies and private joint stock companies)
Holding companies
Co-operatives

The objective of all firms in private enterprise is to make a *profit*.

Sole traders or proprietors

The sole trader is a one-man business. There are many examples such as window cleaners and small independent retail shops. Sole traders are especially found in those industries where a personal service is desirable (retailing) or where quick decisions need to be made (eg farming).

Advantages of sole proprietors

(a) They provide a personal service for customers and staff. They also often provide a convenient service, eg small shops.
(b) They are able to make quick decisions and respond quickly to any changes in demand.
(c) They are independent and their 'own boss'. Therefore they have the incentive to work harder.
(d) They keep all the profits for themselves and do not have to share them with shareholders or partners.

Sole proprietors are said to enjoy the *economies of small-scale production* (see page 37).

Disadvantages of sole proprietors

(a) They do not enjoy the economies of large-scale production such as having large amounts of finance or being able to afford advertising.
(b) They do not have limited liability (see page 72). This means that their personal assets may be sold to pay creditors.
(c) There may be problems if the sole proprietor is ill or wishes to take a holiday.

The sole proprietor obviously owns and controls the firm. Money or capital is raised by the sole proprietor using personal savings, loans from relatives or friends, small bank loans and by 'ploughing back' profits into the firm.

Partnerships

There are two types of partnership: an **ordinary** (or general) partnership and a **limited** partnership. Both types of partnership have between *two* and *twenty* partners. However there are differences.

The ordinary partnership

Advantages

(a) Business affairs still remain private, unlike public joint stock companies (see page 73). They do not have to make public the financial situation of the company such as its balance sheets.
(b) The different partners can contribute their different skills and experiences to the firm, for instance one of the partners may be an accountant, another may be a solicitor and another a surveyor. This allows some degree of specialisation within the firm. This is an advantage over the sole proprietor who has to rely on personal judgement.
(c) They are able to raise more capital than sole traders.
(d) They are still quite small and enjoy the economies of small-scale production.

Disadvantages

(a) Unlike the joint stock companies they do not have limited liability.
(b) Profits have to be shared among all of the partners.
(c) They still tend to be quite small and cannot enjoy the economies of large-scale production.
(d) All partners should be consulted when decisions are made. This may lead to a slowing down of decision-making compared to sole traders. Decisions are binding on all partners irrespective of whether or not they were consulted.
(e) The partnership is dissolved on the death or retirement of a partner.

The limited partnership

This is different from an ordinary partnership because some of the partners will have limited liability. However, at least one of the partners must be an ordinary partner. This means that this partner does not have limited liability and therefore carries the full burden for paying off debts (even out of personal belongings) if the partnership fails. Limited partnerships are not popular in the United Kingdom; most firms wishing to raise more capital will form a *private joint stock company* (see page 73).

Advantages

(a)   The limited partner has limited liability therefore taking less risk and may contribute more capital.
(b)   The limited partner has a share in the profits.

Disadvantages

(a)   Only the ordinary partners have a say in the running of the partnership and making decisions. The limited partner is a type of sleeping partner, in that their contribution is capital.
(b)   The limited partners' share of the profits will probably be less because they are taking less of a risk.
(c)   Limited partners are unable to withdraw even part of their capital unless the ordinary partners agree.

Partnerships are owned and controlled by the partners and capital is raised from contributions by partners and possibly bank loans. Like sole proprietors they do not issue shares and debentures. Profits are divided among partners: the size of the partner's allocation of profits depending on whether he or she is an ordinary or limited partner. Profits and losses are shared equally among the ordinary partners irrespective of the amount of individual capital invested. This is so unless there is some prior agreement in the Deed of Partnership which will give details of the ratio to be apportioned.

Partnerships are especially evident in the professions, eg doctors, dentists, barristers and solicitors where a personal service is still required.

Joint stock companies (or limited companies)

Joint stock companies are easily distinguished from sole proprietors and partnerships because they *issue shares* and have *limited liability*.

The meaning of limited liability

This means that in the event of a company going out of business, shareholders will only lose the money they have invested in the company, and not their personal belongings (house, television, furniture, car, and so on). This dates back to the Limited Liability Act of 1855. It means that investors are more willing to buy shares and therefore provide joint stock companies with finance because there is less risk. Companies can use this money to build new factories, buy more equipment and generally expand the business.

There are two types of joint stock company: the *private joint stock company* and the *public joint stock company*.

The private joint stock company
Often referred to as the private company or the private limited company. They have the following distinguishing features:

(a) since the *1981 Companies Act* private joint stock companies are required to have a minimum of two shareholders, but there is no limit on the maximum number;
(b) shares are *not* offered on the Stock Exchange;
(c) shares can only be transferred with the agreement of all the shareholders;
(d) often family-run businesses, they tend to be smaller but are more numerous than public companies;
(e) they are free from many of the legal requirements of the public company, for instance, their financial affairs are much more private than those of a public company.

The public joint stock company
Often referred to as the public company or public limited company (PLC). They must not be confused with public corporations (or nationalised industries). They have the following distinguishing features:

(a) There is no maximum limit of shareholders but there must be at least two shareholders. Before the 1981 Companies Act there was a minimum of seven shareholders.
(b) Shares are bought and sold on the Stock Exchange.
(c) The affairs of a public company are made public.
(d) They tend to be larger than private companies.
(e) Like private companies they have a separate legal existence and can be sued in a court of law.

Advantages and disadvantages of public joint stock companies
Advantages

(a) Large amounts of capital can be raised because they will probably have more shareholders.
(b) Shareholders have limited liability which encourages them to invest more capital.
(c) Shares can be easily transferred on the Stock Exchange.
(d) Accounts are made public so the public are aware of the company's history.
(e) Shareholders are safeguarded by legal requirements to which public companies have to conform.
(f) They can enjoy the economies of large-scale production.

Disadvantages

(a) They might suffer from the diseconomies of large-scale production.
(b) There may be a divorce between ownership and control. This means that everyday decisions applying to the company may not be made by the owners (ie, the shareholders).

Documents which have to be prepared by joint stock companies

To safeguard the interests of shareholders against fraud and malpractice, companies have to prepare certain documents. These requirements have been laid down by the *1981 Companies Act*. The *Memorandum of Association* includes the name of the company and the words public limited company (PLC) if applicable. Where these words do not exist the company is deemed to be a private company. The objectives of the company and the situation of the registered office must be included. There is also a statement that liability is limited and an outline of the amount (and type) of shares which would be issued. The issued share capital for a PLC must be in excess of £50 000 and at least 25% must be paid up.

The *Articles of Association* explain the internal workings of the company and how it would be controlled. It would include information and details such as the powers of the managing director, how shares are to be issued and transferred, how profits are to be divided and how meetings are to be organised.

Both the Memorandum and Articles of Association are sent to the Registrar of Companies. If there are no problems the Registrar will issue a *Certificate of Incorporation*. This recognises the company and gives it permission to begin trading. It must be displayed in the company's registered main office.

The public company might issue one final document – the *Prospectus*. This invites the public to take up shares in the company. It contains the names and addresses of directors and all details which prospective investors might need to assess the prospects of the company. A copy of the prospectus is also filed with the Registrar.

Under the 1981 Companies Act a business which does not trade under the name(s) of its owner(s) must print on its stationery, and display at its business premises, the identity of the owner(s).

How joint stock companies raise finance

Joint stock companies can raise finance in four main ways – issuing shares, issuing debentures, 'ploughing back' profits (undistributed profits) and loans from the bank. In assisted areas, capital will also be forthcoming from the government in the form of loans.

Issuing shares

Shares in public companies are bought and sold on the Stock Exchange. Investors purchase shares for different reasons. Joint stock companies issue different types of shares because there are different types of investors. Some investors are cautious and look for a safe return on their investment even though this return may be quite small. Other investors are willing to take risks in the pursuit of larger dividends. Cautious investors would probably purchase debentures (see page 76) or preference shares. Investors willing to take a risk might purchase ordinary shares (known as risk capital or equities).

Here is a list of the main types of shares.

(a) *Ordinary shares* (also known as equities or risk capital)
Advantages: In years when large profits are made, the ordinary shareholders

may receive a large dividend because they do not have fixed interest dividends.

They can also have a vote at the Annual General Meeting (AGM) and consequently have some say in the running of the company.

Disadvantages: Since they are last in the queue to be paid out of profits they may be left with very little dividend or even no dividend at all. This would happen in years of poor profits. For this reason ordinary shares are known as risk capital.

Ordinary shares can be profitable but carry a degree of risk. Investors looking for quick profits may purchase them if the company is profitable.

(b) *Preference shares*
Advantages: Preference shareholders have a claim on profits before the ordinary shareholder. They carry less risk.

Disadvantages: Since they are fixed interest dividend shares they may miss out on large dividends in years of good profits. Also, they do not have a vote at the AGM and play no part in the decision making of the company.

Preference shareholders, like holders of cumulative preference shares, may be looking for security rather than the possibility of large profits.

(c) *Cumulative preference shares*
The difference between these and preference shares is that cumulative preference shares will catch up on missed dividends in years of good profits. In Year 1 the company may not have been able to pay dividends to cumulative preference shareholders because of poor profits. However, in Year 2, a year of good profits, the cumulative preference shareholders will receive this year's dividend and, in addition, last year's dividend. Nowadays all preference shares are cumulative shares unless otherwise stated. They carry a fixed interest dividend and have no vote at the AGM. These disadvantages are therefore much the same as for preference shares.

(d) *Participating preference shares*
They have an entitlement to a bonus to be paid out of profits in years when very good profits have been made. The bonus is normally paid after the ordinary shareholders have been paid their dividends. Apart from this their advantages and disadvantages are the same as for preference shares.

(e) *Deferred or founders' shares*
These are sold to the original founders of the company. They receive a dividend after all other shares have been paid dividends. They may be taken up by the founder of the business when they sell it to another company. Eventually they will probably be transferred to one of the other types of shares.

It is sometimes said that an investor aims to have a '*balanced portfolio*' of shares. This means that he or she will possess different types of shares in different companies in an effort to spread the risks involved. In Chapter 12 on the Stock Exchange we will discuss why people buy shares, what is meant by *par value*, *market value* and *nominal value* of a share, buying shares at a *premium* and at a *discount* and the difference between *dividend* and *yield*.

It is not only individuals who buy shares. Indeed, most securities are bought by *institutional investors*: banks, insurance companies, pension funds, investment trusts, unit trusts and savings banks. The workings of these institutions are discussed in Chapter 9 which covers money and banking.

The difference between authorised, paid-up and issued capital
Authorised capital is set out in the company's Memorandum of Association. It is the maximum amount of shares which the company has been given permission to issue. *Issued capital* is the amount of shares which the company actually issues. It may decide to issue the rest at a later date. *Paid-up* capital is what the company actually receives for its shares. It may decide to sell each £1 ordinary share for 60p each and the remaining 40p per share may not be called up for some time.

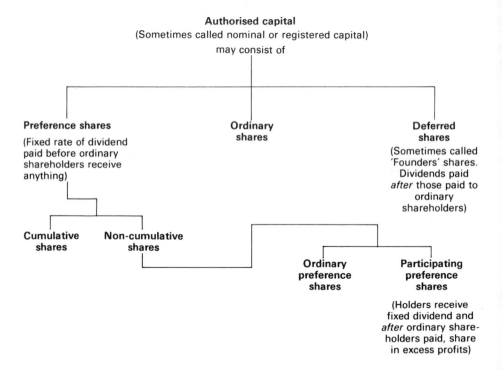

Issuing debentures
Debentures are loans to the company and they carry a fixed rate of interest. Like shares they can be purchased on the Stock Exchange. They must be paid out even if the company makes a loss and are always the first type of security to be paid. Debenture holders are sometimes given extra security by the company which might allocate certain assets to guarantee repayment of the loan. These assets can be sold off to repay the debenture holder if the company is forced out of business. Consequently debentures are a low risk form of investment which pays a consistent but low rate of interest.

'Plough back' profits
When profits are made the company need not pay all of these in dividends to shareholders. It could, and usually does, retain some of the profits in the company to finance spending on machinery, further production, employment and so on. These are called undistributed profits.

Borrowing from the bank
Joint stock companies may be able to raise money by borrowing on a loan account from a bank. They may also be able to borrow on a very short term basis from a bank by going into overdraft on their current account (see page 185).

Ownership and control of joint stock companies
Often in a public joint stock there is a *divorce between ownership and control*. This means that the owners of the company may not be in control of its management.

The owners of a company are the shareholders. However, there are various factors which often mean that they do not have any effective say in the running of the company. For instance:

1 only ordinary shareholders have a vote.
2 the rights of preference shareholders are limited and they do not have a vote.
3 only a small percentage of shareholders bother to turn up for the Annual General Meeting to vote at all.

Consequently shareholders will appoint a *Board of Directors* with a *Chairperson* at its head. The Board exercises some degree of management and the powers of the mass of shareholders may be limited to merely questioning the Board's decisions and in certain cases replacing people on the Board. However, even here, most shareholders are powerless, since the directors tend to be the biggest shareholders and can win votes of confidence. Moreover, the Board may appoint a *Managing Director* to take day-to-day control of the company and make urgent decisions. The managing director may not even be a shareholder. Thus there is a divorce between ownership and control, the owners of the company (the shareholders) having little control over the decision making.

Holding companies

Holding companies are companies which gain control of other companies either by a *merger* or a *take-over*. The *holding company* (or parent company) can take control of the other company (known as the *subsidiary company*) by gaining at least 51% of its ordinary shares. It is important that they control ordinary shares because it is these shares which carry a vote. Indeed, it is often possible to gain control of a subsidiary with a smaller shareholding if only a small percentage of shareholders turn up to the AGM. In this situation the holding company can win any votes which take place at the AGM and thus control the activities of the subsidiary.

There are two main reasons for gaining control over other companies. Firstly, it means that the 'group' can achieve the economies of large-scale production thereby reducing production costs. Secondly, it can create a monopoly. A monopoly is a firm which dominates an industry and can set prices without fear of competition. This is an advantage for the company but not so for consumers.

Holding companies are often criticised. Firstly, as we have already stated, a monopoly might be formed which might set prices at a high level. Secondly, the holding company can gain control of a whole group of companies for a relatively small amount of money.

Consider the following example:

Company B   (capital includes £2 million worth of ordinary shares and
controls   debentures worth £2 million)
  ↓

Company C   (capital includes £1 million worth of ordinary shares and
controls   debentures worth £500 000)
  ↓

Company D   (capital includes £750 000 worth of ordinary shares and debentures
            worth £250 000)

Another company, Company A, might be able to gain control of Company B by purchasing slightly over half of its ordinary shares for £1 000 000. For this amount it has control of the whole group with a capital value of £6½ million. The third criticism of holding companies is that a situation could occur where a company gains control over a group of companies whose assets (premises, land, machinery) are worth a great deal more than the amount that was paid for the company. The holding company might, therefore, decide to close down certain companies in the group and to sell the assets, thus making a quick profit. This is called *asset stripping*.

The co-operative movement

Co-operatives do not technically seek to make a profit. However, they must make a profit to continue in business and are organised for the benefit of consumers/workers. There are two main types of co-operative in existence: the consumer co-operative based on consumer control and producer co-operatives based on worker control.

Consumer co-operatives
The Co-operative Retail Society (CRS)
This is an old established form of co-operative. The movement dates back to 1844 and the 'Rochdale Pioneers'. These were a group of weavers from Rochdale, Lancashire who opened a retail shop with the purpose of buying goods in bulk at low prices and selling them at cheap prices to consumers in the area. The consumer co-operatives have expanded since the early days.

How capital is raised
Unlike joint stock companies, consumer co-operatives have an open membership and the share list is never closed. All shares are worth £1 each. However, there is a

limit to the amount of money any one individual can invest. Shares can be redeemed but not transferred or sold. Liability is limited.

How profits are shared

In the past the co-operative would share its profits only with members in the form of a dividend (the 'divi'). This dividend would be in the form of money, or in the form of goods which usually had a greater value. The dividend was proportionate to the amount of money the consumer had spent with the co-operative. Each member had a number which was recorded at the time of making the purchases.

Nowadays, all consumers, whether members or not, usually receive some dividend in the form of co-operative dividend stamps which can be exchanged for money or goods. However, members are allowed a limited dividend on capital invested.

Who owns and controls the co-operatives?

The co-operative movement is democratic, and the owners (the customers) have a great deal of control. There is only one vote per member no matter how much the individual member has invested. Members of each *local retail society* elect a committee to organise the society's affairs. The committee appoint officials and staff to operate the business. They also elect the membership of regional societies and of *The Co-operative Wholesale Society (CWS)*. This is collectively owned by the local retail societies. It provides the retail co-operatives with the bulk of their requirements, some from their own factories. It is responsible for advertising and it also operates the co-operative Federal Societies which administer such activities as laundries, bakeries and dairying services (it is the United Kingdom's largest farmer). On a national basis they provide such services as the Co-operative Bank, Co-operative Insurance Society and Co-operative Printing Society. The Wholesale Society is controlled by a board of directors consisting of members elected from regional societies. These directors then appoint executives to manage their operations.

Advantages of consumer co-operatives

(a) They are democratic and give a great deal of power to the consumers themselves.
(b) All members have an equal voice in the running of the society.
(c) Profits are shared amongst consumers and trade is encouraged by the payment of a dividend.
(d) Members provide a readily available market for sales and special promotions.
(e) The co-operative has traditional social and political objectives as well as economic objectives. For instance, the co-operatives often organise educational courses.

Disadvantages of consumer co-operatives

(a) The co-operative sells many products produced by non-co-operative firms who are, in effect, their competitors.

(b) In large urban areas, such as London, there may be more than one society.
(c) The local committees of management may have little experience in business affairs since they are drawn from consumer members.
(d) Most members do not attend meetings.
(e) It is questionable how big an attraction dividend stamps are for consumers, and prices do not tend to be generally cheaper than at other types of outlet.
(f) Finally, the co-operative has a traditional and conservative image. In an attempt to counter this criticism it has introduced self-service techniques, issued dividend stamps to all customers, built supermarkets and hypermarkets and undertaken nationwide advertising campaigns.

Producer co-operatives

In the United Kingdom producer co-operatives are not so numerous or popular as consumer co-operatives, although they are quite numerous in Europe. For instance, producer co-operatives have been widely adopted in Danish agriculture. A producer or worker co-operative is a form of co-operation where the employees provide the capital and take the risks. The company is owned by the workers who provide the capital, share the profits, and appoint the managers. However, these are still very small in number. Worker co-operatives have the advantage that the workers feel involved in company affairs and can identify with the company. Moreover, it provides an incentive for workers to work harder because they share in profits and ultimately their jobs depend on the company's success.

Many people suggest that the United Kingdom should increase worker participation in the business affairs of non-co-operative companies. This is not

Forms of ownership in the private sector

	Ownership	Control	Share of profits or losses	Liability	Legal responsibility
Sole proprietor	One person	The owner	The owner	No limit	full
Partnership	2–20 persons (with exceptions)	The active partners	Equally or otherwise by agreement	No limit	fully on the partners
Public limited liability company	Shareholders, minimum 2, no maximum	Directors elected by shareholders	Divided amongst the shareholders according to the type and number of shares held	Limited to amount which each share-holder has agreed to contribute	rests with the Company
Private limited company	minimum 2, (excluding employees)				
Co-operative Society	Shareholders, any number	Committees elected by shareholders (members)	Divided amongst the members according to their purchases	Limited	rests with the society

the same as producer co-operatives but does involve workers purchasing shares and sharing profits, and sometimes workers may be appointed as members of the board of directors. This has similar advantages to producer co-operatives.

Checkpoints

1 The United Kingdom is a mixed economy consisting of both private and public enterprise.
2 The objective of all firms in private enterprise is to maximise profits.
3 There are five main types of firm in private enterprise: sole proprietors, partnerships, limited companies (PLCs and private companies), co-operatives and holding companies.
4 Each of these different firms in private enterprise has different sources of finance, different ways of distributing profits, different methods of ownership and control.
5 Each type of firm has different advantages and disadvantages.

Multiple-choice questions – 4

1 Under private enterprise the problem of what to produce is mainly solved by

    A civil servants
    B consumer wants
    C shareholders
    D limited partners
    E a government minister

2 Co-operative Retail Societies

    A issue shares on the Stock Exchange
    B do not have limited liability
    C exist only to make profits
    D are managed by committees elected by members
    E sell only commodities provided by the CWS

3 Which of the following types of security would usually carry voting rights?

    A preference shares
    B debentures
    C gilt-edged securities
    D local authority bonds
    E ordinary shares

4 Shares carrying a fixed rate of interest and which are paid arrears of dividend when profits improve are called

    A cumulative preference shares
    B participating preference shares
    C founders' shares
    D ordinary shares
    E gilt-edged securities

5 The word 'limited' at the end of a firm's name means

    A It only produces one commodity
    B Shareholders cannot lose the money they have paid for their shares
    C Shareholders are not liable for paying all the debts of the company
    D The capital is limited
    E There can only be 50 shareholders

6 When the public are invited to subscribe to a new share issue, the information concerning the issue is given in the

    A debenture
    B AGM
    C Articles of Association

D Memorandum
E Prospectus

7 The ordinary shares of a company are known as

    A reserve capital
    B founders' shares
    C working capital
    D equities
    E gilt-edged securities

8 Which of the following is *not* a part of the private enterprise sector?

    A public companies
    B public corporations
    C partnerships
    D holding companies
    E Co-operative Retail Societies

9 Which of the following will definitely *not* be an objective of a holding company when gaining control of a subsidiary?

    A to achieve a monopoly
    B to enjoy the economies of scale
    C to increase competition
    D to sell off assets
    E to rationalise the industry

10 An important advantage of a PLC is

    A it cannot be sued in law
    B it is not bound by any Act of Parliament
    C it continues to exist even though shares change hands
    D it is owned by the government
    E it can have up to 50 shareholders

Answers on page 328.

Data response question 4

Study the passage below and then answer questions (a) to (e).

> Havant plc is one of two toy manufacturers in Portsmouth. The company has capital from investments of £450 000 divided into
>
> > £300 000 ordinary shares of 50p each
> > £100 000 cumulative preference shares of £1 each, attracting 7% return
> > £50 000 of loan capital in 6% debentures of £1 each
>
> After all other payments have been made the company has the following amounts available for distribution to shareholders over a three year period
>
> > Year 1 £ 9 000
> > Year 2 £15 500
> > Year 3 £43 000
>
> The company, encouraged by its good profits in year 3, is considering expanding. There are two possibilities:
>
> 1 Take over the other local toy manufacturer, Horndean plc.
> 2 Establish a new toy manufacturing company in a development area over 400 miles away in the North East.

(a) What type of integration is being considered by Havant plc?
(b) What is the main advantage for shareholders of Havant plc of having limited liability?
(c) If Havant plc decides to take over Horndean plc, give two advantages which may be expected.
(d) What factors should be considered by the directors of Havant plc when deciding whether or not to build a new factory in a development area?
(e) Calculate how much the debenture holders, cumulative preference shareholders and ordinary shareholders receive in each of the three years.

5 Public enterprise

British Steel, Port Talbot

In this chapter we shall discuss the public sector and particularly nationalised industries. We shall also discuss local authorities which provide many local services such as local schools, refuse collections, sanitation and so on.

What is the public sector?

The United Kingdom is a mixed economy with both a private enterprise sector and a public enterprise sector. The public sector is that part of the economy owned by the state and controlled by the government. The public sector is also often termed public enterprise.

It includes:

(a) Nationalised industries (or public corporations). These are mainly involved in industrial activity and board members are appointed by a government minister. Examples of nationalised industries are British Steel, British Rail, and British Coal.
(b) Services provided by the government, such as defence forces, education, health and social security services.
(c) Services provided by local authorities.
(d) Bodies and agencies set up by the government, such as the Monopolies and Mergers Commission and the National Economic Development Organisation.

Nationalisation

What happens when an industry is nationalised?

When an industry is nationalised the government does not confiscate the holdings of existing shareholders, but instead they are compensated by being able to exchange their shares for stock in the new nationalised industry.

Arguments for nationalisation

(a) Some industries can benefit from being organised on a national rather than a local level. It is much more efficient to provide services such as postal services, electricity, gas and railways on a national scale. For instance, if railways were provided by local companies, passengers might have to change trains frequently as they passed between areas controlled by different companies, and there might be different gauges between track and different timetables.
(b) Some industries, such as steel, railways and electricity, are best provided on a large scale so that they can take advantage of the economies of large-scale production. If the industry was nationalised it would be provided on a large scale rather than by several smaller private enterprise firms.
(c) Some industries require vasts amounts of finance to operate efficiently. For instance, the steel industry needs to invest millions of pounds every year on new plant and equipment. If the industry is nationalised then finance can be found by allocating some of the revenues of the government, which it receives mainly from taxation. It is unlikely that private enterprise firms would be able to afford such large expenditures.
(d) Some industries are monopolies, which would then have the power to charge high prices and limit the quality and quantity of output. The government might nationalise such industries to prevent such a state of affairs.
(e) Some industries are so important to the well-being of the economy that they should always be owned and controlled by the state which can then organise them to the advantage of the economy as a whole. Such industries include railways, coal, electricity, and steel. These industries are known as 'the commanding heights of the economy'.
(f) Some industries are best provided by the government for reasons of national

People in employment in the UK: by sector¹ (in millions)

	Public sector									Private sector²	Total in employment
	Central government				Local authorities			Public corporations	Total		
	HM Forces	National Health Service	Other	Total	Education	Other	Total				
1961	0.5	0.6	0.7	1.8	0.8	1.1	1.9	2.2	5.9	18.6	24.5
1971	0.4	0.8	0.8	2.0	1.3	1.4	2.7	2.0	6.6	17.8	24.4
1976	0.3	1.1	0.9	2.4	1.5	1.4	3.0	2.0	7.3	17.5	24.8
1981	0.3	1.2	0.9	2.4	1.5	1.4	2.9	1.9	7.2	17.2	24.3
1983	0.3	1.2	0.8	2.4	1.4	1.5	2.9	1.7	6.9	16.7	23.6
1984	0.3	1.2	0.8	2.4	1.4	1.5	2.9	1.6	6.9	17.2	24.1
1985	0.3	1.2	0.8	2.4	1.4	1.6	3.0	1.3	6.6	17.8	24.4
Males	0.3	0.3	0.4	1.0	0.4	0.8	1.2	1.1	3.3	10.9	14.2
Females	—	1.0	0.4	1.3	1.0	0.7	1.7	0.2	3.2	7.0	10.2

1 As at mid-year.
2 Employees, employers, and the self-employed.

safety and security. It would, clearly, be better for the government to provide industries such as nuclear power and the armed forces rather than allow private entrepreneurs to do so.

(g) Some industries are so important to employment in a particular region, or to other industries in the economy, that they should be helped and even nationalised in a time of financial difficulty. For instance, if a major industry was facing being closed down, this would cause a great deal of unemployment in the region. The government might, therefore, seek to nationalise a company rather than allow this to happen.

(h) The Labour Party tends to be more in favour of nationalisation than other political parties. Supporters of the Labour Party believe in more government intervention in the economy to aid the redistribution of wealth and income from rich to poor and to ensure that industry is run for the benefit of all the people in the country.

(i) There are also social arguments for nationalisation on the grounds that some services, such as health services, should be available to *all* members of society, either free or at subsidised prices.

Arguments against nationalisation

(a) Nationalised industries suffer from being too big. They suffer the diseconomies of large-scale production, such as too much 'red tape', little personal service to staff and consumers, slow decision-making and little profit motive among managers and labour force.

(b) Nationalised industries are public monopolies and are therefore equally as bad as private monopolies. They charge high prices for a poor service.

(c) Nationalised industries are constantly in the 'public eye'. The affairs have to be made public, there is an annual debate in Parliament and managers may be interviewed by parliamentary committees. Therefore managers are afraid of making risky and imaginative decisions in case of failure.

(d) The Conservative Party argues more in favour of private enterprise which they believe to be a more efficient economic system. They dislike nationalisation because it involves government interference in the economy.

(e) Nationalised industries are frequently inefficient and unprofitable. They demand large amounts of finance to keep them in business. Thus they are a drain on the taxpayer.

The Conservative governments of Mrs Thatcher *have been committed to* a policy of denationalisation or privatisation. This involves returning public sector assets to the private sector.

Ownership and control of nationalised industries

Nationalised industries are owned by the people of the United Kingdom and are controlled on their behalf by the government of the day.

Each nationalised industry is subject to an *Act of Parliament* which sets up a framework of organisation which is best suited to the requirements of that particular industry. Nationalised industries are known as public corporations.

Normally a *Government Minister* is appointed to take charge of overall policy applying to the industry. The Minister is subject to any parliamentary questions regarding the affairs of the nationalised industry. The Minister will appoint a *board* and a *chairperson* to take over day-to-day control of the running of the industry. The chairperson usually becomes a national figure and often represents the industry on television and in the newspapers. The board submits an annual report on the affairs of the industry to Parliament and a debate will discuss the report and the industry's affairs. The board of the nationalised industry is theoretically free from government interference and can make decisions regarding staff employment, wage negotiations and investment.

Nationalised industries aim to be accountable to the public who are its owners. They aim to achieve *public accountability* by being answerable to the government and Parliament. They are also subject to the advice of *Consumer Councils*. These have been set up to achieve direct consumer participation in the industry's affairs. Consumer members are nominated by such bodies as trade unions and local authorities. Their main role is to deal with consumer complaints and suggestions, and pass these on to the Minister and the board.

The raising of capital and disposal of profits

The nationalised industries receive most of their finance from the government. The government raises the money in two main ways:

(a) by selling stocks in the nationalised industries on the Stock Exchange. These can be purchased by foreign as well as home investors.
(b) by giving subsidies and grants which will be largely financed out of taxation.

The nationalised industry may also 'plough back' any surplus which it may have made. In the event of a surplus most of this money will be handed over to the government who can then use it to help finance overall government spending. Of course some will be used to pay interest on government securities and perhaps even to lower taxation.

The objectives of nationalised industries

Nationalised industries, unlike private enterprise firms, do not exist solely to make profits. Profit-making is important but they are also expected to provide employment, help the assisted areas, help other industries and provide basic goods and services for the benefit of the nation as a whole. Nationalised industries have three main conflicting objectives:

(a) *To make profits* Nationalised industries do not all make losses. It is true to say that in the late 1970s and the early 1980s, certain industries, such as British Steel and Austin Rover, made large losses. However, other industries, such as the Central Electricity Generating Board made profits.
(b) *The social role* Nationalised industries may be expected to provide unprofitable goods and services because of the social benefits this may give to the community at large. For instance, British Rail may be expected to keep open a loss-making line because it is the only transport link a village has with the

outside world. British Coal may keep open an unprofitable mine to prevent further unemployment in an assisted area.

(c) *Wider economic objectives* The government may expect the industry to consider wider economic objectives in its decision-making. A nationalised industry may be prevented from increasing its prices because of inflation. The industry may be forced to purchase British goods to 'prop up' other home industries.

It is often suggested that nationalised industries should be left to be run by their own managers without government interference. However, in reality, management is often obstructed in achieving objectives by government interference.

Local government

What are the local authorities?
Local authorities provide for mainly local needs. They are obliged to provide certain essential services such as education and police and fire services. They also spend money on other services such as recreational facilities and leisure centres. How much they spend on these other services depends on each individual local authority. However, central government ensures that essential services are provided and lays down standards which have to be met.

Local authorities consist of County Councils and these are subdivided into smaller District Councils which deal with really local affairs.

Ownership and control
The control of local government is in the hands of elected representatives (councillors) who are elected by local people at local government elections. The councillors are then appointed to Council committees which appoint the full-time paid officials to run council affairs on a day-to-day basis. For instance, the Education Committee will appoint the Director of Education who then has day-to-day control over education in the area. The Director of Education is answerable to the education committee and ultimately to the council as a whole. The owners of the local services provided are the local people who elect the council representatives.

Local government finance

Local authorities raise money in the following ways.

The issue of local government stocks
Local authorities issue stocks on the Stock Exchange which pay a fixed rate of interest. They can also borrow from the Public Works Loans Board at low rates of interest and borrow from the banks. This provides long-term capital to provide services such as new road building or new school buildings.

Rates
A rate is a type of tax levied by the local authority on the ownership of land and

buildings. Each unit of land and every building is given a rateable value which is roughly equivalent to its annual letting value. The local authority estimates how much money it is going to spend in the coming year and the Finance Committee estimates how much will have to be financed from the rates. It will then decide a rate of so many pence in the pound of rateable value (known as poundage). If a house has a rateable value of £400, for example, and a rate of 50p in the pound is levied then the householder will be expected to pay an annual rate of £200. Householders must pay their rates. It is an offence not to do so, and, after three months of the first notification of rates, householders will receive a final rate demand. Rates can be paid in one lump sum or by monthly instalments. Rates are the most important source of finance for local authorities. The Ratepayers Association (a non-political organisation) enters candidates in local elections to represent the interests of the ratepayer. Rates are due to be abolished by 1990 in England and Wales and by 1989 in Scotland.

Advantages of rates

(a)   Local authorities have a stable source of revenue. They know exactly how much money can be raised from the rates.

Local authority expenditure

Net, England and Wales 1986-87

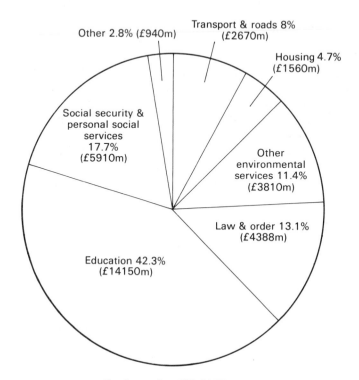

Other 2.8% (£940m)

Transport & roads 8% (£2670m)

Housing 4.7% (£1560m)

Social security & personal social services 17.7% (£5910m)

Other environmental services 11.4% (£3810m)

Law & order 13.1% (£4388m)

Education 42.3% (£14150m)

Total spending £33.4 billion

(b) Householders find it very difficult to avoid payment.
(c) Farm land is not subject to the rates.
(d) It is progressive in the sense that wealthy householders will pay a higher contribution than others.

Disadvantages of rates

(a) The householder's rate bill may increase if he improves his property by, for example, building a new garage. This would increase the rateable value of the property and therefore increase the rate to be paid. This is a discouragement to householders to improve their property.
(b) Rates vary from area to area. The size of rate will depend on the level of local government spending and how many householders there are in a particular area.
(c) Some householders may be paying high rates but are not often using the services provided by the local authorities, such as swimming pools, schools and leisure centres.
(d) People living with parents do not pay rates.
(e) Householders with large families may be paying exactly the same rate, as a householder with no family at all if they live in a house of similar size and location.

Central government grants

Central government will make grants and loans to the local authority. The rate support grant is an important source of revenue for local authorities and it helps keep down the level of rates.

Revenues from the sale of goods and services

When people use leisure centres, squash courts, local football pitches, municipal golf courses, swimming pools, and so on, they pay a charge or fee. These revenues help contribute to the cost of their upkeep and again relieve the ratepayer of some of the burden.

Alternatives to rates

(a) *A poll tax (or community charge)* Everybody within the local authority would pay the same lump sum amount of tax. It would be impossible to avoid but there would have to be exemptions (or rebates available) for children, senior citizens and people on social security. However it would be regressive, for a millionaire would pay the same as a man earning a low income. It would be difficult to collect from that group of people who frequently change accommodation and are difficult to trace. Rebates would involve too much expensive bureaucracy. Some people may attempt to avoid registering and therefore may also lose their voting rights in elections. Households with many adults would lose compared to the present system and many people would be made worse off. The Conservative government re-elected in June 1987 propose to introduce a poll tax (community charge) in England and

Wales in 1990 and in Scotland by 1989. Supporters argue that it is fairer than rates because everybody pays and high income earners still pay higher income tax.

(b) *A local income tax* This could be levied either by the local authority or by the Inland Revenue. Problems would include different workers from different local authorities paying different local income tax. It would also add to the 'Poverty trap' (see page 226), being equivalent to an increase in the basic rate of tax. It would also discourage people from finding jobs. However, it would be progressive (see page 222) for people who are unemployed or very low income earners compared to the present rating system.

(c) *A local sales tax* This could be a percentage tax in addition to VAT (see page 225) but would only be levied at the retail stage. The problem here is that it would be regressive to someone who at the moment does not pay rates or who is a very low income earner. It would also encourage cross-border shopping as consumers in high sales tax areas travel to low sales tax areas for cheaper goods, leading to a waste of time, money and energy for consumers. In addition, local authorities would find it difficult to estimate revenues and the tax would contribute to inflation.

Community charge (poll tax): questions and answers

Answers to the questions that the system will raise

SOME 37 million people would be liable to pay the community charge — more than twice as many as pay rates in England and Wales, Sarah Hogg writes.

However, all those new payers on social security will have to be subsidised by the Government, through higher benefits. Listing everybody, and seeing the tax is paid, are tasks which raise all kinds of problems.

■ Who pays where?
All adults will be liable to pay the community charge in the area where they live, to notify changes of address and to pay the charge in the new area of residence as soon as they move.

■ How are people registered?
It is not proposed to use the electoral register, but to compile a completely separate one. This, like the electoral register, would be based on a household canvass, but then — in theory — continually updated. A separate register is said to be needed because some people — notably foreigners residing here — will have to pay the community charge even though they cannot vote, while others — for example students — may be able to vote even if they are not paying a community charge in their home area. In reality, the register is being kept separate to

avoid the "poll tax" label. However, the electoral register will be available as a cross-check, so the new tax is likely to discourage some people from registering.

■ What if you don't register?
The local authorities will compile the register from a whole variety of sources: their own records, for example, from their own services such as libraries and schools. The will not, however, be allowed access to family practitoner records, social workers' case notes or Inland Revenue or police records. However, when a non-payer is identified he or she can be fined for failing to register — and back-taxed.

■ Where do students pay?
All those over 18 (or 19, if they are still at school) will be charged: students living away from home will normally be charged as if they resided the whole year at their college or university.

■ Who fills in the forms?
A "responsible person" in each household will be required to respond to the regular canvass. In the Green Paper it was proposed to make non-compliance a criminal offence, but this has been watered down to the risk of a civil penalty. The Government has also changed its mind about requiring "responsible people" to

inform the authorities the minute someone joins the household.

■ What about lodgings?
A collective charge will be levied on, for example, boarding houses and other landlords with a shifting population of tenants — but the Department of the Environment is determined to prevent this being used too widely, for fear of reducing "accountability".

■ And second homes?
The community charge idea breaks down here, because the DoE does not want to lose rate revenue on second homes and empty property. So charges for every adult will be levied in the area of people's "main residence"; but for second homes, people will simply be taxed at twice the community charge for the area. Local authorities will, however, be empowered to charge less — for example for caravans and holiday homes.

■ Who escapes?
According to the latest DoE paper, only convicted prisoners and resident hospital patients. But the Government is under pressure to extend this category.

■ What if you can't pay?
Those on social security will be sheltered from the effect of the community charge through the benefits system, but it is still un-

clear how complete this protection will be. Because the community charge may vary widely, it is very complicated to match it through a national benefits system. The Government wants to achieve "accountability" by making as many people as possible pay some part of the charge, but the system is likely to work with some pretty rough justice.

■ Who pays the bill?
Husbands and wives will each be charged individually. However, because many households have only one income-earner, the DoE proposes to make married couples liable for each other's community charge — and may extend this to unmarried couples living together, too.

■ How often will we pay?
It will be assumed that everybody would prefer to pay by instalments (at present only about half of all ratepayers take up this right), and local authorities will try and persuade as many people as possible to pay by standing order.

■ What happens if you don't pay?
If, after the usual business of issuing reminders, local authorities are not getting their money, they can recover it through the magistrates' court. As with rates, the debt can then be recovered by seizing goods. But the DoE also intends to build in authority for payments to be deducted by instalments from a person's earnings. It will also "carry over" the last-ditch authority that exists at present to send people to prison for non-payment of rates.

Privatisation

During the 1980s the Thatcher Conservative government pursued a policy of denationalisation or privatisation.

Publically owned assets which have been sold or are to be sold (as at April 1988)

Already sold (in whole or in part)
Amersham International
Associated British Ports
British Aerospace
British Airports Authority
British Airways
British Gas
British Petroleum
British Rail Hotels
British Sugar Corporation
British Technology Assets
British Telecom
Britoil
Cable and Wireless
Enterprise Oil
Inter Aeradio
Jaguar
National Freight Corporation
Rolls-Royce (aero-engines)
Royal Ordnance Factories
Sealink
Unipart
Wytch Farm

To be sold
British Shipbuilders
British Steel Corporation
Electricity
National Bus Company
Rover Group
Water authorities

Arguments for privatisation

(a) Industries are returned to competitive market conditions and are driven by the profit motive. This leads to more efficiency and public monopolies are destroyed.
(b) Management is freed from government interference in decision-making.
(c) Being part of the private enterprise sector these industries are able to raise more finance from private investors.
(d) Trade unions are no longer able to treat the industry as a 'soft touch' or operate restrictive practices.
(e) The financial burden on the taxpayer is reduced. The government's PSBR (see page 228) is reduced and revenue is generated from the sale.
(f) The market mechanism is allowed to operate freely to allocate resources.

Arguments against privatisation

(a) Public monopolies are being replaced by private monopolies, eg British

Telecom and British Gas. Thus there is no increase in competition.

(b) Returning these industries to private enterprise may mean all other considerations (eg jobs and quality of service) are subordinated to the pursuit of profit.

(c) Only the profitable parts of the public sector can be sold off. Thus the loss-making parts will remain a drain on the tax payer.

(d) Those industries sold off have been sold too cheaply allowing private investors to make speculative profits (eg British Telecom).

(e) The revenues generated by the profitable industries will be lost to the Exchequer forever.

Checkpoints

1 The public enterprise sector of the United Kingdom's mixed economy is owned and controlled by the government. It consists of public services (like education and health), local authority services and nationalised industries (public corporations).

2 Nationalised industries have advantages and disadvantages.

3 Nationalised industries are owned and controlled by the government and their methods for raising finance and disposing of surpluses differ from those of private enterprise firms.

4 Nationalised industries are faced with a great difficulty. They are expected to make a profit while at the same time providing a public service and are subjected to government interference in decision-making.

5 Local government is a distinct part of public enterprise. It raises revenue largely from rates. Rates are subject to much criticism and will be reformed and replaced by a community charge (poll tax).

6 The Thatcher Conservative government embarked on a programme of privatisation (or de-nationalisation) believing that private enterprise is better than public enterprise as a method of allocating scarce resources.

Multiple-choice questions – 5

1   Which of the following is *not* part of public enterprise activity in the United Kingdom economy?

    A   the Bank of England
    B   the Health Service
    C   the BBC
    D   cross-Channel ferry services
    E   postal delivery

2   The total rateable value of property in a local authority is £5 million. After allowing for other sources of revenue the authority has to raise £2½ million. What rate poundage must the local authority set?

    A   10p in the pound
    B   20p in the pound
    C   50p in the pound
    D   150p in the pound
    E   200p in the pound

3   Which of the following organisations is to be found in the state sector of the United Kingdom economy?

    A   Public companies
    B   Public corporations
    C   Co-operative Societies
    D   Discount houses
    E   Insurance companies

4   Which of the following would *not* be a reason for the government nationalising an industry?

    A   to increase dividends for shareholders
    B   to control a private monopoly
    C   to safeguard a strategic industry
    D   to provide the good or service more efficiently on a national basis
    E   to prevent unemployment in the industry

5   Which of the following is a source of local authority revenues?

    A   Corporation tax
    B   Value added tax
    C   Sales of debentures
    D   Surpluses made by state-owned industries
    E   Rate support grant

6   The main difference between a public company and a public corporation is that

A the former is always small, the latter usually much larger
B the former only raises capital through the Stock Exchange, the latter only from the tax payer
C the former is controlled by the government, the latter by shareholders
D the former is part of private enterprise whilst the latter is publicly owned
E there is no difference since both organisations are the same

7 A public corporation comes into existence by means of

A registration under the Companies Acts
B a separate Act of Parliament for each one
C a national referendum
D a decision made by shareholders
E the wishes of the Stock Exchange

8 One of the greatest problems of a nationalised industry is likely to be that

A the government doesn't interfere enough
B the industry will be short of revenue
C it has no social role
D it must not make a profit.
E workers and managers lack incentives

9 Which one of the following statements is an argument in favour of rates?

A people who pay the highest rates use local services more
B they are usually regressive
C different local authorities raise the same amounts of finance
D they provide local authorities with an independent source of revenue
E it encourages people to improve the quality of their homes

10 Which of the following has *not* been privatised by the government?

A British Rail
B British Airways
C British Gas
D British Telecom
E Rolls-Royce (Aero Engines)

Answers on page 328.

Data response question 5

Stags to cash in on Rolls

ROLLS-ROYCE plc

OFFER FOR SALE

by

SAMUEL MONTAGU & CO. LIMITED

on behalf of

THE SECRETARY OF STATE FOR

TRADE AND INDUSTRY

of up to 801,470,588 Ordinary Shares
of 20p each at 170p per Share

of which 85p is payable on application
and 85p on 23rd September 1987

SHARES in Rolls-Royce are expected to be heavily stagged when dealings in the aero-engine manufacturer re-open on 19 May. The City expects that first-day profit-takers will enjoy a premium of between 15p and 30p — a profit of as much as 35 per cent on the 85p part-paid issue price.

With the initial premiums of the British Airways and British Gas issues still fresh in the public mind, the momentum of both the Government's privatisation programme and the current record bull market are likely to generate substantial oversubscription for the £1.36 billion offer.

Only some 40 per cent of the 801 million Rolls-Royce shares on offer are earmarked for private investors. But a clawback from institutions, representing 10 per cent of the offer in the event of it being more than twice subscribed, is more than likely to be triggered.

In order to answer some of these questions you will need to refer to Chapter 12 on the Stock Exchange.

(a) (i) Which issuing house (merchant bank) is supervising the privatisation of Rolls-Royce?
(ii) How many shares are the government selling and at what *final* price?
(iii) How much premium will first day profit taken enjoy (according to the article)?
(iv) What is meant by '85p part-paid issue price' of shares?
(v) How much more per share will shareholders have to pay on 23 September 1987?

(b) What is the meaning of the headline 'Stags to cash in on Rolls'?

(c) (i) Explain the meaning of a *bull market*
(ii) Explain an oversubscription for shares

(d) What are the distinguishing features of a PLC compared with a public corporation?

(e) (i) By what method is this new issue of shares being sold?
(ii) Name two other methods of selling new issues of shares.

(f) What are the advantages and disadvantages of purchasing ordinary shares for the shareholder?

(g) Give two advantages and two disadvantages of privatising a nationalised industry.

6 The market economy: supply, demand and price

The price mechanism is the theoretical basis for the market or price economy which is discussed in Chapter 1.

Preliminary definitions and assumptions

Price and value
Price is not the same as value. The value consumers give to a good varies from person to person. The value of a good can be measured in terms of what a person is willing to give up to satisfy his or her want for that good. The more a person is willing to give up to satisfy the want the greater the value given to the good. Only economic goods (ie, goods which are limited in supply) will have value. Free goods, such as fresh air, are easily supplied and, in consequence, have no economic value.

Prices are the market values of goods and services consumers buy. The price indicates the value of a good or service, measured in terms of a monetary unit. Moreover, prices indicate the different rates at which goods can be exchanged. For example, if a quantity of apples is exactly the same price as an equal quantity of oranges then the value of apples is equal to the value of oranges. On the other hand, if oranges have a price twice that of apples then they have twice the value of apples.

The market
Prices are determined in the market by the forces of supply and demand. Indeed a market can be defined as a situation where demanders and suppliers are in contact with each other. A market need not be a building (like the Stock Exchange) or a traditional Saturday morning market. A market could be a national market for a good and the many buyers and sellers might never actually come into face-to-face contact with each other. The importance of the market is that it is where price is determined.

Assumptions
It would be very difficult to examine the process of the price mechanism in the real world because economic conditions are constantly changing. For instance, governments interfere with the working of the economy by raising taxes and spending, and consumer tastes are always changing.

In order to simplify our analysis we shall assume the following points apply.

(a) *A perfect market* The market consists of many small sellers and buyers and no single seller or buyer can influence prices.

(b) *Perfect knowledge* All buyers and sellers have perfect knowledge about all other buyers and sellers.

(c) *Perfect mobility of factors of production* Land, labour, capital and enterprise are freely available.

(d) *Freedom of entry and exit* Producers can enter or leave the industry at will.

(e) *Laissez-faire economy* There is no government interference in the economy.

(f) *Homogeṇous product* The quality and price of all goods is the same, for instance, that of all oranges is the same as all other oranges.

Students might assume that perfect competition creates a totally unreal and false picture about what actually happens in the real world. To an extent this is true. However, the alternative would be no study of the price mechanism at all. Moreover, many of the conclusions we will reach in theory do actually transmit to the real economy. Let us now examine two factors which determine prices in market: demand and supply.

Demand

The meaning of demand
Demand is the quantity of a good or service which buyers are prepared to buy at a given moment and at a given price. Demand is not the same as a desire, or a need or want. Demand implies the ability to purchase the good or service – it is *effective demand* (or *wants*) backed up by money.

Demand schedules and demand curves
Generally the higher the price of a good or service, the less will be demanded. The lower the price, the more will be demanded. It is possible to compile an individual's demand schedule for a commodity (a demand schedule is a table setting out the quantities that would be bought at various prices). Consider this example of an individual's demand schedule for a particular good.

Price	Quantity demanded
£1.00	5
£0.80	8
£0.60	12
£0.40	18
£0.20	28

We can see here that as the price of the good dropped, the person's demand increased. Of course, there are more consumers in the market and if we add all the individual demand schedules together we can construct a *composite* or *market demand schedule for the good.*

Price	Quantity demanded
£1.00	100
£0.80	180
£0.60	300
£0.40	450
£0.20	650

This information can be shown graphically in the form of a demand curve. It is very important to note that the *demand curve falls downwards from left to right* and it indicates that at high prices there is low demand and at low prices there is high demand.

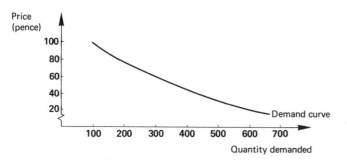

Utility

The theory of diminishing marginal utility attempts to explain the shape of the demand curve and why consumers purchase less when prices are high and more when prices are low.

The distinction between total utility and marginal utility

Total utility refers to the *total satisfaction* derived from consuming a certain good or service. Normally the more of the good or service a person consumes, the greater will be the total utility or satisfaction.

Marginal utility refers to the *satisfaction gained from consuming an additional unit* (the marginal unit) of the good or service. It is apparent that as a person consumes additional units of a good or service the marginal utility of the good or service diminishes. This can easily be explained by an example. A man has been lost in the desert for two days and arrives at an oasis where soft drinks are available. The first bottle of the drink gives the man a great deal of satisfaction, the next bottle gives satisfaction but not as much as the first bottle, the third bottle gives satisfaction but not as much as the second bottle, and so it continues. This state of affairs would apply to most people's consumption of most goods and services.

It is possible for marginal utility to become zero if a point of consumption is

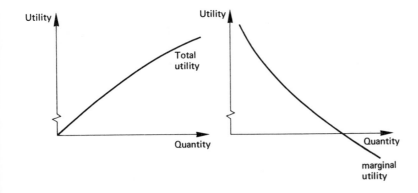

reached where no more satisfaction is gained from further units. Indeed marginal utility may become negative. For instance, if *an individual* drank too many soft drinks the side effects could be very unpleasant. However, rational consumers would never consume a good or service which gave them negative utility although free goods will be consumed up to the point of zero marginal utility.

The principle of equi-marginal utility
An individual will allocate expenditure between two goods so that *the satisfaction of the last penny spent on each is equal*. At this point the individual is maximising utility and has no desire to buy more or less of either good. This can be illustrated by the formula:

$$\frac{\text{Marginal utility of good A}}{\text{Price of good A}} = \frac{\text{Marginal utility of good B}}{\text{Price of good B}}$$

Assume the individual gains 100 satisfaction from good A and 200 satisfaction from good B. Assume the price of good A is 10p and good B 20p. The individual is maximising utility from expenditure because

$$\frac{100}{10} = \frac{200}{20} \qquad 10 = 10$$

However, assume that the price of good B now rises to 40p. The individual is no longer maximising utility because

$$\frac{100}{10} \text{ is more than } \frac{200}{40} \qquad 10 \text{ is more than } 5$$

To get back to a situation where there is maximising of utility, the individual would purchase less of good B which will increase marginal utility, since according to the theory of diminishing marginal utility as the individual purchases less units then marginal utility will rise. This will eventually bring the individual back to a situation where utility is maximised when marginal utility of B is 400.

$$\frac{100}{10} = \frac{400}{40} \qquad 10 = 10$$

This is called the principle of equi-marginal utility and explains consumer behaviour as illustrated by the downward sloping demand curve. As the price increases less of the good will be demanded.

There are several criticisms of the theory of diminishing marginal utility. Perhaps most important of these is that numerical values are being allocated to the consumer's satisfaction in consuming units of goods. This is very difficult to do accurately, and, although we all have a scale of preferences, we probably do not give numerical scores to the goods and services we consume. The theory also ignores the effects of income changes which will also affect demand for goods and services.

Changes in demand
If the price of the good increases or decreases then the consumer will merely *move*

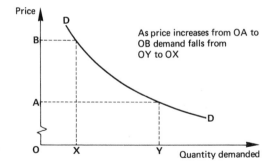

As price increases from OA to OB demand falls from OY to OX

along a demand curve. This means that as the price increases the consumer will demand less and as the price decreases then demand will rise.

However, there could be a *shift* in the demand curve which is caused by changes in the conditions of demand (see below). Normally when we speak of an increase or decrease in demand we are referring to a shift in the curve.

An increase in demand means that at each of the prices there is now an increase in the quantity demanded, which means that the curve shifts to the right.

A decrease in demand means that at each of the prices there is now a decrease in the quantity demanded, which means that the curve shifts to the left.

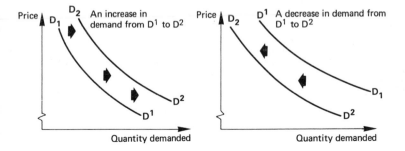

Causes of changes in demand

The demand for a good may alter although there has been no change in price. There are several factors which could cause a change in demand.

(a) *A change in taste or fashion* Consumer tastes and fashions are always changing, especially for clothes.

(b) *Changes in the price of other goods and services* There are two main relationships between goods in which a change in the price of one good will have pronounced effects on the demand for the others. When the goods are *substitutes* (ie, they can be used instead of each other), an increase in the price of one good will cause an increase in demand for the other. For example, if the price of apples increased the demand for oranges will increase. When the goods are *complementary goods* (ie, when they are jointly demanded or demanded together), an increase in the price of one good will decrease the demand for the other. For example, an increase in the price of cars will cause a decline in the demand for petrol.

(c) *Changes in real income* If consumers have more income to spend on goods and services and the increase in their incomes is greater than the increase in prices of goods and services then demand will increase for most goods and services. Moreover, a change in the distribution of income will also change demand. For instance if more income went to young people then demand for goods and services young people purchase, like records and clothes, will increase.

(d) *Advertising* A successful advertising campaign for a certain good will increase demand for it.

(e) *Changes in population* A larger population will mean, all things remaining equal, that demand for most goods and services will increase. Moreover, a change in the distribution of population will also change demand for certain goods and services. For instance more babies in the population will increase demand for prams and nappies.

(f) *Price expectations* If consumers expect the price of a good to increase in the near future they will demand more of the good at the present time. This phenomenon is often seen before the Budget when consumers expect the price of certain goods to increase.

(g) *Availability of credit* If hire-purchase facilities and bank loans were easily and cheaply available then demand for goods and services would increase.

Exceptional demand curves

Giffen goods (named after an economist called Giffen) do not conform to the normal demand curve. Giffen goods include goods of ostentation and goods having snob appeal such as furs, jewellery and works of art. As the price of the goods increases then demand increases.

A demand curve for goods of ostentation

Inferior goods are another type of Giffen good and are goods which will probably be substituted when possible as consumers demand something more desirable. For instance, low-income families may demand certain inferior foodstuffs. However, if the price of the inferior good declines then consumers may purchase less of that good and more of a more desirable foodstuff.

A demand curve for inferior goods

Supply

The meaning of supply
Supply is the quantity of a good or service which is offered for sale at a given moment and at a given price. Supply does not necessarily comprise the entire stock of any commodity in existence but only the amount put on to the market at a given price and at a particular moment in time.

Supply schedules and supply curves
What motivates suppliers in a price economy is profit. Generally, therefore, we would expect more of a good or service to be supplied at a high price, and less of a good or service supplied at a low price.

It is possible to construct a supply schedule for a given good.

Price	Quantity supplied
£1.00	475
£0.80	400
£0.60	300
£0.40	125
£0.20	50

We can see that as price increases the supply of the good increases. This information can be illustrated graphically in the form of a supply curve.

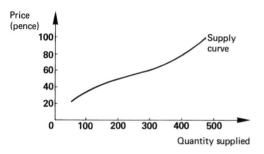

It is very important to note that the *supply curve falls from right to left* and it indicates that at high prices there is high supply and at low prices there is low supply.

Changes in supply

If the price of a good increases or decreases then the supplier of a good will merely *move along* a supply curve. This means that as price increases suppliers will supply more.

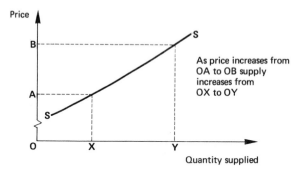

As price increases from OA to OB supply increases from OX to OY

However there could be a *shift* in the supply curve which is caused by changes in the conditions of supply (see below). Normally when we speak of an increase or decrease in supply we are referring to a shift in the curve.

An increase in supply

An increase in supply means that at each of the prices there is now an increase in the quantity supplied, which means that the curve shifts to the right.

A decrease in supply

A decrease in supply means that at each of the prices there is now a decrease in quantity supplied, which means that the curve shifts to the left.

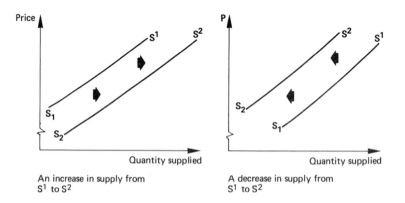

An increase in supply from
S^1 to S^2

A decrease in supply from
S^1 to S^2

Causes of changes in supply

The supply of a good may alter although there has been no change in price. There are several factors which may cause a change in supply.

(a)   *Changes in the cost of production* There are various production costs involved in the production of anything, such as wages, rents, and the price of raw materials. When production costs fall it costs less to produce the same quantity or, looking at it another way, more can be produced and supplied at the old price and the supply curve will shift to the right. An increase in costs will mean less is supplied and the supply curve shifts to the left.

(b)   *Changes in climate* (eg, storms, floods). The weather is especially important to the supply of agricultural goods. A bad harvest will mean that the supply curve will shift to the left as less of the good is supplied. A good harvest will shift the supply curve to the right.

(c)   *Technical progress* New inventions may improve production methods and therefore decrease production costs. Therefore, more can be supplied and the supply curve will shift to the right. A war might mean less technology is available, supply of some goods would, therefore, drop and the curve will shift to the left.

(d)   *Taxation and subsidies* An increase in the taxation of a good is equivalent to an increase in its costs of production. Therefore, this may decrease supply and shift the supply curve to the left. A subsidy will tend to increase supply because it makes production cheaper. Thus the supply curve will shift to the right.

The time factor in supply

There is a difference between supply in the momentary period, the short run and in the long run. In the momentary period supply tends to be absolutely fixed and therefore any change in demand will cause a large change in prices. In the short run, supply can respond to a certain extent by releasing or adding to stocks or labour working more or less overtime. Thus the change in price is not so marked as in the momentary period. In the long run, supply can be extensively increased or decreased and, therefore, the supply changes can to a great extent counteract demand changes and reduce their effects on price.

Equilibrium (or market) price

The meaning of equilibrium price

The market or equilibrium price is determined in the market by the forces of demand and supply. Equilibrium is the point where economic forces obtain economic balance and it exists where there are no influences tending to change any of the factors involved in it. Equilibrium price is the price at which the good or service will be sold in the market.

Let us illustrate equilibrium by using the supply and demand schedules already established.

Price	Quantity demanded	Quantity supplied
£1.00	100	475
£0.80	180	400
£0.60	300	300
£0.40	450	125
£0.20	650	50

Here we can see that equilibrium price will be established at £0.60 where 300 units are demanded by consumers and 300 supplied by suppliers. This information can be illustrated graphically.

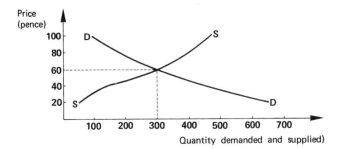

Supply and demand are in balance at a price of £0.60 and at a quantity of 300 units.

What would happen if suppliers tried to charge a price of £0.80 for the good?
If a price of 80p was charged for the good, supply would exceed demand, there would be a glut of the good on the market and this would decrease the price. Price would settle back at equilibrium.

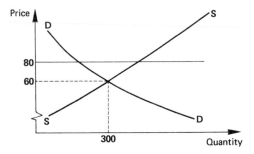

What would happen if the price was £0.40 for the good?
If a price of 40p was charged for the good, supply would be less than demand, there would be a shortage of the good on the market and this would increase the price. Price would settle back at equilibrium.

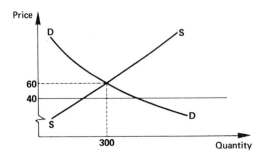

Changes in demand and supply and their effect on equilibrium
Assume an increase in demand

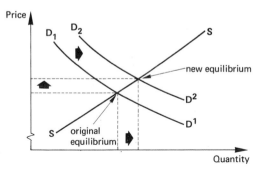

An increase in demand will shift the demand curve to the right. The results will be a higher equilibrium price and a greater quantity supplied. For example, an increase in demand for milk, all other factors remaining equal, will cause an increase in the price of milk and a greater quantity supplied by dairy farmers.

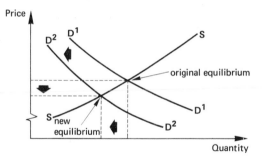

Assume a decrease in demand
A decrease in demand will shift the demand curve to the left. The result will be a lower equilibrium price and a lesser quantity supplied. For example, a decrease in demand for cars, all other factors remaining equal, will cause a decrease in the price of cars and a lesser quantity of cars supplied.

Assume an increase in supply
An increase in supply will shift the supply curve to the right. The result will be a

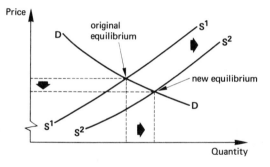

lower equilibrium price and a greater quantity demanded. For example an increase in the supply of petrol, all other factors remaining equal, will cause a decrease in the price of petrol and a greater quantity of petrol demanded.

Assume a decrease in supply
A decrease in supply will shift the supply curve to the left. The result will be a higher equilibrium price and a lesser quantity demanded. For example, a decrease in the supply of coffee will cause an increase in the price of coffee and a lesser quantity demanded.

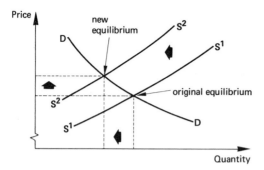

The operation of the price mechanism
What will happen to the price of potatoes if potato blight ruins the crop?
A disease of potatoes will affect the supply of potatoes. The supply of potatoes will diminish which will shift the supply curve to the left. The result will be an increase in the price of potatoes.

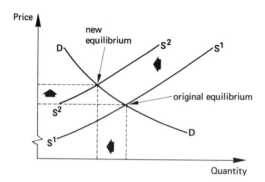

What will happen to the price of petrol if the demand for cars decreases?
A decrease in demand for cars may be due to falling living standards or higher prices for cars. A drop in demand for cars will decrease demand for petrol because they are complementary goods and the price of petrol will drop.

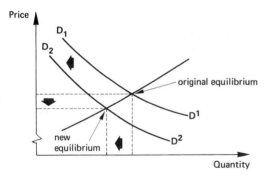

What will happen to the price of coffee if the demand for tea increases?
Tea and coffee are substitutes. An increase in demand for tea will mean that less coffee will be demanded. A drop in demand for coffee will cause lower prices for coffee.

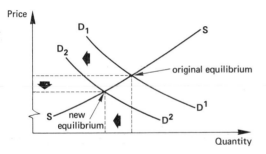

What will happen to the price of synthetic fibres if the demand for crude oil increases?
Synthetic fibres and crude oil are jointly supplied. This means that an increase in the supply of crude oil automatically increases the supply of synthetic fibres. Thus an increase in the demand for crude oil will cause its price to rise and more to be supplied. This will mean that the supply of synthetic fibres will increase and prices of synthetic fibres will drop.

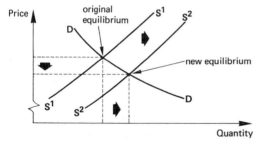

There are many other everyday examples of the price mechanism in operation.

The role of prices in a price mechanism

The price or market mechanism is a means whereby resources (factors of production) are allocated by price which is determined by supply and demand. The price mechanism is the theoretical basis of the market economy, which is discussed in detail in Chapter 1.

(a) *Price is the signal, in such a mechanism, to private entrepreneurs as to where resources should be allocated.* If the price of apples is rising and the price of oranges falling then entrepreneurs will begin to grow more apples and less oranges. The price signal is determined by demand and supply. If demand increases, then, all things remaining equal, price will increase; if supply increases, then, all things remaining equal, price will decline. Prices are determined in the market.

(b) The price also indicates changes in consumer wants. For instance, if people want more apples than oranges, then demand for apples will rise and demand for oranges will fall. The consumer is king in the price mechanism because changes in demand cause changes in price.

(c) Price changes will also bring about changes in supply to correspond with the change in demand. For instance, if people want more apples then the price of apples will rise and suppliers will supply more apples because they have become more profitable. The consumers by changing their demand have caused a change in supply. This is what is meant by the consumer being described as 'king'.

Elasticity

Price elasticity of demand

What is meant by elasticity of demand?

As we have seen, as price falls demand increases. However, the extent to which the quantity demanded changes, in response to a price change, does vary. If a slight change in price causes a big change in the quantity demanded, then demand is said to be elastic. If, however, a fairly considerable change in price makes little difference to the quantity demanded, then demand is inelastic. *Elasticity of demand* means the degree of responsiveness of demand to changes in price.

Different elasticities of demand

Perfectly (or absolutely) inelastic demand

Here demand remains the same whatever the price.

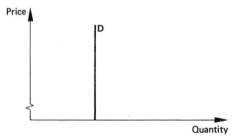

Inelastic demand
If the rate at which demand rises (or falls) is less than the rate at which price falls
(or rises) then demand is inelastic.

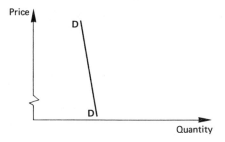

Unity elastic demand
If the rate at which demand rises (or falls) is equal to the rate at which price falls
(or rises) then demand is unity elastic.

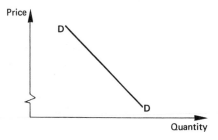

Elastic demand
If the rate at which demand rises (or falls) is greater than the rate at which price
falls (or rises) then demand is elastic.

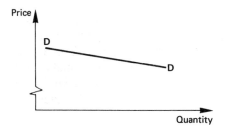

Perfectly (or absolutely) elastic demand
Here demand is infinitely responsive to any price change, however small.

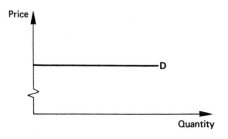

Factors influencing elasticity of demand

(a) *The possibility of substitution* If there are close substitutes for a good, its demand is likely to be more elastic. For example, a rise in the price of beef will cause more people to eat pork, or a rise in the price of tea will cause people to drink more coffee. If there are no close substitutes within the same price range, the demand for a commodity is more likely to be inelastic.

(b) *The case of complementary goods* Complementary goods are those which complement each other, such as bread and butter, pens and ink, and motor cars and petrol. Usually an increase in demand for one causes an increase in demand for the other. If the price of one falls then its demand may be inelastic if the price of the other good has risen.

(c) *Degree of necessity* Necessities tend to have inelastic demand (if they have no close substitutes). Luxuries may have an elastic demand (if they have substitutes). However, luxuries could have inelastic demand if they have no substitutes.

(d) *Cheap commodities* The smaller the proportion of total income spent on a commodity, the more inelastic will be demand for it. For example, a rise in the price of mustard will not stop people buying mustard because they only buy it now and again, and it does not account for a great deal of a person's expenditure.

(e) *Habit* Because of habit, people may be accustomed to buying a particular good or brand of good and may be reluctant to change even if prices increase. Demand is inelastic for such goods (eg, tobacco and alcohol).

Practical use of elasticity

(a) If a manufacturer can estimate the elasticity of demand for goods he or she may be able to increase profits. For example, if demand is relatively inelastic, the manufacturer may be able to increase prices, or if it is very elastic, decrease prices. In both cases more revenue will be made and profit will probably be increased.

(b) If the Chancellor of the Exchequer increases taxes on a good with inelastic demand, demand will remain the same and increase tax revenue. However, if he taxes a good with elastic demand this may cause demand to decrease greatly and tax revenue will be less than before.

The measurement of elasticity of demand
Elasticity of demand is measured by the formula:

$$\text{Elasticity of demand} = \frac{\text{proportionate (percentage) change in quantity demanded}}{\text{proportionate (percentage) change in price}}$$

eg take our original demand schedule on page 100, when price falls from 80p to 60p, demand expands from 180 to 300.

$$\text{Proportionate change in quantity} = \frac{120}{180} \quad \cdots \quad \frac{\text{change in quantity}}{\text{original quantity}}$$

$$\text{Proportionate change in price} = \frac{20}{80} \dots \frac{\text{change in price}}{\text{original price}}$$

$$\text{Elasticity of demand} = \frac{120/180}{20/80} = \frac{2/3}{1/4} = \frac{2}{3} \times \frac{4}{1} = 2\frac{2}{3}$$

The numerical value of elasticity corresponds with one of the categories of elasticity. It enables a producer to know what the elasticity is for the good and act accordingly.

Numerical value of elasticity	Type of elasticity of demand
0	Perfectly inelastic
between 0 and 1	Inelastic
1	Unity
between 1 and infinity	Elastic
infinity	Perfectly elastic

In our calculation above the value of elasticity was 2⅔ when price fell from 80p to 60p. Demand is elastic and the producer would be advised to decrease prices to increase revenues.

Income elasticity of demand
Income elasticity of demand refers to the responsiveness of demand to changes in income. It is measured by the formula:

$$\text{Income elasticity of demand} = \frac{\text{percentage change in quantity demanded}}{\text{percentage change in income}}$$

There are five possible categories of income elasticity. These are:

(a) *negative*: Income increases but demand for the good decreases, as in the case of inferior goods. This has a negative numerical value.
(b) *zero*: Income increases but demand remains the same as in the case of salt and pepper.
 This has a zero numerical value.
(c) *inelastic*: Income increases and demand increases by a smaller proportion, as with necessities such as basic foodstuffs. This has a numerical value of between 0 and 1.
(d) *unity*: Income increases and demand increases by the same proportion. This has a numerical value of 1.
(e) *elastic*: Income increases and demand increases by a greater proportion, as with luxuries. This has a numerical value of more than 1.

Of course a person's income elasticity of demand for a particular commodity will depend on their present standard of living. For instance, a millionaire will probably have zero income elasticity for all goods.
 A knowledge of income elasticity is very important when planning ahead for social and industrial requirements. If a manufacturer knows that demand for the

good being manufactured is income elastic, and an increase in consumers' incomes is anticipated, then the manufacturer can plan to increase production.

Cross elasticity of demand

Cross elasticity of demand refers to the responsiveness of demand for one good to a change in the price of another good. It is measured by the formula:

$$\text{Cross elasticity of demand} = \frac{\text{percentage change in demand for good A}}{\text{percentage change in price of good B}}$$

If good A and good B are substitutes then the answer will be a positive (+) answer because an increase in the price of good B will cause demand for good A to increase. The nearer the goods are as substitutes, the larger the positive answer.

If good A and good B are complements the answer will be a negative (−) answer because an increase in the price of good B will cause a decline in demand for good A. The closer the goods are as complements, the larger will be the negative answer. It is useful for manufacturers to know the cross elasticity of demand for the good they produce because they can anticipate any changes in demand for the good as a result of changes in the price of other goods.

Elasticity of supply

What is meant by elasticity of supply?

Elasticity of supply shows the responsiveness of supply to a change in price We have seen that as price increases for a good then manufacturers will supply more. There is a direct relationship between price and quantity supplied. However, like demand, supply might rise a great deal in response to an increase in price, in which case, supply is said to be elastic. Conversely supply might rise only a little in response to increase in price, in which case supply is said to be inelastic.

Different elasticities of supply

Perfectly (or absolutely) inelastic supply

Supply remains the same despite an increase (or decrease) in price.

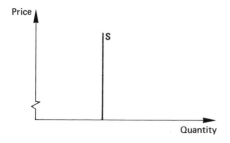

Inelastic supply

If the rate at which supply rises (or falls) is less than the rise (or fall) in price, then supply is inelastic.

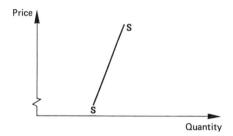

Unity elastic supply
If the rate at which supply rises (or falls) is equal to the rise (or fall) in price, then supply is unity.

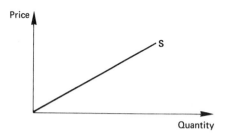

Elastic supply
If the rate at which supply rises (or falls) is greater than the rise (or fall) in price, then supply is elastic.

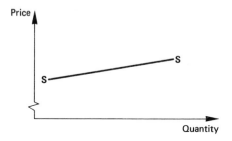

Perfectly (or absolutely) elastic supply
Here supply is infinitely responsive to any price change however small.

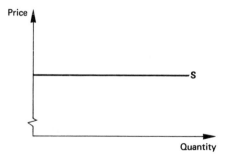

Measuring elasticity of supply

Elasticity of supply is measured by the formula:

$$\text{Elasticity of supply} = \frac{\text{proportionate (percentage) change in quantity supplied}}{\text{proportionate (percentage) change in price}}$$

The numerical value of elasticity of supply corresponds with one of the categories of elasticity.

Numerical value of elasticity	Type of elasticity of supply
0	Perfectly inelastic
between 0 and 1	Inelastic
1	Unity
between 1 and infinity	Elastic
infinity	Perfectly elastic

Manufacturers need to know the elasticity of supply for their goods because they can anticipate the effects on price and supply of any change in demand.

Factors influencing elasticity of supply

If the supply of a good can be expanded or contracted fairly easily in response to any change in price, then it is elastic. If, however, supply remains fairly fixed despite an increase or decrease in price, then supply is inelastic. The following are some factors which will determine the elasticity of supply for a particular good.

(a) *If stocks are carried* If stocks are carried then supply will be relatively more elastic because an increase in demand can be met with an increase in supply.

(b) *If the industry is operating below full capacity* If the industry is operating below full capacity it will be able to use up unused factors of production and, again, an increase in demand will be met with an increase in supply. If, on the other hand, factors of production are already fully employed it will be very difficult to increase supply.

(c) *The ease of attracting factors of production into the industry* If factors of production can be easily attracted to come into the industry then supply will be more elastic.

(d) *The nature of the good and the time period involved* Certain goods are very difficult to increase in supply in the short run whereas others can be fairly easily increased in supply. There are three main time periods: the momentary period, the short run and the long run.

The momentary period

This is the immediate period when demand has changed. All goods would tend to have an absolutely inelastic supply during this period because there is no time for manufacturers to respond. For instance, if the demand for apples increases in the fruit market today, supply will not increase because deliveries were made earlier in the day.

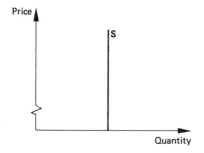

Here supply on any one day (one momentary period) is absolutely fixed or inelastic.

Short run
The short-run period is when there are fixed factors of production, such as land and capital, which cannot be increased or decreased in supply, and variable factors, such as labour and raw materials, which can be increased or decreased in supply. The length of time of the short period varies according to the industry in question. For instance, the short run for fruit will be a few days whereas for steel it may be a period of months or years.

Supply for most goods tends to be more elastic in the short run. This is because workers can work overtime and stocks can be released. How elastic supply is in the short run will depend on the nature of the good. For instance, the supply of manufactured rubber is likely to be more elastic than natural rubber.

In the short run supply can become more elastic as stocks are released and variable factors of production are increased.

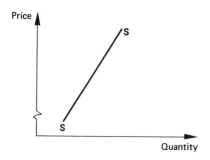

Long run
The long run is when all factors of production become variable, even land and capital. Therefore, supply can be increased or decreased substantially to correspond with the change in demand. For instance, more apple trees have been planted and are supplying fruit, more rubber trees have been planted and are supplying rubber. Again, the long period varies according to the industry. The long run for tomatoes may be one year, but for natural rubber it may be up to seven years. In the long run a new supply curve exists which will have even more effect on price.

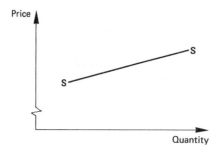

In the long run supply becomes even more elastic since all factors of production are variable and can be increased.

In order to illustrate the effects of the time period on elasticity of supply and on price let us consider this question. 'How will an increase in demand for tomatoes affect their price?'

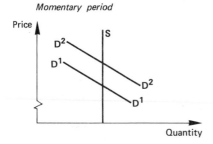

Momentary period
Demand for tomatoes increases in the momentary period. Supply of tomatoes is absolutely inelastic and price increases by a large amount.

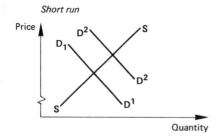

Short run
In the short run more tomatoes can be picked by workers working overtime. Thus price drops a little, compared to the momentary period, since supply is more responsive.

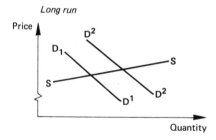

Long run

Long run

In the long run many more tomatoes can be supplied because more tomato plants can be grown. This supply is more elastic and the price of tomatoes falls compared to the short run price.

Checkpoints

1 The market economy is based on the operation of the price mechanism which involves the interaction of demand and supply to determine price.

2 Demand is often presented as a downward sloping demand curve which indicates planned demand at different prices. The shape of the demand curve is explained by the Theory of Utility. Several factors may cause demand to increase or decrease.

3 Supply is presented as an upward sloping supply curve which indicates planned supply at different prices. Several factors may cause supply to increase or decrease.

4 Supply and demand interact in the market place where equilibrium (or market) price is determined. The market price will be the price at which the good or service will be sold. Market price will change if either demand or supply increases or decreases.

5 Prices perform several different functions within the price mechanism, eg allocating scarce resources (factors of production).

6 It is too simple to say that as price increases demand decreases. Elasticity of demand gives more precision to the responsiveness of demand to a change in price. There are four types of elasticity: price elasticity of demand, income elasticity of demand, cross elasticity of demand and elasticity of supply. Elasticity can be calculated in numerical form and will be determined by several different factors.

Multiple-choice questions – 6

1 The diagram below shows a change in the conditions of supply for video recorders in the United Kingdom, in which the supply curve has moved from S¹S¹ to S²S².

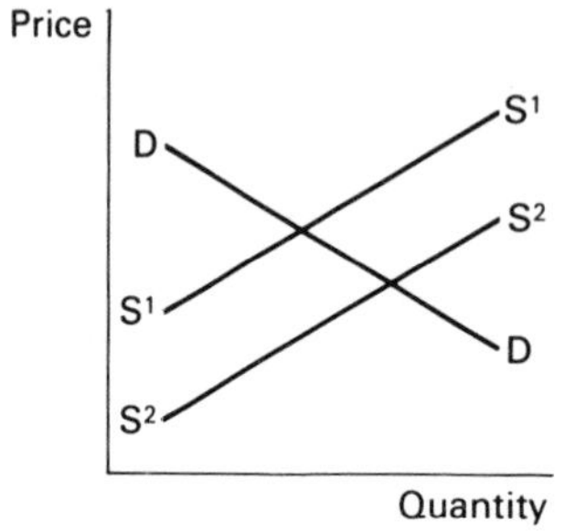

Which of the following is the most likely explanation of this change?

    A a quota is imposed restricting how many video recorders can be imported.

    B an increase in the costs of producing video recorders.

    C an increase in incomes leading to more video recorders being bought.

    D a subsidy to video recorder manufacturers.

    E an increase in the price of video cassettes.

2 Income elasticity of demand is calculated by the formula:

    A $\dfrac{\text{percentage change in income}}{\text{percentage change in quantity demanded}}$

    B $\dfrac{\text{percentage change in price}}{\text{percentage change in income}}$

    C $\dfrac{\text{percentage change in quantity demanded}}{\text{percentage change in income}}$

    D $\dfrac{\text{percentage change in quantity demanded}}{\text{percentage change in price}}$

    E $\dfrac{\text{percentage change in price}}{\text{percentage change in quantity demanded}}$

3 Which of the following products have a complementary demand?

    A apples and oranges

    B crude oil and petrol

    C motorbikes and motor cars

    D video recorders and books

    E video recorders and video cassettes

4   The diagram below shows an increase in demand for apples.

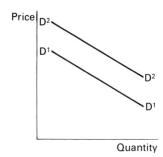

This change could be explained by

   A   a successful advertising campaign to eat more apples
   B   a fall in the price of oranges
   C   more efficient apple production methods
   D   a rise in the costs of producing apples
   E   an increase in imports of apples from the common market

5   A company manufacturing radios found when it lowered its selling price
   from £30 to £20 per unit, the number of radios sold per month increased
   from 100 000 to 140 000. The price elasticity of demand for the company's
   radios was therefore

   A $2/5$
   B $5/6$
   C   1
   D $1^1/5$
   E $1\frac{1}{2}$

6   The following supply and demand schedules are for commodity A.

Price (£)	Demand (tonnes per week)	Supply (tonnes per week)
18	200	750
16	300	500
14	400	400
12	500	300
10	600	100

If supply increases by 200 units at all prices the new equilibrium price for commodity A will be

   A £18
   B £16
   C £14
   D £12
   E £10

7 A movement along a demand curve reflects a change in

   A the price of a substitute product
   B the price of a complementary product
   C price
   D consumer tastes
   E disposable income

8 The diagram below shows a change in the conditions of supply for motor vehicles.

A shift in the supply curve for motor vehicles from SS to S¹S¹ would *not* be caused by

   A a larger tax on new motor vehicles
   B an increase in wages for car workers
   C an increased tariff on imported motor cars
   D an increase in steel prices
   E a successful advertising campaign to purchase new cars

Multiple-choice questions 9 and 10 are based on the table below which gives information about the demand for kiwi fruit and nectarines.

	Kiwi fruit		Nectarines	
	Price (pence per kg)	Quantity demanded per week (kg)	Price (pence per kg)	Quantity demanded per week (kg)
Week 1	20	250	20	200
Week 2	15	300	20	100

9   The cross elasticity of demand between kiwi fruit and nectarines if the price
of kiwi fruit falls from 20p to 15p is

    A ½
    B 1
    C 1½
    D 2
    E 2½

10   The price elasticity of demand for kiwi fruit if the price falls from 20p to 15p
is

    A 0.4
    B 0.8
    C 1
    D 1.4
    E 1.8

Answers on page 328.

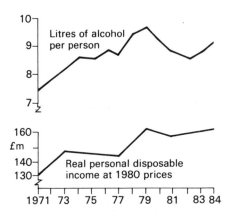

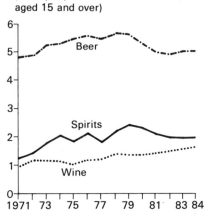

Data response question 6

UK alcohol consumption: by type (litres per person aged 15 and over)

CIGARETTES AND DRINK

Whoopee . . . and woe

THE tax freeze on alcohol and tobacco pleased producers and pubs but was bitterly attacked by the health lobby.

'This is very welcome news, particularly for the lower paid workers,' said a Brewers Society spokesman.

'Whoopee for wines and spirits,' said Mr Nick Gent,

chairman of the Wine and Spirit Association. 'The whole country should pop a cork to celebrate.'

But Action on Alcoholic Abuse said: 'People are encouraged to drink more and absolutely nothing is done to stop the cutback and closures of services trying to deal with the casualties.'

The 'disappointed' British

Medical Association said: 'Countless numbers of people who use the rise in tax to give themselves the incentive to try to stop smoking will be discouraged.'

To answer questions (a) (i) and (b) you will need to refer to page 284.

(a)   (i) What is 'real personal disposable income at 1980 prices'?
    (ii) For which alcoholic drink is demand greatest?
    (iii) Which alcoholic drink is rising in demand?

(b) Explain the inter-relationship between real personal disposable income at 1980 prices and consumption of alcohol.

(c) With the aid of a diagram explain how an increase in tax on cigarettes would affect the
    (i) supply of cigarettes
    (ii) price of cigarettes
    (iii) demand for cigarettes

(d) Both alcohol and cigarettes have a relatively inelastic demand.
   (i) explain this statement
   (ii) draw a demand curve for cigarettes
   (iii) why is this knowledge important to the Chancellor of the Exchequer at Budget time?

(e) Why do some people argue that the Chancellor should increase taxes on alcohol and cigarettes?

(f) Apart from taxation, how else could the government encourage
   (i) sensible drinking habits?
   (ii) reductions in cigarette smoking?

7 The circular flow: national income and economic growth

Factors determining a nation's income and output

The meaning and importance of national income
The national income (Y) is the money value of all goods and services produced in an economy in a particular period of time (usually one year).

The size of Y in a country is very important because it influences the level of employment, the level of prices, the level of output and people's standard of living. Usually an increase in Y will mean more jobs, upward pressures on prices, more output and a better standard of living. A fall in Y will have the opposite effect.

Y is determined by the *total level (or aggregate) demand* in the economy (AD). An economy is in *equilibrium* (ie all opposing forces in balance with no need for change) when

$$Y = AD$$

This is when the supply (or output) of goods and services produced in the economy is equal to the demand for these goods and services. If AD is greater than Y then Y will have to rise. If Y is greater than AD then Y will have to fall. The economy will eventually have to end up at equilibrium.

The circular flow

The circular flow of income in a simple economy where all income is consumed
The operation of forces in an economy can be expressed in the form of a circular flow of incomes and spending between households and firms. A household is a group of people (consumers) earning incomes and spending them on goods and services produced by the firms. In this simple economy we assume that the household spends all income. This spending on consumer goods (termed consumption) (C) is the only component of AD in this simple economy.

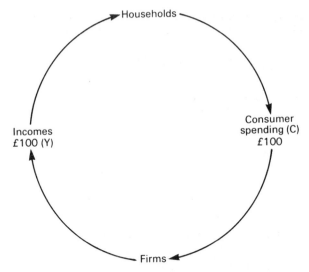

This economy is in equilibrium because

$$Y = AD$$
$$Y = C$$

If Y was greater than C then Y would fall, if Y was less than C then Y would rise.

The circular flow of income in a closed economy

A closed economy exists when there is no international trade. We shall also assume that in this particular closed economy there is no government spending or taxation. Here households have two alternative uses for their income – they can consume it or they can *save it*. Savings are (S). AD consists of C and S.

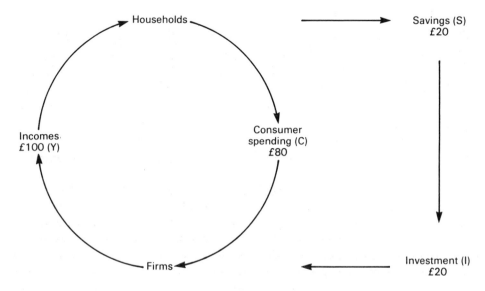

S are lost to Y and will reduce the level of Y. However some (if not all) of S will be used to finance *investment* (I). I is the creation of real capital goods such as machinery and factories, and adds to Y. If S = I then Y is in equilibrium.

In this economy

$$Y = AD$$
$$\text{therefore } Y = C + I$$
$$\text{in equilibrium } S = I$$

However, if S is greater than I then AD and Y will fall. If I is greater than S then AD and Y will rise.

The circular flow of income in an open economy

An open economy is one in which international trade exists. Assume also that there is government spending and taxation.

Thus households need not consume all of their income. Some may be saved (S), spent on imports (M) or taxed (T). S and M and T are known as withdrawals (W) or leakages. An increase in W will reduce the level of Y.

However Y will be added to by *investment* (I), *government spending* (G) and money spent by foreigners on *exports* (X). These are known as *injections* (J).

In an open economy the size of Y is determined by the size of AD which is determined by C + I + G + X.

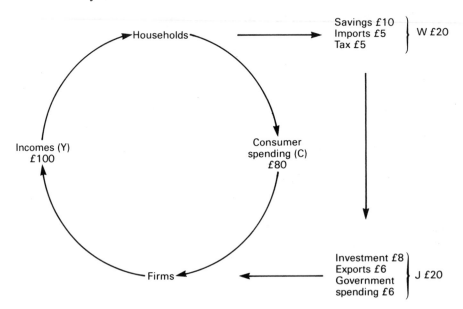

In this economy

$$Y = AD$$
$$\text{Therefore } Y = C + I + G + X$$
$$= C + J$$

In equilibrium J = W. If J was greater than W then Y would rise. If W was greater than J then Y would fall.

The main components of AD
Let us look in more detail at the main components in determining AD. These are consumption (C), investment (I), savings (S), government spending (G), taxation (T), exports (X) and imports (M).

Consumption (C)
Consumption is consumer spending (or expenditure). This is the biggest component of AD and therefore the biggest determinant of the size of Y. C is that spending on domestically produced goods and services. There is a direct relationship between C and Y. As C increases so does Y (and vice versa).

Determinants of C

(a) *The size of income* As Y rises so will C. However, the relationship between Y and C is not so clear cut. An increase in Y will cause C to increase by a proportionately lower amount. The proportion of an increase in Y which is consumed is termed the *marginal propensity to consume* (MPC). MPC will fall as a country's (or individual's) Y increases. The average propensity of Y which is consumed is termed the *average propensity to consume* (APC) and this also declines as Y increases.

$$\text{MPC} = \frac{\text{change in C}}{\text{change in Y}} \quad \text{APC} = \frac{\text{C}}{\text{Y}}$$

(b) *The distribution of income* High income consumers spend more than low income consumers. However MPC and APC both decline as Y increases. A redistribution of Y from high income to low income consumers will increase C.

(c) *Cost of credit* High interest rates on loans will reduce the level of C.

(d) *Availability of credit* If credit is generally available from banks and hire-purchase companies then the level of C will rise.

(e) *Government policy* Government fiscal policy will affect C. If the government operates a progressive tax system and spends money on welfare payments to the poor then C will increase. This is because low income earners have a high MPC.

Savings
Savings is a withdrawal from Y, and an increase in S will reduce the size of Y. S is that part of Y, in a closed economy, which is not spent on C. S includes buying securities and depositing money with financial institutions (banks, building societies, and so on).

Determinants of S

(a) *The size of income* As Y rises then so will S. However, as with C, the relationship between Y and S is not clear cut. An increase in Y will cause S to increase by a proportionately greater amount. The proportion of an increase in Y which is saved is termed the *marginal propensity to save* (MPS). MPS will rise as a country's (or individual's) Y increases. The average proportion of Y which is saved is termed the *average propensity to save* (APS) and this also rises as Y rises.

$$\text{MPS} = \frac{\text{change in S}}{\text{change in Y}} \quad \text{APS} = \frac{S}{Y}$$

(b) *The distribution of income* High income consumers save more than low income consumers. MPS and APS both increase as Y increases. A redistribution of income from low income to high income consumers will increase S.

(c) *Interest rates* High interest rates will encourage individuals to save.

(d) *Availability of financial institutions* The more banks, building societies, and so on, that exist, the more opportunity individuals have to save.

(e) *Government policy* Government fiscal policy will affect S. If the government operates progressive taxes and welfare payments to low income earners then S will decline. This is because low income earners have a low MPS.

Investment (I)

Investment (I) is an injection into Y and any increase in I will increase Y. Investment is that spending on the creation of capital goods such as factories, buildings, machinery. These capital goods can create more capital goods or consumer goods. Gross investment includes the creation of all new capital goods. However some of this investment is to replace worn-out existing capital goods (a process termed *depreciation*). Therefore net investment is gross investment minus depreciation.

Determinants of I

(a) *Expected yields from the investment* This is itself determined by business expectations for the future and existing economic indicators like the level of unemployment, inflation and economic growth.

(b) *The cost of the investment* This is determined by the rate of interest prevailing in the economy. The money for the investment will mean a forgone rate of interest.

(c) *New techniques and inventions* New technology may encourage new industries and firms to develop.

(d) *Government policy* The government itself can stimulate investment by building new roads, schools, hospitals, etc. This may set off a *multiplier effect* which will create even more investment, jobs and incomes. If the government decides to build a new motorway, jobs and incomes are directly created for people involved in its construction. They then spend their incomes on a wide range of consumer goods creating jobs and incomes in other industries.

Then these people demand consumer goods. The process continues eventually creating many more jobs and incomes than those resulting directly from the initial motorway development.

The aim of the following section is to examine the meaning of the terms *national income* and *economic growth*, assess how they are measured and establish what they tell us about a country's economic performance. The facts relating to the national income are presented every year in an official publication, *National Income and Expenditure*. This is a large volume of statistical tables. It illustrates how the economy has performed over the previous twelve months, breaking it down for detailed analysis into different regions and industries. From this information it is possible to draw conclusions about consumers' spending habits, about which sectors of the economy are expanding or contracting and about the distribution of the labour force between different types of industry.

The measurement of national income: income, expenditure and output

The national income is an estimate of the value of goods and services made available as a result of the country's economic activity over a given period.

The total value of goods and services produced in a country during a given year is called *national output* or *national product*. These goods and services could only be produced by employing factors of production which receive incomes. The sum of all these incomes is called the national income and, therefore, national income = national output.

The whole value of output consists of income payments to factors of production. For example, the payment to the baker for a loaf of bread can be broken down into the profit the baker keeps, the wages paid to the assistants, the rent paid for the shop, the interest repayments on capital and the payments for raw materials. In other words, national income = national output = national expenditure.

The total value of national output is what is spent in producing it. One person's spending is income for others. For instance, assume a simple economy with one consumer and one producer (a baker). The consumer buys a loaf of bread for, say, 50p, therefore national expenditure is 50p. The value of national output is therefore 50p. National income will also be 50p because the baker will distribute receipts in the form of profits, wages, rents and interest. Thus it can be seen that national income = national output = national expenditure.

The income method

The incomes received for producing goods and services include the wages and salaries of employees, the incomes of the self-employed, trading profits of companies, trading surpluses of the public corporations and other public enterprises, and incomes from rent. This gives *total domestic income*. Other forms of income, such as receipts of interest and dividends, private gifts or retirement pensions, family allowances and other social security benefits are not included in the national income since they are not payments for the production of any goods or services, but merely *transfer payments* from one section of the community to another.

From total domestic income we subtract *stock appreciation*, which is when the value of stocks has risen, probably because the price of goods held in stock has gone up. This has no direct connection with changes in output and is excluded from national income. We also add on, or subtract, *residual error* which is an allowance for errors made in calculations. The sum of incomes should be equal to the sum of expenditures, but, because of imperfections in compiling the statistics, expenditure may be more or less than incomes. This is known as residual error.

We now have *gross domestic product at factor cost*. To arrive at *gross national product at factor cost* we now add on *net property income from abroad* which is the net amount of flows of property income. The United Kingdom receives a flow of interest, profits and dividends from its overseas investments and there is a corresponding outflow of funds on foreign investments in the United Kingdom. The estimates of gross domestic product (GDP) and gross national product (GNP), however, take no account of an important point which is that part of the country's output will be needed to make good the wear and tear to buildings, plant and vehicles, and to replace worn-out equipment. This is termed *depreciation*. The *net national product* or *national income* is thus equal to the GNP minus *depreciation* (or capital consumption).

The income method

Total domestic income	less Stock appreciation		add Net property income		less Depreciation
Total personal income — transfer payments + undistributed profits + surpluses of public corporations	plus Residual error	Gross domestic product at factor cost		Gross national product at factor cost	National income

The expenditure method

On the expenditure side, the national income is the total paid by final buyers for goods and services, either for consumption or for adding to wealth (investment). Consumption includes all kinds of day-to-day spending on goods and services whether by consumers (consumers' expenditure), or by government departments and local authorities (public authorities' consumption). Investment may be in the form of fixed assets such as factories, machinery and houses, and it is then described as fixed investment or fixed capital formation. Investment may also be in the form of stocks of raw materials and finished goods, or work in progress, when it can be described as capital formation in stocks.

This gives us *total domestic expenditure at market prices*. However, in some cases

The expenditure method

| Investment / Consumer spending | add Exports / deduct Imports | Gross domestic product at market prices | deduct Taxes / add Subsidies | Gross domestic product at factor cost | add Net property income | Gross national product at factor cost | less Depreciation / National income |

the buyers of goods and services are in overseas countries and this expenditure is included in national income as *exports and income from abroad*. On the other hand *imports and income paid abroad* must be excluded from calculations as they do not generate income for the domestic economy. This gives us *gross national product at market prices*. However, this includes taxation and is minus subsidies, so some prices are distorted. To find *gross national product at factor cost* we deduct taxes and add on subsidies. The *net national product* or national income is thus equal to GNP minus *depreciation*.

The national output method

The national income is also the sum of the products of various industries in the country; it is the sum of the values added by each industry which is equal to the value of its total output, minus the cost of materials and services supplied from other industries or imported. This gives the *total domestic output*. We then

The output method

| Total Domestic Product | less Stock appreciation / plus Residual error | Gross domestic product at factor cost | add Net property income | Gross national product at factor cost | less Depreciation / National income |

proceed as for the income method, because we subtract *stock appreciation* and add on or subtract *residual error*. This gives us *GDP at factor cost* to which we need to add on *net property income from abroad* to give *GNP at factor cost*. If we now deduct depreciation we have *net national product or income*.

Gross domestic product (GDP)

The gross domestic product (GDP) is the total value of goods and services produced in this country and may be calculated as follows:

Gross domestic product at market prices is GDP in terms of the prices at which products are sold and therefore includes taxes, less any subsidies provided out of taxation.

Gross domestic product at factor cost is the GDP in terms of what the producer actually receives for the goods. Thus from GDP at market prices, subtract taxes and add on relevant subsidies.

Gross national product (GNP)

Due to many overseas investments the United Kingdom receives an inflow of interest, profits and dividends. Similarly other countries have investments in the United Kingdom and there is a corresponding outflow. The net amount of these flows of property income is added to the amount produced in the United Kingdom (GDP) to give gross national product (GNP).

Gross national product at market prices
= GDP at market price plus exports and property income from abroad, minus imports and property income paid abroad.

Gross national product at factor cost
= GNP at market prices minus taxes plus subsidies.

Problems involved in measuring national income

The danger of double counting

This has already been seen to be a problem and is constantly recurring in this area of study. Transfer payments should not be included in the calculations. In addition, the cost of raw materials must be deducted from the value of the products of industries, and from products and services provided by other industries. Only the value added is included. *Stock appreciation* must also be deducted. This occurs when the value of stocks increases because of inflation, since it represents no increase in real output.

Self-supplied goods and services

Certain goods and services may be provided by a person for himself or herself and it is very difficult to include these in calculations. Many of these self-supplied goods and services will be omitted from calculations altogether. However, an imputed value is given to owner-occupied houses and an estimate is made of the value of food consumed by farmers themselves.

Similarly, some goods and services, for instance, services given by housewives, cannot be valued at all and are omitted. However, this creates a difficulty because a housekeeper's services are calculated in national income.

Moreover, work done in the *black economy* is not included in calculations. In the black economy, payment for work done is not declared to the Inland Revenue, which therefore receives no income and has no record of the work.

Government services
The education and health expenditures are included at their cost since they are obviously no different from similar services for which people pay. All government services are therefore included at cost in national output, despite the argument that in some instances this could amount to double counting because these services are financed out of people's taxation.

Inflation
Do we express statistics in terms of market prices or constant prices? If in terms of market prices, then figures will be distorted by inflation even though national output may have remained the same. To overcome this, statistics are often expressed in terms of constant prices where a particular year's prices are chosen to calculate the value of output. This means that rising prices cannot distort the calculations. *Money national income* is when statistics are expressed in market prices. *Real national income* is when inflation has been taken into account by expressing national income in terms of constant prices. The following formula is used:

National income at constant prices

$$= \text{National income at market prices} \times \frac{100}{\text{Retail Price Index}}$$

Uses of national income statistics

As an important instrument in economic planning
Although economic planning is a feature of socialist economies, such as that of the USSR, Western governments also control their economies.

Consequently, national income statistics provide a great deal of valuable information to both local and national government. The planning and decision-making authorities are able to interpret what is happening to investment, consumers' spending, public authorities' spending, and so on, and see which industries and regions are expanding or contracting.

To compare a country's standard of living over time
It is normally assumed that when national income increases this is a good indicator that the standards of living within the country have improved. However, certain qualifications have to be made to this view.

(a) The rise in national income could be due mainly to inflation. To overcome this problem a base year can be chosen and figures valued at constant prices

Consumers' expenditure (at 1980 prices)

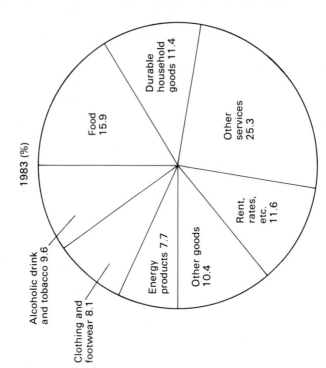

1963 (%)

Food 21.9

Alcoholic drink and tobacco 11.0

Clothing and footwear 6.3

Energy products 7.4

Other goods 9.8

Rent, rates, etc. 11.5

Other services 25.2

Durable household goods 6.9

Total expenditure £95 719 million

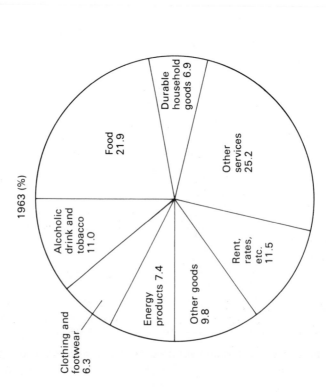

1983 (%)

Food 15.9

Alcoholic drink and tobacco 9.6

Clothing and footwear 8.1

Durable household goods 11.4

Energy products 7.7

Other goods 10.4

Rent, rates, etc. 11.6

Other services 25.3

Total expenditure £144 008 million

and not market prices. National income so revalued is called real national income.

(b) The population may be increasing and one would expect national income to increase. A more reliable indicator would be a calculation relating to real national income per head, which is real national income divided by population.

(c) National income figures do not refer in any way to the distribution of income. Nearly all the income may be in the hands of a few people, and, therefore, it would be difficult to say that standards of living have improved for the majority of the population.

(d) An increase in national income may be due to more investment, which could mean that the individual consumer's standard of living (which normally depends on the quantity and quality of consumer goods he or she enjoys) has not improved in the short term. Of course if the investment is to produce more consumer goods in the long term then future standards of living will improve.

(e) The increase could be caused by a surplus of exports over imports, again not directly improving domestic consumers' immediate standard of living.

(f) An increase in national income may result in more factories, more pollution and a less pleasant environment. Thus there may be social costs involved in improvements in the national income.

(g) The increase in national income may be due to higher defence spending which, again, does not necessarily mean that an individual citizen's standard of living has improved.

(h) The statistics say nothing about the changing quality of production. For instance, a motor car constructed today is much more sophisticated than a motor car built in 1900.

To compare the living standards of two countries

National income figures are used to compare the standards of living between two different countries. Thus if the United Kingdom's national income is greater than that of Nigeria, it is concluded that the United Kingdom has a higher standard of living, but, again, a number of reservations must be mentioned.

(a) The amount of unpaid work may vary between the two countries.

(b) There may be differences in how the statistics are calculated.

(c) The size of the population may be different. Thus it would be better to express national income in terms of real national income per head.

(d) The distribution of income must be taken into account.

(e) There may be differences in the price levels between the two countries. This obviously inflates the national income of one country in comparison to the other.

(f) Differences in taste or climate must be taken into account, such as the fact that the Nigerian spends less on heating than the British person but is no worse off.

(g) The currencies are different and exchange rates have to be used as a common denominator. However, the use of the exchange rate may not reflect differences in domestic price levels and the internal purchasing power of the currency. Moreover, exchange rates change constantly.

(h)   It does not indicate factors such as the number of hospital beds, or doctors, the crime rate and the suicide rate. There is more to quality of life and happiness than the level of GNP. It is often maintained that the average British person would be unwilling to give up his present way of working and much valued social life just to achieve a higher national income.

To measure a country's economic growth

Although economists are not unanimous about what constitutes economic growth, the most common measure is national income. Percentage growth rates are usually expressed in terms of percentage increases in GNP or GDP. Perhaps the best indicator of economic growth is real national income per head but often changes in GNP and/or changes in GDP are taken to illustrate economic growth.

Between 1945 and the early 1980s the United Kingdom's economic growth rates lagged behind comparable countries such as West Germany, France and Japan.

Various arguments have been put forward purporting to explain the United Kingdom's comparatively poor record in economic growth during this period. There is probably no one reason why the United Kingdom did not experience high rates of economic growth and something can be said in favour of all the explanations put forward. These include:

(a)   Too little investment, especially in modern machinery, has meant the use of outdated capital.
(b)   Profits too low and taxes too high, resulting in little incentive for investment.
(c)   Low growth leads to a general lack of confidence and so to continuing low growth because businesspeople will not invest.
(d)   Too much government spending on projects of secondary importance, often for political or social purposes. Public money is being wasted on uneconomic projects.
(e)   Poor or indifferent management in many major industries, coupled with restrictive practices by some trade unions (see pages 299–300).
(f)   Overstaffing in many sectors of government, industry and commerce causing low productivity (output per person).
(g)   There are too few engineers and technologists who are necessary if the United Kingdom's industries are to compete with their principal competitors. This is reflected in a bias by the education system against the study of engineering and science subjects.

However, since the early 1980s the United Kingdom has achieved relatively high economic growth compared with its main competitors (see statistics on page 142).

Does a low rate of economic growth matter?
Some economists maintain that it does not really matter that a country is achieving a low rate of economic growth. They say that there is more to happiness and

Living standards

Real personal disposable income or what people have left in their pockets after allowing for tax and inflation

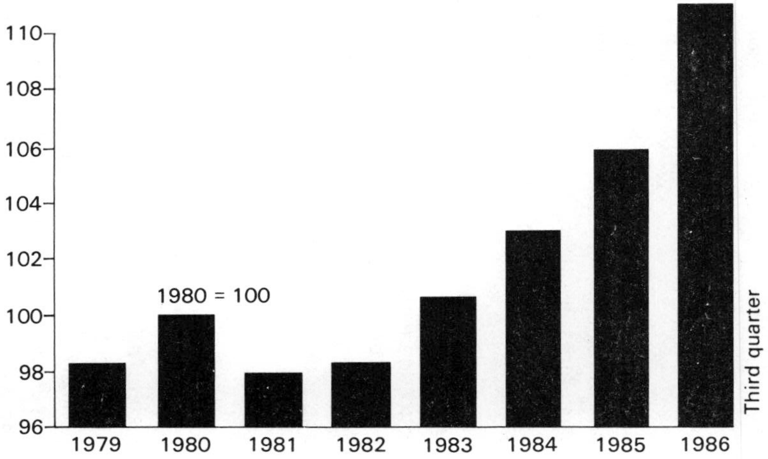

1980 = 100

Growth of the economy

Gross domestic product average estimate 1980 = 100

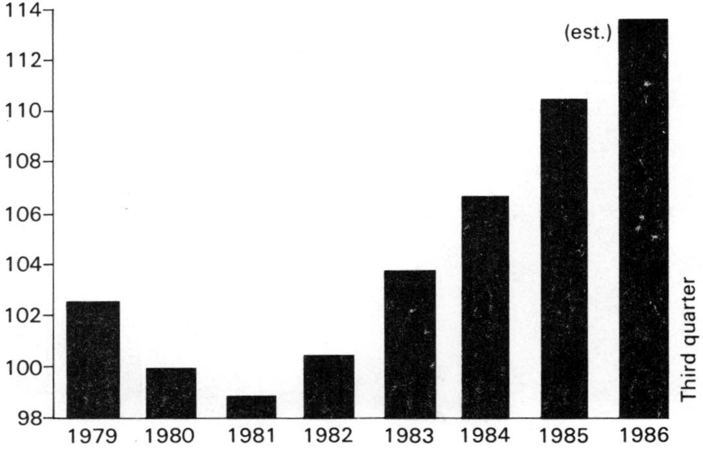

Real GDP growth at constant market prices 1960–86

Per cent a year (rankings out of 12 countries in brackets)

	1960–69	1970–79	1980–86	1982–86	1960–86
UK	3.1 (12)	2.4 (11)	1.4 (8=)	2.6 (3)	2.4 (12)
USA	3.9 (11)	2.7 (9)	2.1 (3)	2.5 (4)	3.0 (10)
Japan	10.1 (1)	5.1 (1)	3.8 (1)	3.6 (1)	6.6 (1)
EC	—	3.3	1.4	1.8	—
OECD	—	3.3	2.1	2.4	—

Growth league table

1960s	1970s	1980s
Italy	France	UK
France	Belgium	Germany
Netherlands	Italy	France
Belgium	Netherlands	Italy
Germany	Germany	Belgium
UK	UK	Netherlands

The economic record: Over the 1980s Britain has grown faster than any other major country in the European Community. This is in sharp contrast to the 1960s and 1970s, when Britain came bottom of the European growth league.

quality of life than achieving a high rate of economic growth. Moreover, if we were to choose to achieve a higher rate of growth this might mean more pollution, more industrial accidents, less leisure time and so on.

The alternative argument maintains that a high rate of economic growth does matter. This is because not only will the average citizen be less well-off than the average citizen from other countries, but it will also mean that the provision of health, education and transport services will be of a lower standard. It will also mean that less help can be given to the poor, unemployed and sick in the form of pensions, benefits, and hospitals. Moreover, the problem will become even worse as we fall further and further behind, which will mean that future generations of citizens will live in a relatively poor country.

Checkpoints

1 National income is the money value of all goods and services produced in a specified time period. The level of national income is determined by the level of aggregate demand. National income determines the level of output, employment and economic growth.

2 In a closed economy and without government interference, aggregate demand consists of consumption and investment. The economy is in equilibrium when investment equals savings.

3 In an open economy aggregate demand consists of consumption, investment, government spending and exports. The economy is in equilibrium when withdrawals equal injections. Withdrawals are savings, taxation and imports. Injections are investments, government spending and imports (I + G + X).

4 The size of the individual component parts of aggregate demand are determined by several factors and the size of C, I, G and X will determine the size of aggregate demand and national income.

5 The size of national income in any one year is measured either by the income method, the output method or the expenditure method. Significant features of the national income calculations are the gross domestic product (GDP) and gross national product (GNP). These can be measured at factor cost or market prices.

6 There are many problems involved in calculating national income such as double counting and the effects of inflation on the statistics. To take into account inflation national income is converted from being calculated in market prices into constant prices.

7 National income statistics are useful to a country because they are used as an instrument for economic planning, they indicate changes in standard of living, they are used to make comparisons with other countries and to indicate the level of economic growth.

8 However, despite its usefulness as an economic indicator, national income has to be used very carefully and reservations have to be made about its reliability.

9 Since the end of World War II the United Kingdom has not enjoyed the same economic growth as comparable countries such as West Germany, France and Japan. The reasons for this are discussed. However, in the 1980s the United Kingdom economy has enjoyed higher economic growth.

Multiple-choice questions – 7

1 Which of the following would be regarded by an economist to be investment?

    A building a new factory
    B buying shares on the stock exchange
    C depositing money in a building society
    D buying shares in a newly privatised company
    E depositing money in a deposit account of a commercial bank

2 Which of the following would increase the level of national income?

    A a reduction in consumer spending
    B a reduction in government spending
    C an increase in taxation
    D an increase in savings
    E an increase in exports

3 Which of the following is a withdrawal from the circular flow of income?

    A Exports
    B Taxation
    C Consumption
    D Investment
    E Subsidies

4 Which of the following will increase consumer spending?

    A higher rates of VAT
    B higher level of savings
    C higher rates of income tax
    D lower interest rates
    E lower repayment period for hire-purchase loans

5 The marginal propensity to consume is

    A the total amount spent on consumption
    B the amount people wish to spend on consumption
    C the proportion of total income spent on consumption
    D consumption during a given period of time
    E the proportion of additional income which is spent on consumption

6 National income is a measure of

    A the size of government revenues
    B the surpluses of nationalised industries
    C payments made to factors of production in the economy
    D total wage increases in a given period
    E the value of exports in a given period

7 If a country's growth rate were 5% it would mean that there has been a 5% increase in

    A manufacturing industry
    B goods and services produced
    C manufacturing output
    D the retail price index
    E government revenues

8 Measures of changes in economic growth can best be seen by changes in the

    A level of unemployment
    B balance of payments statistics
    C real national income per capita
    D retail price index
    E level of earnings

9 From the following figures,

	£000m
total domestic spending at market prices	40
exports and property income from abroad	10
imports and property income paid abroad	16
taxes on spending	6
subsidies	2

the gross national product at factor cost is

    A £30 000m
    B £34 000m
    C £38 000m
    D £42 000m
    E £46 000m

10 In calculating national income which of the following should *not* be included?

    A exports
    B undistributed profits made by a PLC
    C food grown and consumed by a farmer
    D wages of a college lecturer
    E old-age pensions

Answers on page 328.

Data response question 7

National output

1980 = 100

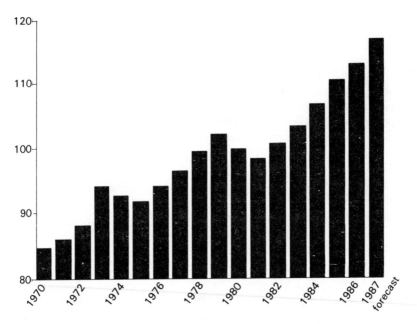

(a) (i) What is the statistical term for how these statistics for national output are presented by the *Economic Progress Report?*
   (ii) Explain the meaning of 1980 = 100 to the presentation of the statistics.
(b) State one year in which national output fell and one year in which national output increased.
(c) Give the two years since 1970 which marked the bottom of the economic cycle.
(d) (i) Give two possible reasons why national output may fall.
   (ii) Give reasons for the fall in national output 1979–1982.
(e) During which periods did the economy enjoy economic growth?
(f) (i) Discuss two advantages of economic growth.
   (ii) Discuss two disadvantages of economic growth.

8 International trade

International trade and protection

Why trade is important to the United Kingdom

International trade is concerned with the buying and selling of goods and services (commodities) between different nations. Only a few countries, such as the USSR or the United States, would be able to provide all their needs themselves. Countries like the United Kingdom rely on others to provide them with supplies of many raw materials and foodstuffs, and the United Kingdom also relies on other countries to purchase the manufactures which she has produced.

Trade is particularly important to the United Kingdom because:

(a) *The United Kingdom has a population of 56 million and produces only a small proportion of its foodstuffs.* Home-produced food must be supplemented by *imports* (purchases from foreign countries) such as tea, coffee, tropical fruits, wheat and so on.

(b) *The United Kingdom cannot satisfy all its requirements of raw materials* such as iron ore, copper and raw cotton which are needed to produce the finished goods (like cars, televisions, refrigerators and textiles) which the United Kingdom manufactures. These raw materials have to be imported from all parts of the world.

(c) *A large number of jobs in the United Kingdom depend on the export (selling to foreign countries) of goods and services.* Many people are employed in producing cars and lorries and providing services for other countries such as banking and insurance. Without international trade a part of this employment would be lost.

It can be seen that without international trade the standard of living of people in all countries, not just in the United Kingdom, would be lower.

The advantages of international trade

The following arguments are often put forward in favour of international trade (or free trade).

A country can produce some commodities but not others

One reason may be that a country's climate is unsuited to producing some commodities. The United Kingdom for instance cannot grow oranges or grapes on a large commercial scale. Alternatively, a country may not possess the necessary raw materials required to produce certain commodities. The United Kingdom, for example, has few deposits of iron ore.

The advantage of specialisation
More goods are produced at lower cost per unit. Consider these two cases.

(a) *A country can produce one commodity better than another* Suppose country X is able to produce a commodity better than country Y and decides to specialise in producing it. Country Y, however, may be able to produce another commodity better than country X. Country Y may, therefore, decide to specialise in this other product. After specialising in producing the commodity to which each country is best suited, the countries will then decide to trade with each other. The United Kingdom for instance can produce wine but perhaps not as cheaply or in such quantities as France. France will therefore provide the United Kingdom with much of its requirements of wine in exchange for, say, high-class manufactures of Scotch whisky which are not readily available in France.

(b) *A country can produce both commodities better than another country* One nation may be able to produce two (or more) commodities better than another country. However, it will only produce the commodity in which its *comparative advantage* is greater and allow the other country to produce the other product. This is called the *theory of comparative costs*. Perhaps an easy way of showing this idea is if we assume a situation where a barrister (Mr Rumpole) is a better barrister and a better gardener than a gardener (Mr Smith). Mr Rumpole can earn £30 000 pa if he specialises in being a barrister, but has to pay Mr Smith £3000 pa for doing his garden. The benefit to Mr Rumpole is £27 000 pa (ie, £30 000 − £3000) while the annual benefit to Mr Smith is £3000. On the other hand, assume that Mr Rumpole decided to spend half of his time being a barrister and half being a gardener. He will only earn £15 000 pa (half of £30 000) and Mr Smith will gain nothing from this situation. Thus we can see that both Mr Rumpole and Mr Smith are better off when Mr Rumpole specialises in the job in which his *comparative advantage* is the greater, even though he is absolutely better in both jobs.

Let us now examine this idea in relation to two countries, country X and Y, which can commercially produce two commodities: cars and freezers.

	Output per person per week	
	cars	freezers
Country X	1	2
Country Y	3	4

It can readily be seen that country Y has the absolute advantage in producing both cars and freezers. The problem is, however, which product does each country give up if it specialises in producing either cars or freezers.

	cars given up to produce one freezer	freezers given up to produce one car
Country X	½	2
Country Y	¾	1⅓

In this situation country X has the comparative advantage in the production of freezers because, to produce one freezer country X has to give up half a car, whereas country Y has to give up three-quarters. It is better, therefore, for country X to produce freezers rather than Y because in doing so it loses less (ie, the opportunity cost is less). Country Y will produce the cars.

After deciding in which commodity they have a comparative advantage, each country will specialise in the production of that particular product. The production of both cars and freezers will, therefore, increase, trading will take place and people in both countries will enjoy a better standard of living.

Criticisms of the theory of comparative costs
As with many other economic ideas, there are criticisms to be levelled at this theory.

(i) It is much more difficult, in the real world, to decide in which goods countries have a comparative cost advantage. This is because there are a large number of goods and many countries.
(ii) The theory ignores political differences between countries which exist from time to time.
(iii) The theory ignores the arguments in favour of protection.
(iv) It ignores the effects of transport costs. For instance, Australia might specialise in cars and the United Kingdom specialise in freezers. However, once transport costs are added any comparative advantage may be lost.
(v) The theory assumes that if country X wants to specialise in producing more freezers it can do so easily by transferring factors of production into freezer production. However, it may be difficult to easily transfer these factors from cars to freezer production. In addition, car workers would have to be retrained to produce freezers.

A larger market and economies of scale
International trade means a larger market for home-produced commodities. Because of the larger market, commodities can be produced on a larger scale. The economies of scale can be enjoyed.

Competition and efficiency
International trade leads to more competition and more efficiency.

Political and friendship reasons
This argument suggests that countries will have more understanding and sympathy towards countries with whom they trade. The idea is that if, for example, the Russians and Americans trade with each other there is a greater possibility that they will become more friendly towards each other. This argument is often put forward in favour of international sporting events, such as the World Cup or the Olympic Games. Conversely, whenever countries have bad relations they normally restrict trade between each other.

Increased value of output
All of the arguments in favour of international trade mean that the value of a country's output (and world output) increases and citizens will enjoy a better standard of living.

Despite these arguments in favour of international trade, governments often restrict international trade by imposing protective measures.

Methods of protection
There are several means of protection used to restrict trade between countries.

Tariffs (import duties or customs duties)
This is a type of tax placed on imports into the country.

(a) *'Ad-valorem' tariffs* This is a tariff based on a percentage of value. For instance, a 10% tariff on an import worth £300 would raise £30, making the selling price £330 for the good. On an import worth £400 the tariff would raise £40, making the selling price £440 for the good.

(b) *Specific tariff* This is a tariff based on an amount per unit. For instance a £20 tariff might be imposed whatever the price or quantity of the import.

Tariffs therefore serve two main purposes: to raise revenue for the government and to raise the price of imports which might lead to fewer imports being purchased.

Import quotas
This is a restriction on the quantity of a good which can be imported. This is a more certain way of restricting imports but it does not raise revenue. It is preferable to use quotas rather than tariffs in an attempt to reduce imports when demand for the import is inelastic (see page 113).

Subsidies
These are made when home producers are subsidised (or given finance) which allows them to sell at a lower price than the import price. Thus when importers endeavour to compete with domestic producers they will find that their prices are more expensive and demand will be lower for the imported commodity.

Exchange controls
When United Kingdom importers purchase foreign goods they normally have to pay the foreign exporter in the currency of the exporter. The Bank of England can control how much foreign currency is available and can therefore restrict imports, if it so wishes, by restricting the amount of foreign currency. Exchange controls were abolished in the United Kingdom in 1979 but are still used by some countries to control the level of imports.

Embargo
This is a straightforward ban on trading with another country possibly due to

poor international relations. These are usually of short duration, caused by acute political differences, but occasionally are of long standing.

Discrimination
This is discrimination by the domestic government in favour of home produced commodities.

Health and safety regulations
These may be designed to keep out imports.

Voluntary export restraint agreements
This is an agreement between two countries to limit exports to each other.

Why are trade restrictions introduced?
Now we have examined the methods of protection we need to know the reasons why such protection may be introduced.

To correct a balance of payments deficit
This occurs when more money flows out of a country to pay for imports than flows in in the form of receipts for exports. A balance of payments deficit is therefore seen as undesirable and protection may be introduced to correct it because protection will discourage imports.

To protect infant industries
When industries are being set up they need protecting from established world competition. Without this protection the new infant industry would decline.

To protect both declining industries and jobs
In the United Kingdom some industries such as textiles, steel and shipbuilding are in decline. It is often argued that these industries need the protection of the state or they will decline further and cause high levels of unemployment.

To prevent 'dumping'
'Dumping' occurs when a foreign producer deposits its surplus production at very low prices in other countries. This will have a bad effect on the industries of the importing country, causing unemployment since people will tend to buy the cheap imports.

To protect 'key' industries
Some industries are so vital to the well-being of the economy that they cannot be allowed to decline. For instance, if there was another war the United Kingdom would need to rely on its agriculture and steel industries. Thus these industries need protection from imports. Also, it may be inadvisable to depend on other countries entirely for supplies of certain very important commodities such as coal or steel.

Criticisms of protection

(a) *Protection means that there is no free trade* The advantages of international trade are, therefore, lost.

(b) *Protection might not work in correcting a balance of payments deficit* Tariffs might be imposed to prevent imports. However, if people still purchase these imports because they have inelastic demand, then the balance of payments will not improve.

(c) *Other countries may retaliate* If country X imposes restrictions on the imports of goods from other countries, then these countries might, in retaliation, impose restrictions on the exports of country X. Again the balance of payments of country X will not improve.

(d) *Inefficient industries are protected* Declining and infant industries may become used to being protected by tariffs from overseas competition. The industries may, therefore, make no attempt to become efficient knowing that they are in a safe position.

The terms of trade

The meaning of the terms of trade
This is the rate at which one country's goods are exchanged against those of other countries. This is usually assessed by comparing index prices of imports and exports (see page 206). A country is said to have a favourable movement in its terms of trade if:

(a) export prices are rising faster than import prices;
(b) export prices are falling slower than import prices;
(c) export prices remain stable whilst import prices fall;
(d) import prices remain stable whilst export prices rise.

A favourable movement in its terms of trade means that a country is able to buy more imports with the same amount of exports.

Measuring terms of trade
The method of measuring terms of trade makes use of two important *index numbers*, the index of export prices and the index of import prices. The terms of trade will be given a numerical value equal to:

$$\frac{\text{index of average export prices}}{\text{index of average import prices}} \times 100$$

The terms of trade in the base year will be equal to 100. If terms of trade improve the index number will increase above 100. If terms of trade deteriorate the index number will fall.

For example, in a certain country in Year 1 (the base year) export and import prices are given the index number 100. Therefore terms of trade are equal to

$$\frac{100}{100} \times 100 = 100$$

However, in Year 2 export prices have risen by 10% and import prices by 5%. Therefore the terms of trade are equal to

$$\frac{110}{105} \times 100 = 104.8$$

The terms of trade for this country have therefore improved compared to the base year since the index number is now above 100.

What determines a country's terms of trade?

This is determined by movements in its export and import prices. These, like all other prices, depend on the interaction of supply and demand. Thus if demand for country X's exports increased, the price of its exports will increase and its terms of trade would improve. On the other hand, if country X increased its demand for its imports, then import prices would rise and its terms of trade would decline.

What has happened to the United Kingdom's terms of trade?

Throughout most of the 1950s and 1960s the terms of trade for the United Kingdom showed an improvement. This trend was in common with most of the Western manufacturing countries, such as the United States, France, West Germany and Japan. This meant that these countries could purchase larger and larger amounts of imports with given amounts of exports. Thus the standard of living in these countries improved. On the other hand the terms of trade of those countries that provided the United Kingdom with imports, mainly primary producers (see page 16), tended to decline. The standard of living of people in the primary producing countries therefore also declined.

However since the early 1970s the situation has changed and the terms of trade for the United Kingdom have deteriorated while the terms of trade for primary producing countries have improved. The reasons for this have been:

(a) Action by the Organisation of Petroleum Exporting Countries (OPEC) which dramatically increased oil prices from 1973.
(b) Shortages of primary products such as foodstuffs and raw materials which forced up prices of these commodities.

The United Kingdom's terms of trade improved again in the late 1970s and early 1980s because the United Kingdom became a net oil exporter (North Sea oil) and oil prices remained high. However, since 1981 oil prices have fallen and so have the United Kingdom's terms of trade.

Terms of trade average
(1980 = 100)

Year	Value
1970	103.9
1975	87.6
1980	100.0
1981	100.5
1982	99.6
1983	98.6
1984	97.4
1985	98.8

The relationship between the terms of trade and balance of payments
It is worth noting at this point that the terms of trade are not the same as the balance of payments or the balance of trade. Refer to pages 154–8 in the next section to be sure that you understand what is meant by balance of trade and balance of payments.

It is easy to assume that since a country's terms of trade are improving the balance of payments for that country must also be improving. However, there are a number of qualifications to be made before we can reach this conclusion.

A great deal depends on the elasticity of demand for exports and imports If demand for exports is elastic (see page 112) then an improvement in terms of trade might have a bad effect on balance of payments. This is due to the fact that if prices of exports increase, total exports decline in volume and consequently the value of exports decline. However, if demand for exports and imports is inelastic then an improvement in the terms of trade should improve a country's balance of payments.

If country X's terms of trade have improved then the terms of trade of some other countries must have declined These other countries may not be able to afford to purchase country X's export of goods and services and again the balance of payments of country X would deteriorate.

The balance of payments

The meaning of balance of payments
The balance of payments is a record of transactions between countries involved in international trade. It is a record of receipts from exports (sales of goods and services abroad) and inflows of capital investment, and spending on imports (purchases of goods and services from foreign countries) and outflows of capital investment. If a country's receipts are greater than its spending then it will have a *balance of payments surplus*. If a country's receipts are less than its spending, however, it will have a *balance of payments deficit*. A surplus is preferred to a deficit because it means that the country is earning more from exports than it is spending on imports.

The balance of payments accounts
The current account
The current account is divided into two parts

(a) *Visible trade* This includes the value (ie, price × volume) of imports and exports of goods. The difference between these is termed the *balance of (visible) trade*. This figure must not be confused with terms of trade (see previous section) or the balance of payments proper.
(b) *Invisible trade* This includes the value (ie, price × volume) of imports and exports of *services*. Such services would include aviation, interest, profits and dividends, shipping, tourism, banking and insurance, government services, and private transfers.

The balance of visible trade is taken together with the balance of invisible trade to give current account balance (see page 156).

Investment and other capital flows

This is a record of inflows of capital investment into the United Kingdom economy and outflows of capital investment out of the United Kingdom economy. An inflow is regarded as a positive (+) item and an outflow is a negative (–) item. Investments can be either long term or short term. The latter are often termed 'hot money' because they constitute capital which can be moved easily.

The balancing item

This represents mistakes and omissions in the figures. The banks know the real values since they handle currency movements. A (+) balancing item means that more currency has entered the United Kingdom than estimated. A (–) balancing item means that less currency has entered the United Kingdom than estimated.

The balance for official financing

When current account balance, investment and other capital flows and balancing items have been calculated, the balance for official financing is calculated by adding these figures together. If the balance for official financing indicates an inflow of money, this is a balance of payments surplus. If the balance for official financing indicates an outflow of money, this is a balance of payments deficit.

Official financing

Every penny of a deficit must be financed by borrowing or running down reserves of gold and foreign currency held at the Bank of England. Borrowing usually takes place from the International Monetary Fund (IMF) (see page 167). Likewise, every penny of a surplus must be allocated to paying off previous loans or added to reserves of gold and foreign currency. Official financing ensures that the balance of payments always balances (on paper at least).

The United Kingdom's performance on its balance of payments in recent years

Visibles

Throughout the 1950s, 1960s and 1970s the United Kingdom experienced problems on its visible trade and normally made a deficit. This was because:

(a) inflation (see page 205) in the United Kingdom made British goods expensive and therefore foreigners were reluctant to buy United Kingdom exports.

(b) many of the United Kingdom's imports are necessities and, despite rising import prices, due to worsening terms of trade and a declining pound, British people have continued to purchase these imports. There has been an inelastic demand to purchase these imports, especially oil.

(c) there was a poor export performance, due to poor after-sales provision and sales techniques.

Current account (1977-86)

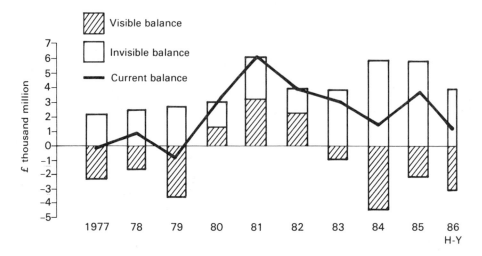

(d) United Kingdom goods have often been unable to compete with imports in the home market because of inferior quality and high prices.

However, in the early 1980s the United Kingdom's balance on visible trade moved into surplus (or 'into the black', as it is called in the press). This was mainly because the United Kingdom had exploited North Sea oil which greatly reduced her imports of expensive oil from the OPEC countries. Indeed, the United Kingdom is now a net exporter of oil. However in the mid-1980s the visible deficit returned, reflecting a deficit on manufacturing trade with the United Kingdom experiencing her first deficit on manufacturing trade for over 100 years in 1983. The size of this deficit increased in 1984, 1985, 1986 and 1987. Refer to page 320 for a fuller discussion on the decline in manufacturing.

Invisibles
There has always been a surplus on the United Kingdom's invisible transactions taken as a whole. A large surplus on private invisibles such as interest, profits and dividends, transport and banking and finance exceeds the deficit on government invisibles.

In most years in the 1950s, 1960s and 1970s there had been a deficit on current account. However because of North Sea oil there has been a surplus on current account in the 1980s. On the other hand the early 1980s have seen the import of manufactures exceed the export of manufactures. This is extremely worrying because North Sea oil will run out one day.

In 1986 and 1987 the current account moved into deficit (£1.7 billion in 1987).

Investment and other capital flows
This varies from year to year.

Analysis of the balance of payments 1981–85 (£ million)

Year	Visible trade	Net invisibles	Current balance	Investment and other capital flows	Allocation of SDRs	Balance for official financing	Official financing		Balancing item
							Reserves drawings (+) additions (−)	Net other transactions	
1981	3360	2866	6226	−7185	158	−801	−1732	2419	−114
1982	2331	1701	4032	−3658	—	374	−137	1421	−1658
1983	−835	3998	3163	−5071	—	−1908	+213	607	1088
1984	−4391	5953	1562	−7184	—	−5622	+408	908	4306
1985	−2068	5831	3763	−3207	—	556	+959	−1758	243

The United Kingdom's imports and exports

Analysis of visible trade 1985: by commodity

United Kingdom	Exports % share	Imports % share
Food and drink	6.3	10.9
Crude materials and oils	2.7	6.4
Fuels	21.3	12.4
Chemicals	12.0	8.1
Manufactures	23.5	28.9
Machinery and transport equipment	31.5	31.7
Other	2.5	1.6
	100.0	100.0

Analysis of visible trade 1985: by area

	Exports % share	Imports % share
EEC	48.8	48.8
Other Western Europe	9.5	14.2
North America	17.0	13.8
Other developed	4.8	7.5
Latin America	1.4	1.9
Middle East and North Africa	7.9	3.1
Other developing	8.5	8.3
Centrally planned economies	2.0	2.2

Exchange rates

Why exchange rates are necessary
An exchange rate is a country's currency expressed in value in terms of other currencies. For instance, the pound sterling might be equal to 1.5 US dollars. If you look in the *Financial Times* on any one day it will give the exchange rate of the pound.

Exchange rates are necessary because when a country sells commodities abroad it normally wants its own currency for those exports in order to pay its workers and shareholders. For instance, if the United Kingdom exports commodities abroad it will require pounds sterling. Thus importers of United Kingdom goods need to buy sterling on the *foreign exchange markets*. As we shall see later, the exchange rates need not remain fixed from day to day.

Methods of organising exchange rates
The gold standard
This was employed in the international economy before 1914 and was briefly restored between 1925 and 1931. Gold was used as the main means of paying

for trade between countries (ie, as a trading currency) and also as a means for countries to hold their national wealth (ie, as a reserve currency). It still fulfils these roles but it now shares them with pounds sterling, US dollars and Special Drawing Rights (see page 169). Gold is no longer so important as a trading unit.

Gold was used because all countries had confidence in its value and it was accepted everywhere. All currencies had an exchange rate in terms of gold, and gold could easily be imported and exported. Moreover, the size of money supply was based on how much gold a country had.

The advantages of the gold standard

(a) Balance of payments automatically corrected itself. If a country experienced a balance of payments deficit this meant that gold had to be exported to pay for it. The country would therefore have less gold, which would mean less money supply and a deflationary policy (see page 214). Prices and incomes would be restricted, making exports more desirable because they are cheaper and imports less desirable because they are dearer. The balance of payments is thus remedied automatically as exports increase and imports decrease.

(b) There is no danger of too much inflation. Because the money supply was based on how much gold a country possessed, it would not be able to oversupply money which would cause too much demand and inflation.

The disadvantages of the gold standard

(a) If a country had a balance of payments deficit at the same time as a high level of unemployment, operation of the gold standard would worsen unemployment. A deficit would cause gold to leave the country and reduce money supply. Demand in the economy would decline causing even more unemployment. This happened in 1926 and the employers tried to reduce wages to improve exports. This caused a *General Strike* among workers throughout the United Kingdom.

(b) In the modern world economy there is not enough gold to finance the volume of world trade. This is called the *liquidity problem*. Therefore gold has been joined by dollars, pounds and Special Drawing Rights to finance world trade.

(c) Most of the gold in the world, yet to be mined, is owned by South Africa and the USSR. Any restoration of the gold standard would give these countries a great deal of power in the world economy.

Because of these disadvantages, gold is unlikely to be restored as the main means of determining exchange rates and financing world trade.

Fixed exchange rates (managed flexibility)
Fixed exchange rates existed in the international economy between 1944 and 1971 and were supervised by the International Monetary Fund (see page 167). The system worked by fixing exchange rates between currencies and it was the responsibility of countries to make sure that exchange rates remained fixed. In the United Kingdom the pound was fixed by two methods. It was also referred to as a

system of managed flexibility because some flexibility was allowed between very narrow limits. It was also called the adjustable-peg mechanism.

(a) *Intervention* The Bank of England, as agent of the government, on its *exchange equalisation account* (see page 190) would purchase pounds if the pound was falling in value (due to a balance of payments deficit perhaps) or sell pounds if the pound was rising in value (perhaps because of a balance of payments surplus).

(b) *Exchange controls* The Bank of England would control how much foreign exchange was available to people who wanted to purchase it. This would control the supply of pounds which would be offered to buy foreign exchange. Exchange controls were scrapped in 1979 as required by the European Community rules.

Advantages of fixed exchange rates

(a) World traders always knew what the exchange rate would be for any currency. This gave them confidence to enter into long term contracts and give credit. It therefore encouraged more trade.

(b) It prevented any speculation in currencies. Speculators in a floating exchange rate system might force a currency's value up or down to make profits. Speculation is prevented by a fixed exchange rate system.

(c) Balance of payments deficits would have to be paid for. Since the currency could not be allowed to decline in value (as it would on floating exchange rates) the deficit would be paid for out of *reserves of gold and foreign currency*. To avoid these being diminished altogether, the country would have to do something to prevent the balance of payments deficit, such as deflation (see page 162) or protection (see page 150).

Disadvantages of fixed exchange rates

Any balance of payments deficit would mean that strains would be felt on gold and currency reserves or borrowing would have to take place. Thus unpopular policies might have to be introduced such as deflation, protection or devaluation. The fixed exchange rate system was seen as too inflexible.

Floating, fluctuating or free exchange rates

These have been in operation in the world economy since 1971 (although not in their purest form because governments often wish to influence exchange rates). The present system is referred to as '*dirty floating*' because the government will always interfere if the exchange rate falls (or rises) too much. Under this system the value of a currency is determined by its supply and demand. If the currency is in demand due, perhaps, to a balance of payments surplus (it is needed to pay for the country's exports) the exchange rate will rise.

Advantages of floating exchange rates

A balance of payments deficit is automatically corrected by a change in the exchange rate. For instance, assume the United Kingdom makes a balance of payments deficit. This means that demand for foreign currency (to pay for imports) is greater than demand for pounds (to pay for United Kingdom exports). The pound will fall in value making United Kingdom exports cheaper and imports more expensive. Consider the following example to prove this

Before devaluation £1 = 4 dollars
After devaluation £1 = 2 dollars

An American firm sells a good to the United Kingdom worth 4000 dollars. Before currency depreciation the United Kingdom importer had to pay £1000, but now he has to pay £2000. Therefore, imports would fall because they have become more expensive. Further assume that a United Kingdom export sells for £1000. Before depreciation $4000 had to be paid for the export. After depreciation $2000 would have to be paid for the same export. Assuming elastic demand for exports and imports, the value of exports will rise and the value of imports will decrease.

Thus a balance of payments deficit is corrected automatically without deflation, protection or strains on reserves of gold and foreign currencies.

Disadvantages of floating exchange rates

(a) There is a great deal of uncertainty in world trade about exchange rates which may be changing on a daily basis. Traders might be reluctant to enter into long term contracts or grant credit. There may be a bad effect on the volume of world trade.

(b) Speculators can force the exchange rate up or down to make profits for themselves.

(c) Governments may come to the conclusion that any balance of payments

Sterling exchange rates against major currencies 1977-85

(1977 = 100)

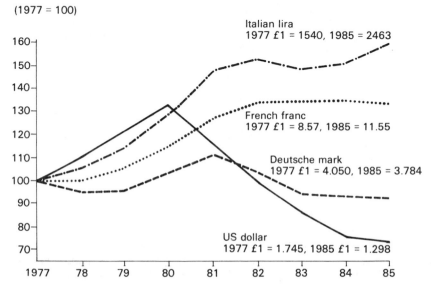

deficit will be automatically corrected by a fall in the exchange rate. Thus the government's economic policies may be too expansionary causing too much demand and inflation. There could be economic mis-management by the government.

Balance of payments surpluses and deficits

What are balance of payments deficits and surpluses? What could cause these states of affairs? Is it good or bad to have a deficit or surplus? If it is bad to have a deficit (or surplus) on the balance of payments, how can it be eliminated?

Balance of payments deficits

A balance of payments deficit occurs when a country spends more on imports of goods and services than it receives in receipts.

Possible causes of a deficit

(a) A high price of home-produced goods and services making exports expensive and imports cheaper.
(b) A high value of the country's currency, again making exports expensive and imports cheaper.
(c) A poor quality or low quantity (perhaps due to strikes) of home-produced goods and services, also poor after-sales services.
(d) Too much domestic demand which 'sucks in' imports.

Why is a balance of payments deficit considered to be undesirable?

(a) A deficit usually indicates that the economy is in a poor situation, depending on the particular cause. It could mean, for instance, that inflation is present in the economy.
(b) A deficit might mean that reserves of gold and foreign currency have to be run down to pay for the deficit.
(c) Loans to pay for the deficit (for example, from the IMF, see page 167) may have to be made and, in future, repaid with interest.
(d) Unpopular measures, like deflation and protection, might have to be introduced to solve the problems causing the deficit.

Curing a balance of payments deficit

A balance of payments deficit can be automatically solved with floating exchange rates by a fall in the value of the currency's exchange rate. However, on a system of fixed exchange rates the following measures might have to be taken to cure the deficit:

(a) *Borrowing from the International Monetary Fund* (IMF) (see page 167).
(b) *Imposition of tariffs and other measures of protection* (see page 150).
(c) *Deflationary policies* Deflation means an attempt to damp down home demand, thereby keeping prices down and leading to less demand for imports and cheaper exports. Such a policy might include *raising interest*

rates, preventing banks from creating credit, higher taxes and making *hire-purchase more difficult* and expensive to obtain.

(d) *Currency devaluation* As a last resort, the country may have to devalue the exchange rate of its currency. As we have seen this would make imports more expensive and exports cheaper and, assuming elastic demand for exports and imports, the balance of payments should be corrected. The United Kingdom devalued the pound in 1949 and 1967. However, there can be disadvantages in taking this course of action. Let us assume the United Kingdom devalued the pound to solve its balance of payments deficit. The devaluation might not work because:

foreigners may not buy more United Kingdom goods even if they have become cheaper; ie, their demand for United Kingdom exports is inelastic;
other countries might also devalue their currencies and erode the advantages of the United Kingdom devaluation;
the United Kingdom might not be able to produce extra goods because of strikes etc; ie, supply is inelastic;
because of the higher price of imports this may cause inflation in the United Kingdom and, therefore, erode the advantages of the devaluation.

Balance of payments surpluses
A balance of payments surplus is when a country's receipts from international trade exceed payments made.

Possible causes of a surplus

(a) Relatively low prices of home-produced goods making exports cheap and imports more expensive. Thus more exports are sold and less imports bought.
(b) Goods and services being exported at the expense of the home market.
(c) Reducing imports by producing goods which previously had to be imported. The United Kingdom's surplus on balance of payments in the early 1980s was mainly due to North Sea oil reducing imports of expensive oil.
(d) Reduced imports due to a lack of consumer demand in the home market.

Is a balance of payments surplus always desirable?
A balance of payments surplus is normally considered to be desirable because more money is flowing into the economy rather than out of it. However, it could be considered undesirable if:

(a) The surplus is large and made year after year. *It must mean some other countries are making deficits* and these countries may have to limit their future trade. Japan and West Germany have usually had a balance of payments surplus since 1950, but they have revalued their currencies at times (see below) to reduce their surpluses.
(b) *The surplus could be inflationary* because it will mean money flows into the economy increasing money supply, and demand will increase, causing prices to rise.

How to cure a balance of payments surplus

If the surplus on balance of payments is considered to be undesirable then the following policies might be introduced (assuming fixed exchange rates).

(a) *Increase consumer demand* in the home market. This will 'suck in' imports.
(b) *Revaluation of the currency* Here the exchange rate of currency would be allowed to rise in value against other currencies. This would have the opposite effect to devaluation. Export prices would rise and import prices would fall. Thus fewer exports would be sold and more imports would be bought assuming elastic demand for exports and imports.

International organisations

EC headquarters, Brussels

There are four main international organisations which need to be examined: the EC, the IMF, the IBRD and the GATT.

The European Community (the EC or Common Market)
Membership

The EC was formed in 1958 by the Treaty of Rome. The original six members were France, West Germany, Italy, Belgium, the Netherlands and Luxembourg. In 1973 the EC was enlarged by the membership of the United Kingdom,

Denmark and Eire. In 1981 Greece joined, and in 1986, Spain and Portugal joined too.

Aims and objectives of the EC
It is hoped that there will eventually be full economic, monetary and political union between the member countries. Thus the EC is something more than an ordinary *customs union* which only has free trade between member countries and tariffs against non-members. By 1980 some of the aims of the EC had been achieved:

(a) free trade between members and a common external tariff against non-members' imports;
(b) a common agricultural policy (CAP);
(c) co-operation between members on transport policy, land reform, regional policy and exchange rates.

Control of the EC

(a) *The Council of Ministers* Each member country sends ministers to meet other countries' ministers. On matters of vital importance unanimous votes are required. Thus any country can veto any proposal which it considers to be against its own national interest. On less important matters a qualified majority is required. There is a system of weighted votes so that the larger countries have a greater number of votes.
(b) *The Commission* Commissioners are appointed by member countries for a period of four years. The United Kingdom, France, Italy and West Germany provide two members each. Commissioners are expected to act independently of their own national interest and formulate proposals for consideration by the Council. It is regarded as the 'Civil Service' of the EC.
(c) *The Court of Justice* This is situated in Luxembourg and consists of one eminent judge from each country. They settle disputes and interpret rules and regulations made by both the Council and Commission. The court is able to award damages and impose sanctions on cases brought before it.
(d) *The European Parliament* Based in Strasbourg, France, its members are elected by electors in each country for a period of five years. Its main role is to consult and debate on policies made by the Council and Commission. With a two-thirds majority vote it can force the entire Commission to resign.

The United Kingdom membership of the EC since 1973
Since the United Kingdom joined the EC in 1973 there has been frequent public debate about whether it should stay in or decide to withdraw. Indeed a referendum (a national ballot) was held in 1975 and the majority of voters decided that the United Kingdom should remain a member. Let us examine the arguments in favour of United Kingdom membership.

(a) The EC has meant that the United Kingdom now has a much bigger market with no tariffs imposed on its goods.

The Community

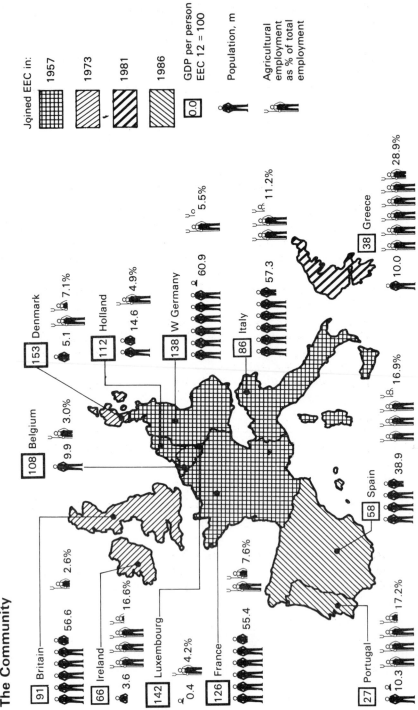

Joined EEC in:
1957
1973
1981
1986

GDP per person
EEC 12 = 100

Population, m

Agricultural employment as % of total employment

Denmark 153
5.1 7.1%

Holland 112
14.6 4.9%

W Germany 138
60.9 5.5%

Italy 86
57.3 11.2%

Greece 38
10.0 28.9%

Belgium 108
9.9 3.0%

16.9%

Spain 58
38.9

Britain 91
56.6 2.6%

Ireland 66
3.6 16.6%

Luxembourg 142
0.4 4.2%

France 126
55.4 7.6%

Portugal 27
10.3 17.2%

(b) The EC now buys most of the United Kingdom's exports and provides the United Kingdom with most of its imports.

(c) The EC countries have done much better economically than the United Kingdom since 1950. By joining the EC the United Kingdom should begin to catch up and improve its standard of living.

(d) The United Kingdom is becoming less important in world affairs. By joining the EC the United Kingdom is an important member of an important group of countries. Therefore it can have some say in world questions.

(e) Competition should encourage United Kingdom industry to be more efficient.

The disadvantages of the United Kingdom membership of the EC

(a) The United Kingdom has to contribute a great deal of money to the EC budget and most of this goes on agricultural support which the United Kingdom does not receive because it has only a small and efficient agriculture industry. United Kingdom taxpayers and consumers are therefore subsidising foreign farmers.

(b) Before joining the EC, the United Kingdom had close trading and political links with the countries of the Commonwealth such as New Zealand and Australia. The United Kingdom should return to these links.

(c) The United Kingdom's food prices have increased because of the common agricultural policy and the high prices needed to support small, inefficient farmers on the continent.

(d) The United Kingdom has lost a great deal of independence and control over its own affairs. Many of the decisions made about our everyday lives are being made in Brussels and Strasbourg.

(e) The United Kingdom has been unable to compete with more efficient countries such as West Germany. This has led to trade deficits with most EC countries and has worsened United Kingdom manufacturing and unemployment.

What do you think about the United Kingdom's membership of the Common Market?

The International Monetary Fund (IMF)

What do countries do if they make balance of payment deficits and need help to pay their debts? The IMF has been set up partly to help such countries.

Origins and development

The IMF was set up at a conference at Bretton Woods (USA) in 1944. The membership consists of 130 countries each of which has voting power determined by the size of the quota of money it has contributed to the fund. The five members with the largest quotas are the USA, the United Kingdom, West Germany, France and Japan.

UK manufacturing trade balance with the nine member states of EEC in 1984

	Imports		Exports		Balance	
	£000	Per cent of total	£000	Per cent of total	£000	Per cent of total
France	4 556 279	17	3 402 730	19	− 1 153 549	14
Belgium/Luxembourg	2 765 706	10.5	2 207 177	12	− 558 529	7
Netherlands	3 447 597	13	2 571 645	14	− 875 952	10
West Germany	9 978 957	38	4 909 782	27	− 5 069 175	60
Italy	3 258 429	12	1 951 787	11	− 1 306 642	15.5
Ireland	1 569 570	6	2 064 540	11.5	+ 494 970	−
Denmark	767 677	3	686 508	4	− 81 169	10
Greece	100 495	0.4	262 959	1.5	+ 162 464	−
Total	26 444 710		18 057 128		− 8 387 582	

The purposes of the IMF

The IMF has six basic objectives:

(a) to promote international monetary co-operation through the fund which provides the machinery for consultation;
(b) to promote the growth of international trade and maintain high levels of employment;
(c) to promote exchange stability. Exchange rates however may only be altered in cases of 'fundamental disequilibrium balance of payments';
(d) to eliminate exchange restrictions which might hamper world trade;
(e) to make the resources of the Fund available when countries have balance of payments difficulties;
(f) to prevent balance of payments disequilibrium between member countries (ie, to avoid large surpluses and deficits by member countries).

In 1971 the fixed exchange rate system was abandoned and floating exchange rates were restored. Thus some of the objectives of the IMF, such as objective (c), have become somewhat less important. However, the IMF remains an important international institution.

The United Kingdom and the IMF

In the 1970s the United Kingdom had many problems with its balance of payments and was forced to borrow from the IMF. In a sense countries do not borrow from the Fund but instead buy other members' currencies and gold with their own currency. Thus countries may purchase up to 125% of their own quota in amounts known as 'tranches'. They are charged interest on the borrowings and often give an undertaking with regard to future economic policies to overcome their balance of payments problems.

Special Drawing Rights

When the IMF was set up, one of the main problems it identified in the international economy was that of international liquidity. It was felt that there was not enough money to finance the volume of international trade. Countries could pay their debts in either the currency of the creditor country, gold, pounds sterling or US dollars. In 1967, therefore, the IMF created a new international asset known as Special Drawing Rights (SDRs) which may be used to settle balance of payments deficits. In order to make the system operate smoothly, however, member countries are required to accept some proportion of SDRs in payment for their debts.

The International Bank for Reconstruction and Development (IBRD) or World Bank

How do the richer countries of the world help the poorer countries? The operations of the World Bank are part of the answer. The World Bank, the sister organisation of the IMF, was set up in 1946. It is financed from subscriptions by member countries of the IMF, by bond issues and from revenues from past borrowings.

Although initially instituted to finance reconstruction in Europe after the Second World War, the World Bank has become increasingly important in its role of helping less developed countries of the world especially in Africa, Asia and South America. It operates by making loans, primarily to governments and their agencies, although private enterprise firms can also borrow.

Loans are intended to help less developed countries achieve economic growth but great emphasis is paid to helping countries build up agriculture, education, transport and electric power stations. The World Bank closely monitors the use to which the loan is being put and is always available to help and advise.

In 1960 the *International Development Agency* (IDA) was set up to help countries with severe economic problems. The loans are very long term (for instance fifty years) and no interest need be paid.

The General Agreement on Tariffs and Trade (GATT)

When we discussed free trade it was argued that free trade is supported by many economists and that since the Second World War (which ended in 1945) there have been moves towards achieving free trade between countries. An important organisation set up to help achieve this is the General Agreement on Tariffs and Trade (GATT).

GATT was set up in 1948. Member countries pledge themselves to the expansion of trade between countries with a minimum of barriers to trade, a reduction of import tariffs and quotas and the abolition of preferential trade agreements. There have been successive rounds of negotiations to achieve these objectives from the first meeting in 1948 to the *Kennedy Round* (named after President John Kennedy of the USA) in the 1960s, the *Tokyo Round* in the 1970s, and the *Uruguay Round* launched at the end of 1986.

Subsidies are severely criticised by GATT, which considers that subsidies on domestic and exported goods should be reduced or eliminated. It also seeks to promote the interests of less developed countries and the elimination of tariffs on commodities of particular concern to these countries. GATT has encountered problems with non-tariff barriers and the setting up of economic blocs making preferential agreements with each other. Examples of non-tariff barriers include government agencies purchasing only from home firms, or legislation which prevents imports. For example, Japanese anti-pollution laws virtually prohibit imports of cars from the United Kingdom.

The European Free Trade Association (EFTA)

Before joining the Common Market in 1973, the United Kingdom and Denmark belonged to EFTA. Other members included Austria, Norway, Sweden, Portugal, Finland, Iceland and Switzerland. EFTA is not a *customs union*. It does not have a common external tariff against non-members. EFTA is merely committed to free trade between members and has no wider economic or political objectives (like the EC) beyond this. The EFTA countries now have free trade agreements with the EC countries.

Checkpoints

1 International (or free) trade is regarded as being very advantageous to countries. It enables countries to specialise in producing commodities in which they have a comparative cost advantage and leads to more output, more variety and a better standard of living. International trade has other advantages apart from the benefits of specialisation.

2 Despite these advantages protectionist measures, aimed at reducing international trade, have often been introduced. Such measures include tariffs and quotas. There are several arguments in favour of protectionism although protectionism may not always work.

3 The terms of trade show changes in export prices relative to import prices. Whether an improvement in terms of trade improves the balance of payments depends on elasticity of demand for exports and imports.

4 The balance of payments is a record of a country's international trade in one year. It shows all receipts and expenditures and consists of current account (visibles and invisibles), investment and other capital flows and the balancing item. These give the balance for official financing (which is the balance of payments statistic). Official financing indicates what happens to a deficit or surplus.

5 The United Kingdom's record on balance of payments is discussed and also the structure of United Kingdom trade. The latter refers to which commodities the United Kingdom exports and imports and with which countries the United Kingdom trades.

6 Exchange rates are required in international trade to convert from one currency to another. The international economy has tried three main alternative methods of organising exchange rates: the gold standard, fixed exchange (managed flexibility) rates and floating exchange rates. Each system has advantages and disadvantages. At present the system of exchange rates is referred to as 'dirty floating'.

7 A country may have a balance of payments surplus or deficit. In both cases such a situation may be seen as a problem and measures may have to be taken to overcome the surplus or deficit. A balance of payments deficit is especially seen as a problem and measures such as protection, deflation and devaluation may have to be introduced.

8 Four main international organisations are discussed: the European Community (EC), the International Monetary Fund (IMF), General Agreement on Tariffs and Trade (GATT) and the World Bank. The objectives, workings, advantages and disadvantages of the EC and IMF are especially significant.

Multiple-choice questions – 8

1   Which of the following would be most likely to result in a rise in the external value of a currency? A significant increase in

    A   imports
    B   interest rates
    C   unemployment
    D   inflation
    E   taxation

2   Which of the following restrictions on trade would involve restricting the amount of the commodity imported to a specified amount?

    A   customs duty
    B   exchange control
    C   subsidies to domestic producers
    D   tariff
    E   quota

3   If the United Kingdom has a deficit on its overall balance of payments which one of the following must be negative?

    A   balancing item
    B   visibles
    C   balance for official financing
    D   balance on current account
    E   investment and other capital flows

4   A deterioration in the terms of trade of a country means

    A   import prices are relatively higher than export prices
    B   export prices are relatively higher than import prices
    C   the balance of payments must deteriorate
    D   the value of imports will fall
    E   the value of exports will rise

5   Which of the following is an example of a United Kingdom invisible export?

    A   British tourists visiting Spain
    B   the upkeep of the British Embassy in Moscow
    C   sales of United Kingdom manufactured goods in the USA
    D   French ships being insured at Lloyds of London
    E   British goods being transported by an Australian airline

6   In what section of the balance of payments would an increase in overseas investment in the United Kingdom be recorded?

A private transfers of money
B investment and other capital flows
C invisible imports
D balance of trade
E interest, profits and dividends

7 The following figures relate to a country's dealings with other countries in a
particular year

	£m
imports of goods	2000
exports of goods	1000
invisible imports	3000
invisible exports	2000

The country's current account is

A £1000m in deficit
B £2000m in deficit
C balanced
D £1000m in surplus
E £2000m in surplus

8 When a country revalues its currency, this must result in

A a deterioration in terms of trade
B an improvement in the balance of payments
C a deterioration in current account
D imports becoming more expensive
E exports becoming more expensive

9 One of the main advantages of membership of the European Community is
that member countries have all

A abolished tariffs between each other
B banned all imports from outside the European Community
C agreed to fix exchange rates between each other
D decided to raise food prices as high as possible
E been able to buy North Sea oil at below cost prices

10 A given combination of resources will give the following output of wheat and
wine in two countries: Country A and Country B

	Wheat		Wine
Country A	24	or	16
Country B	12	or	12

If output maximising co-operation arose, which of the following must be true?

    A Country A would specialise in wheat
    B Country B would specialise in both commodities
    C Both would want to specialise in wheat
    D Both would want to specialise in wine
    E Country A would not co-operate because it is better at producing both commodities than Country B

Answers on page 328.

Data response question 8

	Visible balance £ million	Invisible balance £ million	Current account balance £ million
1980		+ 1568	+ 2929
1981	+ 3360	+ 2799	+ 6159
1982	+ 2331		+ 3937
1983	− 835	+ 3969	+ 3134
1984	− 4384	+ 5596	+ 1212
1985	− 2111	+ 5713	

(a) (i) What was the visible balance in 1980?
  (ii) What was the invisible balance in 1982?
  (iii) What was the current account balance in 1985?
(b) To which of the categories given in the table above would the following transactions belong (state if an export or import)?
  (i) The sale of Rolls-Royce aero-engines to Australia?
  (ii) The flow of interest profits and dividends from Nissan (Sunderland) back to Japan?
  (iii) A Japanese tourist visiting the United Kingdom?
  (iv) A Stock Exchange dealer purchasing a computer manufactured in the USA?
(c) What factors might explain the change in the record on visibles between 1980 and 1985?
(d) What other statistics are required before the balance for official financing can be calculated?
(e) What would be the effect of a large fall in oil prices on
  (i) Current account?
  (ii) Sterling exchange rate?
  (iii) Fiscal revenues?
(f) Assume an economy makes a consistently large surplus on balance of payments.
  (i) Give possible causes of the surplus.
  (ii) How could the government reduce the surplus?
  (iii) Why would a government wish to reduce the surplus?

9 Money and banking

Money

Characteristics of a good monetary medium
Money must have the following qualities.

(a) *Portability* Money must be portable or easily carried about. It would be very difficult to use anything large and bulky as money.
(b) *Divisibility* Money must be able to be divided into smaller amounts to enable small purchases to take place. The use of large goods or animals would not facilitate divisibility.
(c) *Acceptability* Money must be accepted as having some value. Labour must accept money in payment for services provided, and retailers must accept money as payment for their goods.
(d) *Durability* Money must last a long time. It must not die, wither away or be easily defaced. Anything which is alive or perishable would not be a very good form of money.
(e) *Scarcity* Money must be limited in supply to have any value. If money grew on trees then it would cease to have any value.
(f) *Stability* The value of money should not fluctuate wildly.

Stages in the development of money
Modern sophisticated economies rely on division of labour (specialisation) to increase output of goods and services. Such economies need money to facilitate easy exchange and this mainly takes the form of notes and coins in circulation and bank deposits subject to withdrawal by cheque. However, economies have not always been so advanced and money has taken a variety of forms. Let us now look at stages in the development of money.

Barter
Barter is the exchange of one good for another. It is used in undeveloped economies (ie, poor economies) today, to exchange the surplus of one good for other goods. Barter has several disadvantages.

(a) *It is very slow and cumbersome* In advanced economies, which rely on specialisation, exchange would be slowed down.
(b) *It depends on the 'double coincidence of wants'* If someone wants to exchange a bicycle for a guitar, they have to find a person with a guitar who requires a bicycle. It may be very difficult to find such a person.

(c) *There is a problem of amounts* How many radios would exchange for a television? How many televisions would exchange for a motor car?

(d) *There is a problem of divisibility* If the good which a person has to exchange is large and bulky, it may be difficult to divide it up to facilitate exchanges.

The use of one good as money

In some economies, money may take the form of one good. For example, sea shells have been used as money in South Pacific islands and cattle were used as money in the Zulu economy. There may be problems in using a good as money because the good does not have the necessary qualities to act as a monetary medium.

Coins

Early coins were made from precious metals such as gold and silver. This was to make them acceptable to the people and indeed precious metals conformed to the qualities of good money. Such coins had an intrinsic value (value in themselves) which was reflected in their face value (extrinsic value).

The main problem with using gold and silver as a basis for coins was that the amount of coinage was dependent on how much gold and silver a country had. This would be too restrictive in the modern economy where a great deal of money is needed to finance the large amount of exchanges.

Today's coins are made from alloys of copper and nickel, or bronze, and have a face value worth more than the value of the metal they contain. (They have an extrinsic value greater than the value of the metals they contain.) These coins are therefore called *token coins*. They are acceptable because people have confidence in them. To enforce their acceptability (which ensures that exchanges of goods and services takes place smoothly), modern coins are *legal tender*. This means that notes and coins of the Bank of England must be accepted in settlement of debt in the United Kingdom. Legal tender also limits the amount of coin which can be paid at any one time.

Note: cheques and credit cards are not legal tender and as such need not be accepted as settlement of debt.

Bank notes

Modern bank notes have their origins in the receipts for deposits given by goldsmiths in the seventeenth century.

At first the receipt would be for the whole amount deposited, but eventually several different receipts for the amount were given. These receipts would be acceptable as a method of payment.

Before 1914 the bulk of bank notes were *convertible notes* because they could be converted into their gold equivalent. Still written on modern bank notes is the sentence 'I promise to pay the bearer on demand the sum of five pounds' (in the case of other notes the amount would be different). This refers to the payment of the gold equivalent on demand in return for the bank note.

However, in today's economy the vast majority of notes are *inconvertible notes*. This means that they are not convertible into gold and this makes the 'I promise to pay . . .' statement worthless. That proportion of note issue which is inconvertible is called the *fiduciary issue*. The fiduciary issue is so large because a large money supply is needed to finance the large amount of exchanges which take place in the modern economy. Modern notes, like modern coins, are *token money* because their face value (extrinsic value) is greater than their intrinsic value. Acceptability is enforced on Bank of England notes because they are legal tender.

Bank deposits subject to withdrawal by cheque
In recent years the United Kingdom has been described as a 'cashless society'. This means that increasingly most payments are in the form of cheques (and, indeed, credit cards). Over 90% of business transactions (in value) are financed by cheque. The cheque is not money, it is merely a representation of money which is in a bank current account. A cheque is a transfer order enabling transfer of money from one bank current account to another. Cheques are not legal tender and cannot be enforced in payment of debt. An even more recent innovation than cheques are credit cards which are an extension of bank account deposits. We shall discuss cheques and credit cards in more detail on pages 178–81.

What is money in the modern economy?
Money is anything which is generally acceptable in payment for debts. In a modern economy this would include notes and coins of the Bank of England and bank deposits subject to withdrawal by cheque. Thus not all the means of making payments are money because they may not be generally acceptable. This may include postal orders and money orders, bills of exchange and stamps.

Official definitions of the money supply
The government defines money supply in various ways.

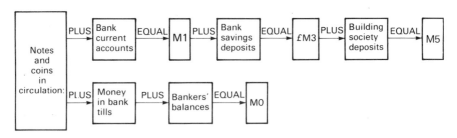

What the Treasury means by 'money'

Cheques and the clearing system
A cheque is not to be considered as money. Money in this connection is the current account bank deposit and the cheque is an instruction to transfer money from the drawer's account to the payee's account.

Drawer, drawee and payee
The drawer is the person who makes out the cheque and signs it. The payee is the

person into whose account the money is to be paid. The drawee is the banker of the drawer.

Crossed cheques and open cheques

A crossed cheque has two parallel lines drawn across its face. This means that the cheque must be cleared into the payee's bank account and the person presenting the cheque to the bank cannot receive cash. An open cheque is a cheque which can be cashed immediately at the bank. A crossed cheque is therefore much safer in case of theft, loss or forgery.

Cheque cards

These are issued by the bank and make cheques up to a value of £50 more acceptable when presented with the cheque.

A cheque card

The advantages of cheques

Cheques are much more convenient than bundles of notes. Cheques can be made safe and secure by being crossed. They can be made out at any time and in any place thus eliminating the need for cash. Cheques can be safely and conveniently sent through the post, and are only of value after being signed by the drawer.

The clearing house system

When a cheque is made payable and given to the payee, the cheque has to be cleared. This means the account of the drawer must be debited by that amount whereas the account of the payee must be credited. This can be quite a complicated procedure (see page 180).

Other methods of payment

Credit cards

The customer can make purchases by credit card up to his or her *credit limit*, a figure which has been agreed between the customer and the credit card company in advance. The details of the purchase are printed on a receipt (or voucher) issued by the retailer and signed by the customer. There are three copies:

(a) the top copy is kept by the customer as a receipt and a record for checking the statement when it arrives;

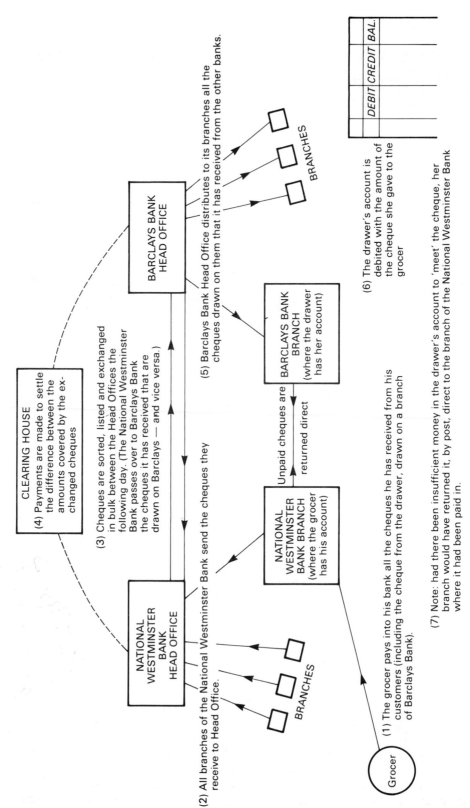

The clearing of cheques

CLEARING HOUSE
(4) Payments are made to settle the difference between the amounts covered by the exchanged cheques

BARCLAYS BANK HEAD OFFICE

(5) Barclays Bank Head Office distributes to its branches all the cheques drawn on them that it has received from the other banks.

BRANCHES

BARCLAYS BANK BRANCH
(where the drawer has her account)

Unpaid cheques are returned direct

(6) The drawer's account is debited with the amount of the cheque she gave to the grocer

	DEBIT	CREDIT	BAL.

NATIONAL WESTMINSTER BANK HEAD OFFICE

(3) Cheques are sorted, listed and exchanged in bulk between the Head Offices the following day. (The National Westminster Bank passes over to Barclays Bank the cheques it has received that are drawn on Barclays — and vice versa.)

(2) All branches of the National Westminster Bank send the cheques they receive to Head Office.

BRANCHES

NATIONAL WESTMINSTER BANK BRANCH
(where the grocer has his account)

Grocer

(1) The grocer pays into his bank all the cheques he has received from his customers (including the cheque from the drawer, drawn on a branch of Barclays Bank).

(7) Note: had there been insufficient money in the drawer's account to 'meet' the cheque, her branch would have returned it, by post, direct to the branch of the National Westminster Bank where it had been paid in.

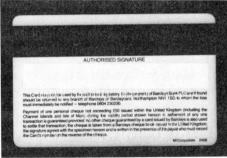

A Barclaycard

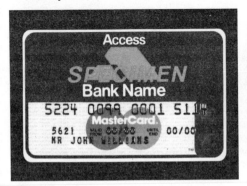

An Access card

(b)   one copy is kept by the retailer as a record of the transaction;
(c)   one copy is sent to the headquarters of the credit card company and details of
      the purchases are added to the customer's account.

A statement of all expenditure is sent once a month by the company to the customer. The customer is obliged to pay at least a minimum amount of the debt and interest will be charged on the amount outstanding. However, if they wish, customers can pay all of the debt and therefore incur no interest charges. Customers are given three weeks to pay the statement. The monthly interest rate is calculated twelve times a year and the actual annual rate of interest will be quite high. Credit cards are not legal tender.

Postal orders
Postal orders are issued by the Post Office for varying sums up to a value of £20. Postal orders are a popular way for clients of football pools firms to pay for their coupon entry. The value of the order can be increased by fixing postage stamps in the space provided. The Post Office makes a charge (called poundage) the size of which depends on the value of the postal order. Postal orders are issued blank and the sender is recommended to fill in the name of the payee and the office of payment. They can be crossed, like a cheque, which means the postal order must be paid into a bank account. Postal orders are marked 'not negotiable' which means that only the rightful owner can cash it, in other words, the ownership of the postal order cannot be transferred to another person. Postal orders are not legal tender. A counterfoil is attached to the postal order and should be kept by the

sender in case of loss. Postal orders have the following disadvantages compared to cheques:

(a) the time and inconvenience in purchasing postal orders and filling them in;
(b) most traders will have cheques anyway;
(c) blank postal orders can easily be stolen and cashed;
(d) for large amounts they will be more expensive than cheques.

Money orders
These are issued for sums up to £50. The sender fills out a special form which states the amount of the order, the name of the payee, where payable and whether open or crossed order. This form is handed, together with the money, to the Post Office who will arrange for payment to be made. The payee will be required to produce proof of identity and supply the name of the drawer. Overseas money orders are very similar.

National Giro (see page 198)

Bills of exchange (see page 194)

Methods of payment provided by commercial banks
Apart from cheques, commercial banks operate other methods which allow customers to make payments.

(a) *Banker's orders* (or standing orders) When a customer wishes to make a regular payment of the same amount to a creditor he can arrange a banker's order. A banker's order authorises the bank to make these fixed payments on a regular basis (usually monthly) until the customer cancels the order. Banker's orders are especially used for building society mortgage repayments, insurance premiums, hire-purchase instalments, and household rates. They save the customer the time and trouble of remembering to pay these bills and the expense of postage.
(b) *Direct debits* These are similar to standing orders but the exact amount of the payment may not be known. Therefore the customer will authorise the bank to pay the bill at regular intervals but the amount will not be specified. This method of payment could be used for gas bills, electricity bills or phone bills.
(c) *Bank giro* (or multiple credit transfer) Where a business (or individual) has a number of creditors to pay, it can avoid the cost and trouble of writing out several cheques by using a bank giro. The firm writes out one cheque to cover all of the amounts and hands this to the bank, together with a list of creditors and their bank account details. The bank will then see to it that the payments are made. Private customers may use this when they have a large number of bills to pay at any one time.
(d) *Banker's drafts* Sometimes a cheque may not be acceptable to a creditor because they do not have confidence in the ability of the drawer of the cheque to pay. In this case, usually when a large amount of money is involved, the bank will issue a bank draft, which is like a cheque of the bank drawn on

itself. This will be readily acceptable to the creditor who will have confidence in the bank's ability to pay. The bank's customer will of course write a cheque for the same amount payable to the bank. Banker's drafts are widely used in international trade where not much may be known about purchasers of goods.

The functions of money
Money should perform the following four functions:

A medium of exchange
We have already discussed the disadvantages of barter as a medium of exchange. Money should be a convenient and acceptable way of making exchanges without the drawbacks of exchanging goods for other goods. In a modern economy notes and coins and bank accounts subject to withdrawal by cheque are the main forms of money. Thus a teacher would accept money as payment for his or her work knowing that money would be accepted by retailers and producers in return for goods and services. Retailers would accept money because they know that their workers would accept money as wages and their suppliers would accept money as payment. Indeed, a modern and complex economy, dependent as it is on specialisation and exchange, relies on a good monetary system to facilitate easy and convenient exchange.

A measure of value and unit of account
Money allows goods to be given a value in terms of a price. The higher the price of a good or service, then the greater the value that consumers in general give to that good or service. The use of barter had obvious disadvantages in fulfilling this function. For instance, how could the values of different goods be compared in a system operating by barter? It would be very cumbersome and complicated. Money serves as a *standard* by which we can make comparison of values.

Moreover, money can be used as a unit of account. It is easy to keep accurate records of expenditures and receipts in money. Again, barter would have disadvantages as a unit of account.

A store of value
If money is acceptable throughout the economy and people have confidence that its acceptability will continue, then some people may store (or save) any surplus wealth in the form of money. In the past, when goods were used as money, there were problems in storing wealth because the good might deteriorate or perish. Similarly, animals might die causing a loss of wealth. One drawback to storing wealth in the form of money, is that inflation might cause the value of the stored money to decline. For instance, £100 in 1978 was worth a great deal more, in terms of what it could buy, than £100 in 1988. To compensate people for this loss of purchasing power, people who are storing money will probably be paid a rate of interest. Many people store money with institutions such as building societies, insurance companies and banks.

Not all surplus wealth will be held in institutions because money is also a *liquid asset* and people will keep some of their wealth in cash or liquid form, such as in a current account. There are three main motives for holding money in a very liquid form:

(a) *Precautionary motive* Money may be held in a liquid form in case of some unexpected expense like a car repair bill or a social event.
(b) *Transactionary motive* People require money to finance everyday exchanges and transactions.
(c) *Speculative motive* Some people will need some money in liquid form while they are considering where best to invest the money to receive the best return and interest.

A means of deferred payments
Money should be acceptable and durable, so that a buyer of goods and services may be able to postpone making immediate payment for purchases. The seller will accept this arrangement because of confidence that money will still have value when payment is eventually made. Indeed, in modern business transactions three month periods of credit are granted on bills of exchange (see page 194). Hire-purchase allows consumers to postpone payments and pay back over time. Inflation would limit confidence in money as a means of deferred payment. Thus interest would be charged on the amounts of money on which payment is deferred to compensate for any loss of value in the amount of money finally received by the creditor.

Commercial banks

Symbols of the main clearing banks

Commercial banks have their origins in the activities of the seventeenth century goldsmiths who accepted deposits of valuables, and in return gave receipts which developed into an early form of bank notes. Like modern banks, the goldsmiths kept some of their deposits in liquid form (ie, near money), to meet any demand by depositors and the remainder was invested or given in the form of loans in order to make a profit. The goldsmiths developed into private banks, probably partnerships with no shareholders. Unlike modern banks, the private banks were able to issue their own bank notes. Eventually the private banks were able to form into joint stock companies, issue shares, and have limited liability.

Through the years the numbers of banks dwindled as some banks went bankrupt and others merged together. Today there are four big commercial banks ('the big four') – Barclays, Lloyds, Midland and National Westminster. Other important banks include Coutts, the Co-operative Bank, the Royal Bank of

Scotland and the TSB Bank. All of these banks have numerous branches throughout the United Kingdom.

Commercial banks have several alternative names, including:

(a) *clearing banks* because they clear cheques at the London Clearing House;
(b) *joint stock banks* because they issue shares;
(c) *high street banks* because their branches are probably found in the main street of most towns.

The functions of commercial banks

Acceptance of deposits

When a commercial bank accepts deposits, it regards these as its liabilities because they are owed by the bank to its customers. There are four main types of deposit:

(a) *Current accounts* Current accounts give a cheque book which enables the account holder to be repaid on demand. Cheques are a very convenient system of making payments. The holder of the current account can enjoy the use of a variety of services provided by the bank. The disadvantages of the current account is that no interest is payable on the balance of the account. However, some banks are beginning to introduce a new type of current account which does pay interest.

(b) *Deposit accounts* The deposit account receives interest on the deposit balance and the holder can deposit funds at any time. However, deposit accounts have no cheque books and the account holder will have to give notice of withdrawal for large amounts.

(c) *Savings accounts* Mainly intended for the small saver who may be saving for a specific target, such as a holiday. They earn a low rate of interest and only small amounts are repayable on demand.

(d) *Budget accounts* The depositor calculates the annual amount he or she will have to pay for regular bills such as electricity, gas, telephone, insurance and hire purchase. A fixed monthly amount is then paid from the current account into the budget account from which the bills are paid, probably by standing order.

Making loans

Loans, or advances (ie, money owed to the bank) are a very profitable asset for the bank. Advances take two main forms:

(a) *Overdrafts* An overdraft is when a current account holder overspends on his or her account. If, for instance, someone has only £100 in their current account and yet they cash a cheque for £200, their current account has become overdrawn (or 'gone into the red') by the sum of £100. The customer will be charged interest on a daily basis on the amount of the overdraft. It is usual practice to get the bank's permission before having an overdraft. It may be that the bank has refused permission for a customer to have an overdraft. If that customer then proceeds to write a cheque for more than the amount in the current account the cheque might 'bounce'. This means it will not be honoured by the bank and will be referred to the payee with the words 'refer to drawer' written on the cheque. 'Bouncing' a cheque, ie deliberately writing a cheque knowing that there are no funds to cover it, is a serious offence.

(b) *Personal loan accounts* A loan account is a loan for a specific amount to be paid back, plus interest on the total amount, over a fixed period of time by equal monthly instalments. The money is credited to the current account. If the amount of money is only required by the customer for a short period of time it may be cheaper to have an overdraft than a loan.

Acting as agents of payment

Banks fulfil this function in a variety of ways:

(a) *by clearing cheques*: see page 180;
(b) *standing orders*: see page 182;
(c) *direct debits*: see page 182;
(d) *bank giro* (credit transfer): see page 182;
(e) *banker's drafts*: see page 182.

Other services provided by banks

(a) custody of valuables;
(b) advice on investments, stocks and shares;
(c) advice on insurance and tax affairs;
(d) issue of foreign exchange and travellers' cheques;
(e) night safes where businesspeople can deposit cash after the bank has closed;
(f) cash cards, enabling customers to make computerised withdrawals and deposits by inserting the card into a cash dispensing machine and entering a personal computer code which accesses their account;
(g) act as executors of wills and trustees of estates;
(h) factoring: the bank agreeing to purchase the debts of a business account client in return for some say in the running of the firm;
(i) the provision of mortgage loans mainly for house purchase.

Liquidity and profitability

Banks require to hold both liquid assets (assets which are quickly and easily converted into cash to repay depositors' demands for cash) and profitable assets. However the more liquid the asset then the less profitable it is, and the less liquid the asset the more profitable it is. The bank's liabilities are its deposits (mainly current accounts and deposit accounts). In order to steer a middle course between these two conflicting considerations of liquidity and profitability, the banks keep certain assets in liquid form. Let us assume that they keep a 10% of minimum reserve asset ratio. This means that 10% of all assets have to be kept in liquid reserve asset form which include:

(a) holdings of Treasury bills;
(b) holdings of bills of exchange;

Functions of commercial banks

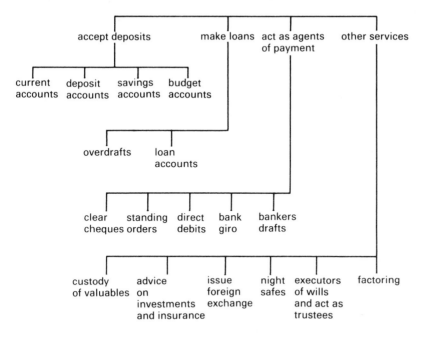

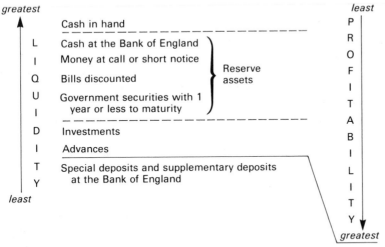

Liquid and profitable assets

(c) reserves held at the Bank of England;
(d) money at call with the discount houses;
(e) holdings of government securities with less than twelve months to mature.

Cash in tills (notes and coins) are not included as part of minimum reserve assets even though they constitute the bank's most liquid asset.

By keeping 10% of its assets in liquid form the bank feels that it can maintain liquidity and use the remainder of assets to make profits.

How commercial banks create credit (money)

The money supply consists of notes and coins in circulation and bank deposits. The government itself can create money by issuing more notes and coins. However, banks can also create money by creating bank deposits. The bank realises that when it receives a deposit, not all depositors will require their money back at once. All that the bank has to do is keep back some of the deposits in reserve asset form to meet the demands of depositors. As an example, assume there is a 10% minimum reserve asset ratio. In its most sophisticated form an initial deposit of £1000 can support the creation of £9000 of additional deposits.

Bank's liabilities		*Bank's assets*	
Initial deposit	£1 000	Reserve assets	£1 000
Created deposits	£9 000	Loans	£9 000
	£10 000		£10 000

In other words, the bank has treated all of the initial deposit as reserve assets which has enabled it to create loans of £9000. Reserve assets at £1000 are 10% of total assets standing at £10 000. Thus the bank is confident it can meet any demands on it by depositors. *Every loan creates a deposit*!, that is to say, the bank makes loans to customers by creating extra deposits. The bank credits the account of the borrower with the amount of the loan.

Restrictions on the ability of banks to create money

There are two main restrictions.

The clearing house operates as a restriction

Assume one bank creates too much credit for its customers and the other banks do not do the same for their customers, then the bank will be in debt with the other banks at the end of the day's clearing at the London Clearing House. This will mean, if this continued, that the bank's reserves at the Bank of England will soon diminish and this would act as a brake on the bank's creation of credit.

A restrictionist monetary policy

See page 191.

The Bank of England

The Bank of England is the *central bank* in the economy, that is to say it is at the centre of the banking system. Its origins can be traced back to 1694 when it was set up by King William III to raise money to fight the French. It was granted special privileges and was the most important of all the banks. Its pre-eminence was established by the 1844 Bank Charter Act which effectively gave the bank the sole right to issue bank notes. In 1946 it was nationalised and is now the government's main agent in enforcing its monetary and banking policies.

The Bank of England

The functions of the Bank of England

Issues notes
The Bank Charter Act 1844 conferred on the Bank of England the sole right to issue bank notes. The Bank of England now has a monopoly in note issue (with the exception of a small number of banks in Scotland and Northern Ireland). Bank of England notes and coins are legal tender.

The banker's bank
The commercial banks use the Bank of England in a similar way to the way their own customers use them. A very important part of this function is the fact that the Bank of England keeps the reserves of the commercial banks (these are part of minimum reserve assets). These balances held at the Bank of England would be used to settle inter-bank debts after a day's clearing at the London Clearing House.

External responsibilities
The Bank of England has close contacts with the central banks of other countries. It provides a variety of services for other central banks such as keeping some of their reserves of sterling, gold and foreign currency. International organisations such as the International Monetary Fund (IMF) and the International Bank for

Reconstruction and Development (the World Bank) also keep some of their reserves at the Bank of England.

Lender of the last resort
This function enables the Bank of England to help the money market (discount houses, see page 193) carry on in times of difficulty. The discount houses receive much of their finance in the form of 'money at call and short notice' from the commercial banks. Due to pressures caused by the Bank of England monetary policy (see page 191) the commercial banks may call in their loans and thus leave the discount houses short of finance. To survive the discount houses may be 'forced into the bank' which will lend money to them at a high rate of interest called the *penal rate* (which until August 1981 was known as the *minimum lending rate*). This explains the reluctance of discount houses to borrow from the Bank of England unless absolutely necessary.

The government's bank
This function includes a variety of services provided by the Bank of England for the government.

(a) *Management of the exchequer account*
     This account deals with government revenues from taxation and government spending required for road building, schools, health and so on.
(b) *Management of the National Debt*
     This is the debt owed by the government of the United Kingdom to individuals and organisations at both home and abroad. Foreign governments may also hold some of the debt as a part of their reserves. The debt comprises sales of government securities (gilts), both long term and short term, issued to finance government spending. An important example of a security sold by the Bank of England is a Treasury bill (see page 194). The Bank of England will also organise payment of debt interest to holders of securities. The management of the National Debt is one of the Bank of England's oldest functions dating back to 1694 when the Bank was set up.
(c) *Protection of gold and foreign currency reserves*
     These reserves are required as a 'cushion' in the event of a balance of payments deficit. They would be used to help finance the deficit. These reserves would probably be added to in the case of a balance of payments surplus. The Bank of England also administers government regulations as regards supply and demand for foreign exchange and arranges loans (possibly from the IMF) to supplement the reserves.
(d) *Management of the Exchange Equalisation Account*
     The Exchange Equalisation Account attempts to stabilise the external exchange rate of the pound sterling. If the pound is dropping in value relative to foreign currencies then the Exchange Equalisation Account will purchase pounds and, according to the laws of the supply and demand, the price of the pound will remain at its higher level. On the other hand, if the pound is rising in value then the Exchange Equalisation Account may sell

pounds to keep its price down to the lower value. Under a system of floating exchange rates the account would very rarely be used.

(e) *Operation of the government's monetary policy* (see below).

Operating government monetary policy

As we have seen the money supply consists mainly of notes and coins in circulation and bank deposits subject to withdrawal by cheque. We have also seen that commercial banks can create money (credit) by creating bank deposits. The Bank of England may wish to restrict the banks' powers to create money, because this may cause too much demand and therefore inflation may result. There is one school of thought, called the monetarists, who see too much money as the main reason for inflation.

There are two types of monetary policy which may be pursued by the government:

A restrictionist or deflationary monetary policy

This policy would attempt to reduce inflation and would also probably mean that the balance of payments improves, as less demand will mean fewer imports. However, such a policy could cause the disadvantages of worsening unemployment and preventing growth of national income (ie, output of goods and services) by the United Kingdom economy.

An expansionist or a reflationary monetary policy

This policy would attempt to reduce unemployment and stimulate national income because this would create a higher level of demand in the economy. However, such a policy may have the disadvantages of worsening inflation and causing a deterioration in the balance of payments as more imports come into the economy.

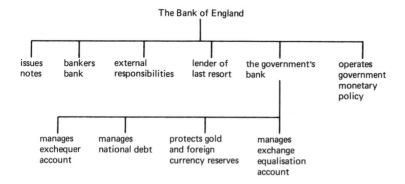

Functions of the Bank of England

The weapons or instruments of monetary policy

Let us assume the government is operating a *restrictionist* monetary policy. Such a policy, up to August 1981, involved:

(a) *The minimum reserve asset ratio* This was the basis of the whole system of monetary control. The banks were required to keep a 10% minimum reserve asset ratio (formerly 12½%). They were not allowed to diminish their reserve assets to below 10% of total liabilities. This obviously controlled how much money banks could create (as shown on page 188). The Bank of England by diminishing the banks' reserve assets can reduce their ability to create credit.

(b) *Raising minimum lending rate (MLR)* If MLR was increased then interest rates throughout the economy rose. This made money and credit very expensive and had the effect of reducing demand for money.

(c) *Open market operations* This is when the Bank of England sells government securities (eg Treasury bills). These are bought by discount houses, commercial banks and the non-bank sector (foreign investors or indeed private individuals). If they are purchased by commercial banks' customers, then cheques are drawn on the commercial banks and the Bank of England runs down the bank reserves that it holds. This means that the commercial banks have fewer reserve assets and therefore cannot create so much credit.

(d) *Funding* This is when the Bank of England sells long term securities or converts short term debt into long term debt. It has virtually the same effect as open market operations, but is more long-lasting.

(e) *Special deposits* These are called in by the Bank of England from the commercial banks. They will have the effect of depleting the banks' minimum reserve assets which will mean that commercial banks have less power to create credit.

(f) *Directives* These are orders or commands from the Bank of England to the commercial banks not to create loans and overdrafts and thereby create deposits.

Since August 1981 the Bank of England has been operating new monetary control arrangements. These include the following changes.

The requirement of the banks to maintain a specific minimum reserve assets ratio was abolished;
Banks are required to keep ½% of eligible liabilities with the Bank of England (eligible liabilities are the bank's deposits);

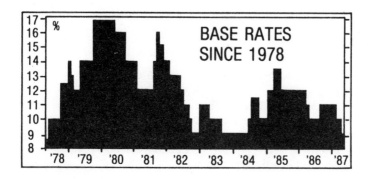

The Bank of England has ceased to announce MLR. Instead, the Bank of England will influence interest rates through open market operations and individual banks can now decide on their own base rates.

In this section we have discussed monetary policy in terms of a restrictionist policy. The introduction of an *expansionist* policy would mean that measures exactly opposite to those of the restrictionist policy would be taken. This means that interest rates would be lowered, securities would be bought back in open market operations and funding, special deposits would be released and directives to banks *not* to lend would be cancelled.

Other financial institutions

It is possible to make a distinction between institutions dealing in short term lending (the money market) and those dealing in long term lending (the capital market). The institutions of the money market and the capital market are illustrated in the following diagram.

Financial Institutions

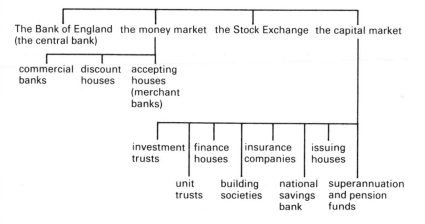

The money market
This consists of those institutions which lend money to government and companies at 'call or short notice' or up to three months. It consists mainly of:

(a) *commercial banks* (see pages 184–8);
(b) *discount houses*;
(c) *accepting houses* or *merchant banks*.

Discount houses

(a) *Membership* The discount houses consist of eleven members of the London Discount Market Association. There are as follows: Alexander Discount Co; Allen Harvey and Rose; Carter, Ryder and Co; Clive Discount Co; Jessel,

Toynbee and Co; King and Shaxson; Gerrard and National Discount Co; Gillet Brothers Discount Co; Seccombe Marshall and Campion; Smith St Aubyn and Co; the Union Discount Co of London.

(b) *Functions* The main function of discount houses is the 'discount', a variety of IOUs issued by the government, local authorities, banks and companies. 'Discounting' means buying a security at less than face value, holding it until it matures and receiving the full face value. There are two main securities in which dealings take place: Treasury bills and bills of exchange.

(c) *Treasury bills* Treasury bills are short term securities with a life of 91 days and sales enable the government to finance short term borrowing requirements. The government sells Treasury bills each week in denominations of £5000, £10 000, £25 000, £100 000, £500 000 and £1 000 000. Discount houses and other financial institutions submit bids for these bills. The lower the price offered, the higher the rate of interest paid on the bill by the government. For instance, if the bid price is £98 for every £100 worth of treasury bills then the annual rate of discount (interest) will be $4 \times 2\% = 8\%$.

Discount houses 'underwrite' the weekly Treasury bill issue. This means that they will purchase the whole amount if needs be. In return, the Bank of England will act as 'lender of the last resort' (see page 190) when discount houses run short of funds. Ownership of Treasury bills can be passed on to another owner within the three months.

(d) *Bills of exchange* Bills of exchange (industrial bills) are used to finance both

domestic and international trade. When a firm A sells goods to another firm, B, it will not expect to be paid immediately. It would be normal practice for firm A to be paid by firm B in three months' time. Therefore Firm A will send Firm B a bill of exchange which specifies how much is owed and when it is to be paid. Firm B (the drawee) signs (accepts) the bill and sends it back to Firm A. Firm A now has a written acknowledgement of debt by Firm B. It is a kind of post-dated cheque. Bills of exchange can be transferred to another owner within the three months. Indeed, Firm A may need the money urgently before the bill matures. Firm A may sell the bill at a discount to a discount house who will then receive the full face value of the bill when it matures by presenting it to Firm B. Commercial banks will also discount bills of exchange. Sometimes it may be necessary for the bill to be accepted (guaranteed) by an accepting house in cases where the firm signing the bill (the drawee) is not well known. This is dealt with in the section which follows, on Accepting houses.

Discount houses, therefore, provide short term loans to the government, local authorities and companies. Indeed, they agree to underwrite the Treasury bill issue. They also provide a means whereby the government can influence interest rates in the economy.

(e) *Discount houses' finance* Discount houses receive much of their finance by borrowing from commercial banks. These loans are called 'money at call' or short notice. This is because the commercial banks can call in these loans immediately whenever they require the money. Commercial banks regard these loans as part of their minimum reserve assets. This may leave the discount houses short of funds. They will be able to borrow money from the Bank of England in its capacity as 'lender of last resort'. This facility is offered by the central bank because the discount houses agree to underwrite the Treasury bill issue.

Accepting houses (merchant banks)

(a) *Accepting bills of exchange*
The main business of accepting houses is to accept commercial bills. This means that for a commission they will use their good name to guarantee that a bill will be paid on maturity. This is important when the drawee of the bill is not a well-known (possibly foreign) company. Thus the seller of goods may be reluctant to accept the bill of exchange and moreover it may be difficult to discount on the London discount market. The accepting houses by lending their good name will make the bill easily discounted on the discount market. The accepting house guarantees payment of the bill, should the drawee default.

This function grew out of the origins of merchant banks who tended originally to specialise in certain types of trade, and therefore had an intimate knowledge of all companies involved in this trade. This knowledge allowed them to accept bills for the firms which were little known. There are now seventeen members of the Accepting House Committee including Hill, Samuel and Co; Samuel Montagu and Co; Morgan Grenfell and Co and Rothschild and Sons.

(b) *Expansion of services*

Today merchant banks fulfil several other functions:

   (i) *Issuing houses* They act as issuing houses and arrange for new issues of stocks and shares on behalf of government and firms. See page 237 for a discussion of the new issue market.

 (ii) *Market-makers* Since 'Big Bang' on the Stock Exchange many merchant banks have become market-makers, joining up with established brokers (see page 239).

(iii) *Extension of banking functions* They have undertaken some of the traditional functions of commercial banks such as accepting deposits (including current accounts) and making loans. Commercial banks have also become more involved in accepting bills.

(iv) *Medium-term lending* They make loans to companies especially those considering becoming public companies. They provide loans and export finance. Medium-term loans are usually for periods of between six months and five years.

Merchant banks today are involved in a variety of business including advice on a wide range of company problems (mergers, dividend policy, new issues), hire-purchase provision, factoring, insurance, property development and management, buying and selling gold and foreign exchange.

The capital market

The capital market consists of those institutions which are concerned with making longer term loans to government and companies. The source of most of the capital for these institutions is the savings of individuals with financial institutions such as investment trusts, insurance companies and building societies. These funds are then channelled by these institutions to the government and companies to finance borrowing.

The institutions of the capital market include the following:

Investment trusts

These are limited liability companies which specialise in the investment of funds. There are about 300 investment trusts and their managers are experts in the field of investment. In purchasing a share in an investment trust an investor is really investing in a large number of different companies. Investment trusts raise money by selling their own shares on the Stock Exchange and pay out dividends to shareholders from the variety of dividends they receive from their range of holdings in other companies.

Unit trusts

Unit trusts differ from investment trusts because they require government authorisation, function under trust deeds and are supervised by trustees. Unit trusts, unlike investment trusts, do not sell shares on the stock exchange. In place of share capital, units are sold which give the owners the right to part of the benefits which derive from the trust's assets. Units can be sold to, or bought from, the trust managers and their value reflects the value of the trust's assets.

Finance houses
Mercantile Credit, Lombard Banking and the United Dominions Trust are examples of finance houses. They provide a major source of medium-term loans. There are well over 1000 houses but most of the business is in the hands of about 20 which belong to the Finance Houses Association. The majority of assets are in the form of hire-purchase agreements for durable or semi-durable goods of which half are commercial vehicles, a quarter are furniture and the rest are radios, televisions and other electrical goods. Other advances are made to commercial companies. The majority of liabilities are in the form of deposits. Most of these deposits come from banks and other financial institutions. Companies also provide a large quantity of funds but deposits from individuals are relatively small. Hire-purchase has been subject to substantial government interference in an effort to control consumer demand.

Building societies
There are over 600 building societies registered as members of the Building Societies Association. The biggest society is the Halifax, and other examples include the Abbey National, the Nationwide and the Woolwich building societies. Liabilities are in the form of share deposits. Ninety per cent of liabilities are in the form of share accounts which pay interest. These are not marketable but withdrawable (theoretically) on notice. There are four million investors and the average holding is small. Eighty per cent of assets are mortgages, chiefly on private houses. Interest is payable on these loans which are repaid by instalment over periods up to 25 years. Within a year repayments are made and new mortgages are advanced.

Building societies' interest rate policy has a significant effect on the building industry in that house building depends on the availability of mortgages which depends on the inflow of funds which depends on the level of interest rates being offered to depositors.

Insurance companies
There are about 500 insurance companies and about half are members of the British Insurance Association. Their activities fall into two main categories: life insurance and general insurance (fire, accident etc). Life premiums finance long term investments (because of the long time before paying out to the insured). General premiums finance mainly liquid short-term loans (because of the need regularly to meet claims). General insurance has twice the amount of business overseas as in the home economy, therefore contributing to balance of payments on invisibles. They are the largest of the institutional investors.

National Savings Bank
Established in 1861 as the Post Office Savings Bank, the National Savings Bank operates 21 million accounts at some 21 000 post offices. There are two types of account. Small withdrawals can be made on demand from ordinary accounts. Withdrawals from investment accounts are subject to one month's notice and attract a higher rate of interest. Deposits are handed over to the National Debt Commissioner for investment in government stock.

Superannuation and pension funds
These funds of local authorities, public corporations and companies are fast growing. A quarter are placed with life assurance, the rest being self-administered. Some funds are handled by full-time investment managers; others rely on consultants. Most of the investment goes into government stocks but increasingly funds are being invested in company securities.

Issuing houses
A group of merchant banks, essentially concerned with the raising of new capital from the public for the formation of new public companies, they advise their clients and underwrite (guarantee) the raising of the whole amount of capital.

The market for securities (the Stock Exchange)
See Chapter 12 on the Stock Exchange.

The National Giro
The National Giro is the United Kingdom's fastest growing bank with over 850 000 customers. It is operated through the United Kingdom's 21 000 post offices and is therefore a convenient form of banking. From March 1981 National Giro was able to clear cheques.

Money can be paid into a Giro account by paying in cash at any post office. When a customer pays in cheques to his or her account the cheques are sent to Giro's headquarters in Bootle (Merseyside) in pre-paid envelopes. Other people, even non-account holders, can pay money into a Giro account. Withdrawals take the form of Giro cheques which can be paid to non-account holders. Account holders can cash a cheque up to a value of £50 at any two named post offices. After six months of being a Giro account-holder the customer receives a cheque guarantee card which enables them to cash cheques at any post office up to a value of £50. Free statements are sent to the account holder every time he or she pays money in or after every ten withdrawals. There are no charges so long as the account remains in credit. If the account goes 'into the red' a charge will be made for each debit item.

Other services offered by National Giro include:

(a) Deposit accounts which earn interest. Money can be easily transferred from current accounts into deposit accounts.
(b) Budget accounts. Instalments will be paid into a budget account and bills will be paid from the account. Interest will be charged if the account is overdrawn.
(c) Standing orders
(d) Direct debits
(e) Personal loans on which interest will be charged.
(f) Overdrafts
(g) Post cheques: Current account holders with cheque guarantee cards can draw out local currency from 80 000 post offices in 24 countries. It is possible to cash up to two post cheques per day up to a total value of £100.

Checkpoints

1   Money should have several characteristics such as scarcity, portability, divisibility and durability. It has developed from barter to the use of bank accounts subject to withdrawal by cheque, and credit cards. There are several forms of money (or near money) but only notes and coins are legal tender. Money is anything which is generally acceptable.

2   The government now has specific definitions for money such as M0, M1 and £M3. The government use these indicators to show how much money is in the economy at a particular time.

3   Money performs valuable functions in the modern economy such as acting as a medium of exchange, a measure of value, a store of value and a means of deferred payment.

4   Commercial banks perform a variety of functions such as accepting deposits, making loans and acting as agents of payment, and give such services as providing foreign exchange and advice on investments.

5   Commercial banks need to keep both liquid and profitable assets.

6   Commercial banks can create deposits (money) by keeping some of their assets in liquid form. The government may be concerned about this ability to create money because it may help cause inflation.

7   The Bank of England is the 'central bank' and issues bank notes, is the bankers' bank, has external responsibilities, is the lender of the last resort and is the government's bank. A very important function of the Bank of England is to operate monetary policy by using weapons such as interest rates, special deposits and open market operations. Monetary policy determines the level of demand, and thereby output, employment and inflation, in the economy.

8   The money market consists of institutions such as discount houses, who mainly discount Treasury bills and bills of exchange, and merchant banks who mainly accept bills and act in the new issue market.

9   The capital market consists of other institutions such as investment trusts, unit trusts, finance houses, building societies and insurance companies.

10   The National Giro is a fast growing bank operated by the Post Office. It is in direct competition with the commercial banks.

Multiple-choice questions – 9

1   Which of the following assets held by commercial banks is *not* included in the reserve assets ratio?

    A   money at call with discount houses
    B   loans and advances to customers
    C   government securities with under one year to maturity
    D   Treasury bills
    E   balances held at the Bank of England

2   A Treasury bill is a document which is

    A   a short term loan from one discount house to another
    B   a short term loan to an exporter
    C   a long term loan to the government
    D   a short term loan to the government
    E   a short term loan from the government to a clearing bank

3   If the Bank of England wishes to reduce inflation it may

    A   purchase government securities on the open market
    B   exert downward pressure on interest rates
    C   call for special deposits from commercial banks
    D   issue fewer long term securities and more Treasury bills
    E   direct clearing banks to increase overdrafts to customers

4   An employer will normally pay salaries directly into the bank accounts of employees by using

    A   standing orders
    B   direct debit
    C   individual cheques
    D   bankers' drafts
    E   bank giro credits

5   A clearing bank keeps a cash ratio of 10% and has £25 million in cash. What is the maximum level of deposits that it can maintain?

    A   £2.5m
    B   £5m
    C   £50m
    D   £250m
    E   £500m

6   Of all methods of payment the only recognised legal tender is

    A   cheques
    B   bank notes and credit cards

C bills of exchange
D bank notes and cheques
E bank notes and coins

7 When acting as lender of the last resort the Bank of England lends money to the money market through the

A discount houses
B clearing banks
C merchant banks
D commercial banks
E National Savings Bank

8 Open market operations is the buying and selling of

A ordinary shares by clearing banks
B government securities by public corporations
C government securities by the Bank of England
D government securities by foreigners
E ordinary shares by institutional investors

9 The creation of credit by a commercial bank will

A reduce the level of overdrafts given by the bank
B reduce the bank's assets
C increase the size of the cash reserve ratio
D increase special deposits
E increase deposits held by the bank's customers

10 Which of the following would *not* be part of a government's restrictionist monetary policy

A increased interest rates
B sales of Treasury bills
C increased special deposits by clearing banks with the central bank
D government directives to banks to reduce lending
E increased income tax

Answers on page 328.

Data response question 9

Charge of the plastic brigade

THERE are now over 30 million credit cards in circulation in the UK, from the giants of Access and Visa to the various in-store cards from the shopping chains.

In 1980, credit cards accounted for just three per cent of consumer spending. Seven years on, that figure has almost doubled to 6.8 per cent.

And only last week, the Department of Fair Trading referred credit cards to the Monopolies Commission and threatened Barclays' new Connect card with the same shake of the fist.

Here, Money Mail looks at the wonderful world of plastic credit, charge, cash, discount and town cards as well, and explains how and when they connect with each other.

by ROGER BEARD

THE credit card industry has long been criticised for charging high interest rates for those Access and Visa cardholders who do not pay up immediately.

Now it has again come under the microscope of the Monopolies Commission, seven years after a similar investigation.

Curious

Sir Gordon Borrie, Director General of Fair Trading, expects the commission to examine seven areas, after his referral of the matter last week:

Are the companies making monopoly profits as suggested by their 50 per cent return on capital?

Is the interest rate too high; is the interest-free period fair?

Is the credit card market sufficiently open to new competition? Are retailers being charged too much? Should they pay a percentage or flat fee? And is the 'no discrimination clause' anti-competitive?

They will come back with their answers in two years' time.

Sir Gordon feels particularly that annual rates of 23.1 per cent which Access and Visa are moving down to, are excessive compared with base rates of nine per cent. The old 26.8 per cent rate was fixed in 1985 when base rates were 14 per cent.

What is curious is that store credit cards, some with interest rates well above Access and Visa, have been excluded from the inquiry. He is prepared to move to protect 22 million cardholders but leaves out nine million others exposed to an even higher rate on the grounds that as individual store groups they are not part of any monopoly.

Charge cards such as American Express and Diners Club International are also excluded from the investigation, basically on the grounds that they contain no interest element.

Prefer

Access and Barclaycard estimate that over 40 per cent of credit card users paid on the nail to avoid interest charges. The rest pay interest on their credit spending sprees.

A recent survey found that over 73 per cent of the population preferred to pay cash, and close to half had no idea of what interest rate they were paying.

A Connect card

Why three into one will go

TODAY sees the launch of Connect, the Barclays Bank 'cashless society' card. Yet it almost crashed on its own launch pad — after having cost £10 million to develop — because the bank told, rather than asked, the retailers what they wanted.

Connect has three main functions: It is a debit card, a cash withdrawal card and cheque guarantee card rolled into one.

Retailers were told that they would have to accept the Connect card under the same conditions as the Visa system, of which Barclays is the senior member — a two per cent commission on the sale value against a flat fee of 10p on a cheque.

'No deal' said the powerful Retail Consortium, which includes most of the High Street household names. By the middle of last week, they had reached at least a partial agreement, that there would still be a commission rate but at a discount.

Service

They have yet to agree on the original Barclays proposal that any shop accepting the Visa credit card would also have to accept Connect, although the bank is reported as affirming that it would not demand membership of one scheme while negotiating terms of the other.

Even now, the pioneer of the triple card which may make both cheques and cash redundant, is not out of the wood. It may debit the customer's account electronically at the point of sale, but who will service the system?

The shop staff's union has voted by 40,000 to ban overtime and co-operation with the new card, and the bank has retaliated in kind. It has nothing to do with Connect, but everything to do with the union's five per cent. wage claim.

The attitude to Connect of the Office of Fair Trading may also cause trouble. Sir Gordon Borrie's initial view was that any insistence on the bank's part that Visa traders should also take Connect amounted to an intended exercise of monopoly power.

(a) What proportion of consumer spending was accounted for by credit cards in
  (i) 1980? (ii) 1987?
(b) Give two reasons why Access and Visa are being referred to the Monopolies Commission.
(c) Name two types of credit card which are not being referred to the Monopolies Commission. What reasons are given for non-referral?
(d) What advantages and disadvantages do credit cards have for
  (i) consumers?
  (ii) retailers?
  (iii) credit card companies?
(e) What three functions will be performed by Connect?
(f) Why are many retailers opposed to introducing Connect into their shops?

(g) How is Barclays Bank attempting to persuade retailers to accept Connect?

(h) Apart from retailers, which other group is causing problems for Barclays in its attempts to introduce Connect?

(i) Why might the government be concerned with a consumer credit explosion?

10 Inflation

Definitions

Inflation can be defined as a *'persistent and generalised increase in the level of prices'*. Inflation is normally measured in terms of changes in the *retail price index* which is discussed on page 207.

Hyper-inflation (galloping inflation) is the term used to describe severe rates of inflation which can undermine the economic and political stability of an economy. Throughout the 1970s and 1980s countries such as Argentina and Brazil had dramatically high rates of inflation (ie, between 100 and 200%). Germany in the 1920s experienced hyper-inflation. Money became virtually worthless and the economy collapsed.

The fear of any government is that *'creeping inflation'* (ie, relatively low rates of inflation) will develop into the much more serious hyper-inflation.

Deflation (the opposite to inflation) This means that prices are declining and that the value of money is increasing. Economists often talk about deflationary policies. These are policies aimed at preventing inflation, see page 214.

Disinflation This is a slowing down of the rate of inflation. Very often people refer to deflation when what is really meant is disinflation.

Reflation This is when the rate of inflation increases. Reflationary policies

Inflation

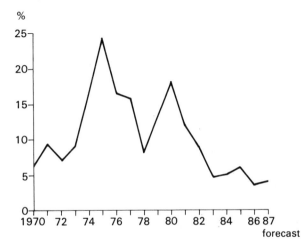

are those policies aiming to increase demand and output in the economy. Reflationary policies are the opposite to deflationary policies.

Slumpflation (or stagflation) A relatively recent phenomenon in the economy of the 1970s is what is called 'slumpflation'. This is when inflation and unemployment co-exist in the economy at the same time. It used to be believed that the twin evils of inflation and unemployment were opposites. If inflation was apparent in the economy then there would be little unemployment and vice versa. Indeed, Professor A W Phillips observed a relationship between the rate of change of money wages (and therefore inflation) and the level of unemployment. This relationship resulted in the now famous 'Phillips' Curve'. However, the economic experience of the 1970s, when there was high unemployment and high inflation, reduced the credibility of the Phillips' analysis curve.

Slumpflation is due mainly to the rise in oil prices, most apparent between 1973 and 1974 and 1979 and 1980. These oil price rises have two effects. Firstly, they cause inflation, as oil-consuming countries have to pay the high prices and pass them on in the prices of their own goods and, moreover, trade unions then want higher wages to maintain their living standards and to keep up with rising prices. Secondly, the high oil prices will cause unemployment among manufacturing countries. Firms will have to lay off labour in attempts to cut costs, and demand for manufactures will diminish as more money is spent on oil. Thus inflation and unemployment exist at the same time.

The natural rate of unemployment Since the demise of the 'Phillips' Curve' some economists now refer to a natural rate of unemployment where both inflation and unemployment can exist at the same time (ie they are not alternatives). Thus any attempt to cure unemployment by expansionary fiscal and monetary measures will increase inflation. Unemployment will temporarily fall but will go back to its previous higher level (ie, its natural level). This is because workers who have been tempted into work by higher wages, brought about by expansionary economic policies, find that because of the higher inflation their real incomes have not increased at all. They decide not to offer themselves for work and volunteer to be unemployed. This view is very contentious and subject to criticisms.

How inflation is measured

Inflation is measured by changes in the retail price index (RPI) which records changes in the general level of prices paid by consumers for all the goods and services they buy.

What are the index numbers?

An index number is a means whereby changes in a large number of related variables can be averaged, and the average change expressed through movements in a single number.

A group of commodities is selected and their prices noted in one particular year which becomes the *base year* for the index and to which the number 100 is given. If the prices of these commodities rise by 1% in the ensuing twelve months then the index number for that year will be 101.

Example

Year 1			Year 2		
Commodity	Price	Index	Commodity	Price	Index
A	2½p	100	A	5p	200
B	10p	100	B	15p	150
C	75p	100	C	100p	133.3
		300			483.3

Price index = 3 ⌐300 = 100   Price index = 3 ⌐483.3 = 161.1

From the above example we can see that, on average, prices rose by 61.1% between Year 1 and Year 2. Prices in future years will be expressed as percentages of those in Year 1 and averaged in a similar manner.

The problem of weighting

The example given is misleading because it does not take into account the difference in importance between the goods. Consumers spend much more of their incomes on certain goods and services and these should be given greater importance in the index. For instance more consumers spend more of their income on bread than on hi-fi equipment. Commodities should be given a weight which reflects their relative importance in consumer spending. For instance, if consumers spend 10% of their income on commodity A, 30% on commodity B and 60% on commodity C then the weights should be 1: 3: 6. The price indices for each commodity are now multiplied by the weight given and the average obtained by dividing the total by the total of weights.

Example

Year 1

Commodity	Price	Weight	Index	Weighted index
A	2½p	1	100	100
B	10p	3	100	300
C	75p	6	100	600
		10		1000

Price index = 10 ⌐1000 = 100

Year 2

Commodity	Price	Weight	Index	Weighted index
A	5p	1	200	200
B	15p	3	150	450
C	100p	6	133.3	799.8
		10		1449.8

Price index = 10 ⌐1449.8 = 144.9

From this example we can see that the weighted index has given us a different result. The average price movement was an increase of 44.9% as compared with 61.1% in the unweighted index. This is largely because commodity C has been given a greater weight in the index and its rise in price was relatively smaller than commodities A and B.

The retail price index (RPI)

The retail price index began in 1914 and was called the cost of living index. It measures changes in the prices of goods in the following way.

(a) A base year is chosen and the average level of prices is represented by the number 100. The most recent base year is 1987.

(b) A representative sample of the population (average families) is asked to carefully record expenditure over a month. This enables the Department of Employment to ascertain which goods and services are predominant in their expenditure, and which to include in the index.

(c) The Department of Employment, through its 200 local offices, collects information about prices of items in the eleven groups of the index. For instance, for changes in food prices five local retailers are visited including a Co-operative Society branch.

(d) A long list of items is included in the index and this average basket is divided into eleven broad groups: food; alcoholic drink; tobacco; housing; fuel and light; durable household goods; clothing and footwear; transport and vehicles; miscellaneous goods; services; and meals bought and consumed outside the home.

An index is calculated for all items in each group and also for each main group. The index is of course weighted. The weights are revised each January based on spending in the previous three years.

(e) The prices of items in this basket of goods are recorded every month and the new prices are expressed as percentages of the base date.

(f) The index is then calculated and published monthly.

Problems with the RPI

(a) The index is based on the spending habits of the 'average family', but it is difficult to define what this means.

(b) Weighting is a problem because consumer spending is always changing due to changes in taste, season, income and population changes.

(c) The quality and performance of goods are always changing and this is not really indicated by changes in prices. For example, a washing machine may have increased by 10% in price but its performance may be vastly superior.

(d) New goods and services are continuously arriving on the market and some goods and services are no longer in demand. The index needs to take this into account in its weighting procedure.

(e) When the Department of Employment is engaged in its survey of food prices in local shops it should bear in mind that most purchases now take place in chain-stores and supermarkets and a greater weight to prices of goods and services purchased in these outlets should be given. Moreover, the index tells us nothing about the quality of service provided in each retail outlet.

(f) The base year is a problem because the further we move away from the base year the more unreal does the basket of goods and services become. The base year should not be an abnormal year of very high or low price increases.

(g) It is very difficult to compare an index of prices between countries because the index in each country will be composed of a different basket of goods.

(h) Mortgage repayments and the cost of credit (interest rates) are not included in the index but these are very important items of expenditure.

What price a new index?

In the year to May, Britain's retail price index rose by only 2.8%—the lowest rate since 1968. But how accurate is the official thermometer of inflation?

How well the retail price index measures inflation is not just a matter of academic interest. The RPI is the basis of a wide range of pricing decisions from wage negotiations, through the uprating of social-security benefits and pensions, to the indexation of financial assets. It affects government spending: if the rate of inflation is overstated by one percentage point, that part of state spending statutorily linked to the RPI will be more than £500m a year higher than it would otherwise have been; public-sector wage settlements will tend to be higher too.

The RPI tries to measure the average change in the prices of goods and services people buy. In fact it is not really a "retail" price index at all: it includes not only goods bought from shops, but also things like owner-occupiers' mortgage interest payments, rents, rates and electricity.

It was the inclusion of mortgage interest which prompted the government, in September 1984, to reconvene the Retail Price Index Advisory Committee (RPIAC). This is effectively the RPI's guardian angel; it represents employers, trade unions, the retail trade, academe and the government.

The treatment of the costs of owner occupation has long been one of the most controversial components of the index. At present, the index recognises these costs in three separate ways: it includes mortgage interest rates net of income-tax relief; house prices, to the extent that they affect the total level of mortgage debt outstanding; and other housing costs, such as repair and maintenance.

The Treasury would like to remove mortgage payments from the index. The reason, it says, is that the cost of borrowing to buy a house is quite different from the prices of other goods and services. Only part of mortgage-interest payments represents the cost of shelter; a big chunk is really an investment in a (hitherto) appreciating asset, rather than a part of the cost of living.

The Treasury also dislikes the way that the inclusion of mortgage rates makes it look as though inflation gets worse each time monetary policy is tightened by raising interest rates. Similarly, a reduction in income-tax rates appears to cause higher inflation, because the value of tax relief on mortgage-interest payments declines.

In recent years, swings in the mortgage rate have played havoc with the RPI. Mortgage-interest payments at present have a weight of 5.4% in the index, so a one percentage-point rise in interest rates will increase the index by about

½%. During the three years to 1985, the inflation rate yo-yoed between 3½% and 7%. Strip out mortgage-interest payments, and that shrinks to a steady 4-5% (see chart).

The cost of home ownership cannot simply be dropped from the index, however. Of the big five economies, only Britain includes the mortgage rate in its cost-of-living index. America, Japan and West Germany all use the "rental-equivalent" approach. That involves measur-

Retail price index
% increase on previous year

Total index

Excluding mortgage interest payments

1983   84   85   86 latest

Sources: Department of Employment; HM Treasury

ing the rental income forgone by living in a house rather than letting it. This was the method Britain used until the RPIAC recommended a switch to mortgage-interest payments in 1975. The trouble with it is that in Britain rents are so distorted by government controls that they are useless as a measure of the "shelter value" of owner-occupied houses.

An alternative is the "user-cost" approach. This takes account of mortgage-interest rates, but also of the capital gains or losses on the house, of interest forgone on the part of the house which is owned outright and of physical depreciation. The Institute for Fiscal Studies has recalculated the RPI to take account of capital gains. It can make a big difference: in the two years 1978 and 1979, when house prices rose by 50%, the official retail price index rose by 23%; this figure falls to 18% if capital gains are taken into account. However, estimates

% increase over 12 months		
end year	RPI	TPI
1979	17.2	14.9
1980	15.1	16.4
1981	12.0	15.6
1982	5.4	5.8
1983	5.3	4.4
1984	4.6	3.3
1985	5.7	4.6
1986 (May)	2.8	0.9

of the full "user cost" would at best be guesses, as none of its other components has a hard cash equivalent.

Now the Treasury has lost its battle with the RPIAC to get mortgage payments stripped out of the RPI. It was fought off by strong opposition from trade unions and consumer groups, who argued that all the alternatives are flawed, and who were suspicious of any tinkering with official statistics.

The government cannot win. On the one hand the RPI is frequently dismissed as misleading; on the other, attempts to change it produce accusations of fiddling

Weights, 1986

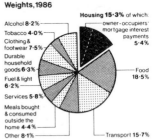

Alcohol **8·2%**
Tobacco **4·0%**
Clothing & footwear **7·5%**
Durable household goods **6·3%**
Fuel & light **6·2%**
Services **5·8%**
Meals bought & consumed outside the home **4·4%**
Other **8·1%**

Housing **15·3%** of which:
owner-occupiers' mortgage interest payments **5·4%**
Food **18·5%**
Transport **15·7%**

the figures. A compromise solution might be to follow the example of the United States. For the two years before America switched from using mortgage-interest payments to "equivalent rent" in 1983, the government published the two indices side by side.

Previous attempts to change the index suggest two morals: first, pick a measure the public can understand; and second, if you want to be believed, pick one measure and stick with it. Remember the tax and price index which the Treasury invented in 1979? No? That is because it broke both rules. It is meant to measure the rise in gross wages needed to keep up with changes in taxes as well as prices. The RPI includes indirect taxes, such as VAT and rates, but excludes income tax. So when the government financed a cut in income tax in 1979 by raising the VAT rate, inflation as measured by the RPI appeared to shoot skyhigh.

The TPI—which is unaffected by a switch between different sorts of taxes—was meant to show that pay packets were not being eroded as quickly as the RPI suggested—and thereby encourage lower pay claims. However, when, in 1981, the TPI started to rise faster than the RPI it was quickly pushed into obscurity. Now it is lagging behind the RPI—it rose by only 0.9% in the year to May—the government is wistfully eager to revive it.

However, the RPI is useful in that it is the best, albeit imperfect, measure of the rate of inflation and changes in the value of money. It is useful to government, employers and trade unions to know changes in the RPI, for instance, to help them decide wage increases. It is an extremely politically sensitive figure and one of the most important economic indicators.

What causes inflation?

People often complain that the government should identify what causes inflation and take the appropriate measures to cure it, but there is no one cause of inflation. There are three major theories which propose to explain the reason for the occurrence of inflation.

(a) *'demand-pull' inflation*;
(b) *the monetarist view of inflation*;
(c) *'cost-push' inflation*.

Demand-pull inflation

This is usually explained by the phrase *'too much money chasing too few goods'*. It means that there is too much demand in the economy which exceeds supply of goods and services and therefore prices are 'pulled up'. This situation is usually, but not always, associated with full employment in the economy.

Demand-pull inflation may be caused by large budget deficits (see page 228). This is when government spending in the economy is greater than revenues from taxation. As a result the government has to borrow. This will stimulate demand in the economy. Proposed remedies for demand-pull inflation are discussed on page 214.

The monetarist view of inflation

Closely associated with this theory is the *monetarist* view which believes inflation is caused mainly by a high supply of money. In the words of Professor Milton Friedman *'inflation is a purely monetary phenomenon'*. The monetarist case is based on the *quantity theory of money* which is as follows.

$$MV = PT$$
Where   M is the quantity of money
        V is the velocity of circulation (the rate at which money circulates)
        P is the price level
        T is the level of transactions or output

It is felt by monetarists that, in the short run at least, V and T do not change much. Therefore any change in M, the quantity of money, will cause prices, P, to rise.

Cost-push inflation

Cost-push inflation is a situation where rising costs 'push up' prices. The causes

Fear of inflation as credit soars by record level

By Anne Segall, Economics Correspondent

FEARS THAT BRITAIN is in the grip of an inflationary credit boom rose yesterday after news of a record £4.7 billion increase in bank lending last month with most of the extra money going to house buyers, consumers, financial companies and property developers.

City experts began to draw parallels with the early 1970s, arguing that the Government has little hope of slowing down the credit bandwagon without raising borrowing costs.

Although underlying inflationary pressures are much lower now than then, warning bells should be ringing at Westminster, they say.

The surge in bank credit was accompanied by evidence yesterday that consumer spending is growing strongly, with the tax cuts announced in the Budget finally feeding through to pay packets.

According to the Department of Trade and Industry, spending in the shops rose by 3.1 per cent between May and June, taking the retail sales index up from 125.4 to 129.3, within a whisker of the peak level reached in April.

Even brisker

During the second quarter spending was 5.7 per cent higher than a year earlier.

Bank lending always rises strongly in June as customers dig deep to finance half-yearly intertest charges. But even allowing for this, the underlying growth in lending last month was a startling £3.9 billion.

Since the beginning of the year banks have lent an extra £2.4 billion a month on average, causing the Bank of England some concern. There are fears that credit conditions have become too lax at a time of mounting competition.

of inflation are to be found, not on the demand side, but on the supply side. There are a number of ways in which costs may be 'pushed up'.

(a) An increase in wages not matched by equivalent increases in productivity (ie, output per man hour). These increases in wages are probably due to strong trade union pressure.

(b) Rising import prices, for instance the rise in oil prices in the 1970s caused inflation.

(c)   Increases in indirect taxation (see page 223) such as VAT. In all of these situations increasing costs will push up prices. This may set off a 'wage-price spiral' because prices rise and wages will rise to compensate. This will cause a further increase in prices and a further increase in wages, and so it goes on.

This view of inflation gains much support from a group of economists called the *Keynesians* who agree fundamentally with this view, put forward by Professor J M Keynes. For possible remedies for this type of inflation see page 215.

The Keynesians and the monetarists disagree fundamentally on the possible causes of inflation. This is important because they also differ on possible remedies. The Conservative governments of Mrs Thatcher since 1979 accept the monetarist view of inflation.

Why is inflation evil?

Inflation is regarded as an evil phenomenon by governments all over the world. At first sight this may be considered to be surprising because if prices are rising by 10% and people get a 10% increase in wages then they are no worse off. However a number of distortions may occur of which the most important are:

Fixed income earners will have a lower standard of living

Fixed income earners are people such as senior citizens, students receiving grants and the unemployed. These people depend on the government for their incomes. In periods of inflation it is unlikely that the government will increase the money incomes of these people (ie, what they actually receive in terms of money) in line with the inflation rate. This means that real incomes (those incomes in terms of goods and services they can buy) will decline and these people will have a lower standard of living.

Workers who belong to relatively weak trade unions will also have a lower standard of living

Those workers who belong to powerful trade unions will probably achieve increases in money incomes which are equal to or greater than the inflation rate. Thus their real incomes increase and they are better off despite the rising inflation rate. Similarly, certain parts of management will be shielded from inflation by high wage rises or increasing perks (fringe benefits like being given a company car or a low interest mortgage). However workers in weaker trade unions, such as nurses, will probably not achieve increases in money wages equal to price rises which will lower their real incomes and standard of living.

Inflation will have an adverse effect on a country's balance of payments

Rising export prices will mean a lower demand for exports. If demand is elastic for exports then the value of exports will decline. Moreover, if prices of domestically produced goods are higher than those of imported goods then more imports will come into the country and the value of imports will increase.

UK success in beating inflation compared with Europe

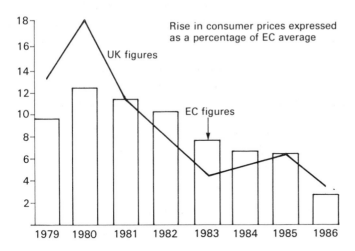

Rise in consumer prices expressed as a percentage of EC average

UK figures

EC figures

Consumer price inflation 1960–86

Per cent a year (rankings out of 12 countries in brackets)

	1960–69	1970–79	1980–86	1982–86	1960–86
UK	3.6 (6)	12.5 (11)	8.1 (9)	5.5 (6)	8.0 (10)
USA	2.3 (1)	7.1 (3=)	6.1 (5=)	3.8 (5)	5.0 (3)
Japan	5.4 (12)	8.9 (7=)	3.2 (1)	1.9 (1)	6.1 (7)
EC	3.5	9.3	8.4	6.9	6.8
OECD	2.9	8.3	6.9	5.1	5.9

Inflation discourages savings and investment

Unless the rate of interest is higher than the level of inflation the value of people's savings will decline. This will mean that they may not save so much with building societies, insurance companies and commercial banks. Instead, people may decide to 'hedge' against inflation by purchasing goods which keep their value even against inflation, such as gold, jewellery and works of art. Much of this hedging is in unproductive goods.

Moreover, the decline in saving will mean that there are fewer funds for industry to borrow and invest in new machines and factories. This will have a bad effect on a country's output and employment. Indeed, businesspeople may not wish to invest if inflation is high. It makes them pessimistic about the future.

Hyper-inflation can have undesirable economic and political consequences

Extremely high levels of inflation may mean that money loses its value and there may be a loss of confidence in the banking system. Also, there may be a dramatic decline in output and a rise in unemployment due to less investment. This may lead to political instability as people turn to extremists to solve the inflationary problem.

Is there anything to be said in favour of inflation?
Although inflation is seen as a major economic evil there are certain advantages in inflation.

(a) 'Creeping inflation' may stimulate businesspeople to invest because they may regard it as a sign of an expanding economy and rising demand.

(b) More people will fall into higher tax brackets and therefore the government will receive more tax revenue. This, of course, is not an advantage to the tax payer and also, it must be remembered, inflation will mean that the government will have to spend more.

(c) A country's national debt repayments will decline in value in real terms. The national debt is what a country owes to governments, institutions and individuals who have bought government securities. The interest repayments on these loans will decline in value in real terms.

What are the remedies for inflation?

Remedies for demand-pull inflation
If inflation is demand-pull inflation then the way to overcome it is to reduce the level of demand in the economy. Such a policy may involve:

(a) *An attempt by government to reduce its budget deficit* (Public Sector Borrowing Requirement) This may involve less government spending, more taxation and less borrowing. This would be termed a deflationary fiscal policy because it is an attempt to deflate the level of demand. For a deeper discussion of such a policy see page 228.

(b) *Reduction of money supply* See monetarist remedies for inflation (below).

(c) *Restrictions on hire-purchase* Many consumer durables (consumer goods which tend to have a long life) are purchased on hire-purchase. The government could make hire-purchase more difficult to obtain by raising interest rates, increasing the amount of deposit required and reducing the period of time during which the credit is to be repaid.

Monetarist remedies for inflation
Monetarists would advocate a reduction in the quantity of money in the economy. This would involve the government itself reducing how much money it prints. Moreover, it would involve a restrictionist (or deflationary) monetary policy to prevent the commercial banks creating too much credit. What such a policy would involve is discussed in depth on page 191.

All of these remedies involve an attempt to reduce the level of demand in the economy. However, critics of such remedies (notably the Keynesians) argue that by deflating the economy another problem will be aggravated and may become worse. Unemployment will undoubtedly increase as a result of deflation. Keynesians would argue that the 'cure is worse than the disease'.

Remedies for cost-push inflation

Keynesians argue that inflation is cost-push inflation and therefore the remedy is to have a *prices and incomes policy*. There are basically two types of prices and incomes policy. Firstly a policy which is compulsory, backed by an Act of Parliament (as in 1972–74 in the United Kingdom). Secondly, a policy which is based on persuasion and consultation, such as the so-called 'Social Contract' of 1976–79. The aim of a prices and incomes policy is to control increases in both prices and incomes in an attempt to prevent inflation. Sometimes such a policy can take the form of a complete standstill on prices and wages and this is called a *'freeze'*.

Advantages of a prices and incomes policy

(a) It controls trade union power to raise wages and the ability of firms to increase prices.
(b) It does not have bad effects on unemployment or output as does the monetarist solution.
(c) It is a fair way of making sure that powerful groups in society do not receive large wage increases at the expense of weaker groups.
(d) Control of prices suppresses inflation (*suppressed inflation*).

Disadvantages of a prices and incomes policy

(a) Monetarists would argue that it is not really solving the main causes of inflation. It is not effectively reducing the level of demand, merely temporarily suppressing inflation.
(b) Many trade unionists would argue that it interferes with free collective bargaining whereby trade unions can achieve a wage increase which reflects the economic situation in each particular industry.
(c) If the policy is one of agreed percentage increases then lower-paid groups of workers argue that they are falling further behind. For example, assume a 10% wage increase across the board. Ten per cent of £10 000 is greater than 10% of £5000, and so the lower-paid workers remain significantly worse off. However, if the policy involves a flat-rate increase of, say, £500, the higher-paid workers argue that wage differentials are being eroded. This means that lower-paid workers are receiving a proportionately greater wage increase.
(d) Prices and incomes policies tend eventually to break down and this means that trade unions use these times to ask for massive wage increases to 'catch up' on ground lost while the policy was in force. There is a 'free for all'.
(e) Prices and incomes policies are unfair. The policy must begin sometime and this may involve certain groups of workers not achieving as high a wage increase as they might have hoped for. Also what about special cases? Certain groups of workers would argue that they are a special case for an increase because they are so important to the economy or to defence. Moreover, what about other forms of incomes such as dividends, rents and interest? To be fair to wage earners these incomes should also be controlled. Wage earners often

complain that such policies are merely wage policies and not 'prices and incomes' policies.

Prices and incomes policies have often been tried but in the past have always broken down. Certain trade unions feel that they are not serving their best interests by being party to such a policy. On the other hand some economists (J K Galbraith, for instance) argue that there should be a permanent prices and incomes policy.

The Conservative governments of Mrs Thatcher since 1979 have introduced mainly monetarist remedies for inflation. They have also pursued deflationary fiscal policies. There has been no prices and incomes policy.

Checkpoints

1   Inflation is a persistent and general increase in the level of prices. It must not be confused with deflation, disinflation, reflation and stagflation.
2   The natural rate of unemployment idea suggests that unemployment and inflation are not alternatives but can co-exist.
3   In the United Kingdom inflation is measured by the retail price index by using index numbers. There are problems such as weighting and choosing a base year.
4   There are three main schools of thought about the causes of inflation: demand-pull inflation, monetarist views and cost-push inflation.
5   Inflation is regarded as a bad state of affairs for a number of reasons including that fixed income earners may suffer, that the balance of payments may deteriorate and that inflation discourages investment.
6   The remedy for demand-pull inflation would be to deflate the economy and reduce demand by deflationary monetary and fiscal policies.
7   The remedy for inflation according to monetarists is to reduce the amount of money in the economy (deflationary monetary policies).
8   The remedy for cost-push inflation is based largely on a prices and incomes policy.
9   All of the proposed remedies for inflation are problematic.

Multiple-choice questions – 10

1   Changes in the value of money are measured by changes in the

    A   terms of trade index
    B   retail price index
    C   level of interest rates
    D   level of national income
    E   level of earnings

2   Which of the following must be a consequence of inflation?

    A   interest rates will rise
    B   exchange rates will rise
    C   the value of money will fall
    D   the balance of payments will deteriorate
    E   unemployment will increase

3   The following are assumed to be initial causes of inflation. Which would be described as 'cost-push'?

    A   an increase in imported raw material prices
    B   an increase in money supply
    C   an increase in unemployment benefits
    D   a reduction in income tax
    E   a reduction in deposits needed for hire-purchase

4   Which of the following is likely to cause 'demand-pull' inflation?

    A   increases in wage rates
    B   a fall in the exchange rate
    C   an increase in VAT
    D   an increase in oil prices
    E   an increase in PSBR

5   The government decides that the economy needs reflating. Which of the following would *not* be appropriate?

    A   sales of government securities on the open market
    B   reducing the level of VAT
    C   reducing income tax
    D   reducing excise duties
    E   increasing government spending

6   Which of the following would most benefit from a period of high inflation?

    A   fixed income earners
    B   savers
    C   debtors

D creditors
E exporters

7 The attempt by government to reduce the level of economic activity during a period of excessive demand is known as

A inflation
B deflation
C reflation
D recession
E expansion

8 In Year 2 the index of retail prices was 110 while in Year 3 it was 130 (Year 1 = 100). Which one of the following conclusions can be drawn from this information about Years 2 and 3?

A the value of money rose
B prices rose less than wages
C there was a balance of payments deficit in Year 3
D the annual inflation rate was 30%
E the value of money fell

9 Inflation may have beneficial effects on an economy if it results in

A more imports being purchased
B large wage demands made by trade unions
C a fall in the purchasing power of the pound
D higher profits stimulating more investment
E a reduction in the external value of the pound

10 A subsidy on a commodity is likely to

A reduce its retail price
B reduce production
C reduce the value of money
D reduce consumer spending
E increase imports from abroad

Answers on page 328.

Data response question 10

Disappointing fall in inflation

By Steve Levinson
Economics Correspondent

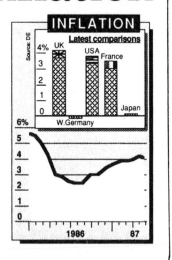

A DISAPPOINTING set of inflation figures yesterday served as a reminder that price pressures are building up, and Britain's inflation rate remains high by international standards.

Inflation dipped from 4.2 per cent in April to 4.1 per cent in May, but a much sharper drop, to less than 4 per cent, had been expected due to the impact of the last cut in mortgage rates which was included for the first time.

The mortgage rate reduction alone knocked 0.25 per cent off the Retail Price Index, but even with this advantage prices overall rose by 0.1 per cent in the month. Expectations in the City had been for a fall in prices in May and an annual inflation rate of about 3.8 per cent.

The main reason for the poorer than expected figures was a 3 per cent increase in seasonal food prices. The poor weather during May pushed up vegetable and fresh fruit prices.

The Department of Employment also highlighted higher costs for home-killed lamb and cars.

(a) From the graph rank the countries in order of highest inflation to lowest inflation countries.

(b) What economic term would be used to describe West Germany's record on prices during this period?

(c) What happened to the United Kingdom inflation rate between April and May?

(d) Which factors influenced the level of prices between April and May?

(e) Discuss the meaning of the terms

    (i) the retail price index

    (ii) the City

(f) Why is an inflation rate which is high by international standards a cause for concern for the United Kingdom?

(g) What policies can a government implement to reduce inflation?

11 Fiscal policy: government spending, taxation and PSBR

The meaning of fiscal policy

Fiscal policy refers to governments' policies towards taxation, government (or public) spending and public sector borrowing. Fiscal policy is an important aspect of government economic policy and it can be used to affect the level of demand in the economy which will in turn affect the level of employment, the level of inflation, the state of the balance of payments, the level of national output and economic growth. In this chapter we shall deal with fiscal policy by examining its two major parts: taxation and government spending.

Taxation

Reasons for having taxation

Before 1914 taxation was not as heavy as it is today. The government of those days pursued a policy known as laissez-faire (leave well alone) which meant that they did not choose to interfere with the economy or the state of society. The taxation which did exist was mainly to finance defence and although the Welfare State began after 1900, and consequently taxation increased to meet that burden, it was still relatively low compared with today's levels.

At present taxation has many more uses and defence is not now the most important. The principal purposes of taxation are to:

(a) achieve the government's social objectives such as re-distribution of income (from rich to poor) or help finance the Welfare State to assist the sick, the old, the disabled and the unemployed.
(b) achieve the government's economic objectives such as the control of inflation, the encouragement of economic growth, the reduction of unemployment and the reduction of balance of payments deficits.
(c) discourage certain types of consumption such as smoking, drinking alcohol and consuming energy.
(d) finance government spending, which has a number of objectives (see page 228).

Qualities of a good tax

The economist, Adam Smith, who wrote *The Wealth of Nations* in 1776, said that a good tax should fulfil four principles:

(a) *A good tax should be equal* An individual should be called upon to pay according to his or her ability to pay. Smith felt that a proportional tax would comply with this principle. (*A proportional tax* is levied when every taxpayer, rich and poor, pays the same tax percentage.) However, we might now say that *a progressive tax*, where the rich pay a higher percentage tax than the poor, best meets this requirement.

(b) *A good tax should be certain* People should be certain about how the tax works and how much has to be paid as well as when it must be paid.

(c) *A good tax should be convenient* People should be able to pay without any inconvenience to themselves. The Pay As You Earn (PAYE) system of income tax collection complies with this principle.

(d) *A good tax should be economic* The costs of collecting and administering should not exceed the revenues gained.

In addition to Smith's four principles, a modern-day Chancellor of the Exchequer might add several other conditions with which a good tax should comply.

(a) The tax should be impartial. Two citizens, equal in income and size of family, should be taxed the same.

(b) It should not be a disincentive to hard work and therefore should not penalise people for working hard.

(c) The tax should be consistent with government policy. If, for example, the government is fighting inflation, it should not pursue a policy of taxation which increases demand too much in the economy.

(d) It should be easily adjustable, and it should therefore be reasonably easy for Parliament to change the rate when necessary.

Direct and indirect taxation
Taxes tend to fall into two categories: direct and indirect. *Direct taxation* is a tax levied directly on an individual's income whereas *indirect taxation* is levied on consumers' expenditure or outlay.

Direct taxation
Examples of direct taxation include income tax, corporation tax (on companies' profits), capital gains tax (a tax on the profits of sales of certain assets), wealth tax (proposed by certain economists, which would be a tax on ownership of wealth) and inheritance tax (a tax on gifts replacing Capital Transfer Tax). Direct taxation is collected by the Inland Revenue.

Advantages of direct taxation

(a) Direct taxes tend to be progressive. People in the higher income groups pay a greater percentage of tax than poorer people, ie, income tax is graduated so that high-income earners pay a larger percentage. Also, a projected wealth tax would only apply to those owning more than a certain level of wealth.

(b) Direct taxes tend to be cheap and easy to collect. Consider, for example, the

PAYE system which is used to collect income tax from most wage and salary earners.

(c) Direct taxes are important to government economic policy. If the government is fighting inflation it can, for example, impose high levels of income tax to restrict consumer demand. If the government is concerned about unemployment, it can reduce the levels of income tax to increase consumer demand and increase production.

Disadvantages of direct taxation

(a) Direct taxation may be a disincentive to hard work. High rates of income tax, for example, may discourage people from working overtime or trying to gain promotion at work. Some economists blame the 'brain drain' (ie, the emigration of highly-qualified persons such as scientists and doctors) on the United Kingdom's high levels of taxation.

(b) Direct taxation discourages savings because, after paying tax, individuals and companies have less income available to save. This means that investment, which relies on the level of savings, is low and this could lead to less production and employment.

(c) This type of taxation encourages tax evasion. To avoid paying tax certain individuals may emigrate or employ tax consultants or accountants to advise them on how they could avoid paying so much tax.

(d) There is no element of choice about paying the tax, it is unavoidable.

Indirect taxation

Examples of indirect taxation include customs duties, motor vehicle tax, tobacco tax and value added tax. Indirect taxes are collected by the Customs and Excise Department and are sometimes called excise duties.

Advantages of indirect taxation

(a) The government can use it to discourage certain types of consumption. The high rate of tax on tobacco might, for example, reduce the number of cigarettes that an individual smokes.

(b) Indirect taxation is a good way of raising revenue when levied on goods with an inelastic demand, such as necessities.

(c) Visitors to the United Kingdom will in some cases also be liable. When foreign visitors spend money on goods and services in United Kingdom' shops this will increase tax revenues.

(d) Consumers have a choice as to whether they pay the tax. They can avoid paying the tax by not consuming the good which is being taxed.

(e) Indirect taxation does not have a disincentive effect on work.

Disadvantages of indirect taxation

(a) Indirect taxes are regressive. A regressive tax is a tax which causes a poor person to pay a higher percentage of his or her income as tax than a rich person. For instance, the tax ingredient of the price of a new television set would be the same for the poor and the rich person, but as a percentage of the poor person's income it is far greater.

(b)   These taxes are not impartial. In recent years, certain groups of consumers such as drinkers, smokers and drivers have complained that they are being heavily penalised by taxation.

(c)   Indirect taxes may contribute to inflation. The imposition of an indirect tax on an item will increase its price which is, in itself, inflationary. However, this may set off an inflationary spiral as trades unions demand higher wages to maintain their real incomes.

Different types of taxes
Direct taxes

(a)   *Income tax* Income tax is levied on an individual's income and it is paid PAYE (pay as you earn). Allowances are given against income including a personal allowance, or a married person's allowance. The remainder of the income is taxed at progressively higher rates.

Basic rate income tax

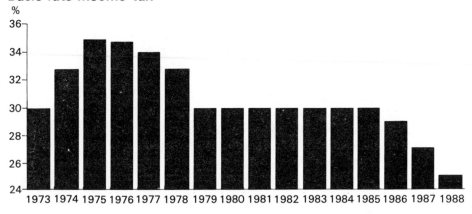

There is a difference between *marginal rates of tax* and *average rates of tax*. Marginal tax is the proportion of tax on the last pound of income. Average tax is the total tax as a proportion of total income. Marginal tax is more than average tax because although a person may be earning £30 000, and therefore marginal tax is 40%, he or she has also to take into account the tax free sum due to allowances and levels of income where he or she was paying less tax.

(b)   *Capital gains tax* A capital gain is an increase in the value of an asset arising from some change in demand or supply. If a person buys an asset and resells it at a profit, the capital gain might be subject to capital gains tax. It is a progressive tax and there are exceptions. For example if a person sells the house in which he or she lives, this is not subject to capital gains tax. It is especially applied to sales of securities and investment property.

(c) *Inheritance tax* A progressive tax, this applies to gifts of wealth made at any time including at death. An exemption is when the husband or wife leave wealth to the surviving spouse. Inheritance tax replaced Capital Transfer Tax in 1987.

(d) *Wealth tax* This has never been introduced but is often advocated by certain economists and politicians. There is a great deal of uncertainty about how it would operate. How often would it have to be paid? What is wealth and who would assess its value? The main objective is to achieve a more equal distribution of wealth in the United Kingdom.

(e) *Corporation tax* Corporation tax is levied on companies' profits. Standard rates of corporation tax are 35% although it will be lower on firms situated in the assisted areas and enterprise zones. Firms with profits of less than £100 000 pay 25% corporation tax.

Indirect taxes

The most important indirect tax is *value added tax*. Value added tax (VAT) was introduced by the government in the United Kingdom in 1973. It is a tax on the sale of certain commodities. Some goods are exempted such as foodstuffs, children's clothes, and services provided by schools and hospitals. The seller is required by the government to add on VAT when selling to the buyer, and it is levied at each stage of the distribution process. The rate of VAT levied is decided by the government and may be changed at any time. As it is an indirect tax, added to the cost of purchases, the government can use it to regulate demand in the home market.

Look at the following table (assuming VAT to be 10%).

Purchase price		Selling price before VAT[a]	VAT liability[b]	VAT credit	VAT paid
£		£	£	£	£
0	Farmer sells to manufacturer	100	10	—	10
110	Manufacturer sells to wholesaler	200	20	10	10
220	Wholesaler sells to retailer	250	25	20	5
275	Retailer sells to consumer	300	30	25	5

Thus the consumer will pay £330 for this commodity ((a) + (b)). Note that tax is calculated by charging 10% on the selling price but deducting tax already paid.

VAT is chargeable at a standard rate of 15%. Some goods and services may get relief from VAT and are *zero-rated*. This means that no tax is chargeable on these goods but a trader supplying zero-rated goods can reclaim VAT on inputs from the Customs and Excise Department. This applies to most types of food, books, newspapers, exports, fuel (but not petrol), young children's clothes and footwear, drugs and medicines.

Zero-rating should not be confused with *exemption*. A trader in exempt goods

VAT rates in EC countries, March 1987

	Reduced rate (%)	Standard rate (%)	Luxury rate (%)	Zero-rated items
Belgium	6 or 17	19	25 or 33	Minimal
Denmark	—	22	—	Minimal
France	5.5 or 7	18.6	33.3	None
W Germany	7	14	—	None
Greece	6	18	36	—
Ireland	10	25	—	Wide variety (incl. some food)
Italy	2 or 9	18	38	Minimal
Luxembourg	3 or 6	12	—	None
Netherlands	6	20	—	None
Portugal	8	16	30	Variety (incl. food)
Spain	6	12	33	None
UK	—	15	—	Wide variety (incl. food)

Research by Mike Kell, Institute of Fiscal Studies

does not charge any tax on goods but cannot reclaim any tax charged on inputs, such as betting, finance, education, health.

The results of taxation

(a) *On incomes* Higher taxes reduce disposable income (what people have to spend from income after taxation). Direct taxes do this by directly reducing income. Indirect taxes reduce income by increasing prices of goods and services. There is a phenomenon known as the 'poverty trap' where some people at the lower end of the income scale can become worse off by getting a job or pay increase. This is because they may lose benefits (social security, free school meals, etc) and at the same time start paying basic rate of income tax and national insurance. They become worse off. This is sometimes called the 'unemployment trap' when it prevents people getting jobs. How could the 'poverty trap' be relieved?

(b) *On savings and investment* Higher direct taxation reduces individuals' and firms' abilities to save and invest. To a certain extent this depends on how much of the increase in taxes is financed from savings and how much from consumption. It has been argued that higher indirect taxes provide an incentive to save because prices are high. However, on the whole, savings and investment are reduced by higher taxes.

(c) *On prices* Higher direct taxes have a deflationary effect on prices by reducing demand. However, trade unions may request higher wages to compensate for higher taxes and the effect of this will be inflationary. Indirect taxes have an inflationary effect because prices will be increased. The extent of the inflationary effect will depend on the elasticity of demand. If demand for the good is inelastic then prices will increase to a great extent, whereas if demand is elastic, prices will increase only slightly.

(d) *On effort* Higher direct taxation will have a disincentive effect on effort as leisure becomes more attractive compared to work. On the other hand, it could be argued that higher taxes will mean some people work harder to maintain living standards.

(e) *On the economy* Higher taxation will, other things remaining equal, reduce the level of demand in the economy which will have a deflationary effect on prices and output. Balance of payments should improve but unemployment will probably worsen as there is less demand in the economy.

Government spending

Total government spending
as % of GDP

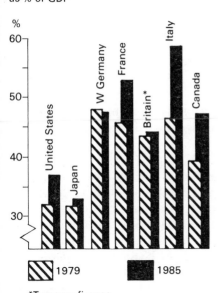

*Treasury figures

The term public spending or public expenditure refers to the money paid by the government for the benefit of the community as a whole. An important part of it – spending on pensions, subsidies, education and health – directly improves the standards of living of the British people.

Public expenditure includes money spent by government departments and local authorities on goods and services, in addition to expenditure by nationalised industries. It also includes money called transfer payments, ie, money transferred from one part or section of the nation to the other, from rich to poor. Much direct expenditure by public authorities, however, is to provide and operate services such as roads, railways, fuel and light, hospitals, schools, police and fire stations.

Objectives of government spending

Public or government spending has the following objectives:

(a)   *To provide public goods and services* for the benefit of the people of the United Kingdom, such as defence spending or spending on education, or roads.

(b)   *To provide certain goods and services at prices below the costs of production for social reasons* This would apply to subsidised food prices and the provision of goods, such as medicine, at low prices.

(c)   *To redistribute income* Much of the revenue is raised by progressive direct taxation and spent in the form of transfer payments such as pensions and social security payments.

(d)   *To increase economic efficiency* Some proportion of public expenditure is allocated to commerce, industry and agriculture in an attempt to make these industries more competitive and efficient, such as the subsidies to Austin Rover.

Where the money goes and where it comes from

Most of the revenue is gained from taxation, and indirect taxation is becoming increasingly more important. A proportion of revenue comes from National Insurance contributions and from rent and interest.

Budgetary policy

Budgetary policy refers to the fiscal policy of the government of the day. Governments are faced with three possible budgetary policies.

Budget deficit

A budget deficit is when government spending is greater than government revenues. The deficit is made good by the public sector borrowing requirement (PSBR). The PSBR is financed by sales of government securities to both foreign and British institutions and individuals. Interest has to be paid on this debt. The increasing size of the PSBR has been blamed for the high level of demand and inflation. The larger the budget deficit, the greater the PSBR and in consequence this will increase inflationary tendencies. Most governments since 1945 have run budget deficits, although recent governments (for example the Thatcher Conservative governments since 1979) have attempted to reduce the size of the deficit by lowering government spending. Indeed the outturn for 1987–88 saw a budget surplus achieved.

Budget surplus

A budget surplus is when government spending is less than government revenues. This will have a deflationary effect as it will lower the level of demand in the economy. This might cause unemployment in the economy and lower output.

A balanced budget

A balanced budget is when government spending is equal to government

Chancellor's arithmetic (1988/9)

Where the money comes from
All figures in £ billion

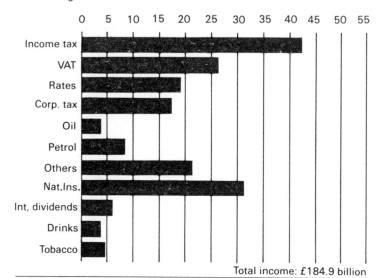

Total income: £184.9 billion

How the money is spent

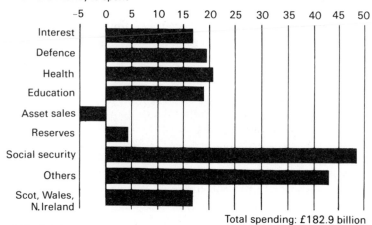

Total spending: £182.9 billion

Chancellor's income	£184.9 bn
Expenditure	£182.9 bn
Public and market borrowing	£1.2 bn
Budget surplus	£3.2 bn

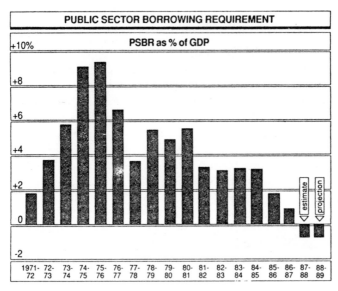

PUBLIC SECTOR BORROWING REQUIREMENT

PSBR as % of GDP

revenues. This will have neither an inflationary or deflationary effect. However, it is extremely difficult for a government to balance its budget.

The budget statement

Budget day occurs once a year, usually during Spring. The Chancellor of the Exchequer outlines his forecast for the economy over the coming year. He sets out his proposals for changes in taxation and other related areas, such as government spending and the forecast size of PSBR, in order to achieve the economic and social objectives of the government of the day.

Public spending in the 1970s and 1980s

Government spending increased during the 1970s. There were several reasons for this:

(a)   The two World Wars of the twentieth century increased government spending dramatically, and although, after peace was declared, spending was reduced, it did not fall back to pre-war levels.

(b)   Although as a percentage of total government spending, expenditure on defence has fallen over the years, it still accounts for a significant proportion of government spending. Sophisticated and expensive defence requirements account for a large percentage of expenditure and this is likely to be even greater with further scientific development of weapons.

(c)   *Law and order* The United Kingdom has a population of approximately 57 millions. In recent years, public spending on law and order has increased, reflecting an increase in crime and the need for personnel to administer the vast amount of recent government legislation.

(d)   *The expansion of services provided by the State to protect the community* As well as defence and law and order, this includes the extended provision of education and social security benefits.

(e) *State intervention to achieve specific social and economic objectives* Recent governments have been committed to a fairer distribution of income among the United Kingdom's population. Transfer payments, such as pensions, student grants and social security allowances, have therefore increased rapidly in recent years. Payments related to economic objectives, such as the help given to the assisted areas and large firms (eg Austin Rover) have accounted for some increase in government spending. The presence of higher levels of unemployment has also accounted for such expenditures.

(f) *Expansion of Civil Service* More Civil Servants have been employed to administer the increase in the Welfare State and other services provided by the government.

(g) *Inflation* The existence of inflation will obviously make government expenditure seem large when compared on an annual basis. Thus when making comparisons of government spending between different years, it is better to compare figures in terms of constant prices and not market prices, see page 137.

(h) *Increases in debt interest* The government has been spending more than it has received from tax. To finance this expenditure the government has been forced to borrow, and, of course, is obliged to pay interest on this 'National Debt'.

During the 1980s the Thatcher Conservative governments have attempted to restrict increases in government spending. This is due to a belief that high levels of government spending contribute to inflation and reduce incentives to work hard.

The results of government spending

(a) It accounts for the redistribution of income by way of transfer payments. Money has been taken from the rich (progressive taxation) and given to the poor in pensions and social security benefits.

(b) The government has provided medical services, roads, schools, and so on, and these have undoubtedly improved the standard of living of most people. However, those in the higher income groups may complain that their standard of living has declined due to the tax burden.

(c) It is said that incentives have been blunted by high rates of tax and government spending. Unemployed people do not have the incentive to find jobs or people in employment to work hard.

(d) Government spending helps prevent unemployment because it provides jobs to build roads, ships, aircraft, and so on. These people spend their incomes on other goods and services and create jobs in other industries, and so the process continues. This is called the *multiplier effect*. However, too much government spending is seen by many economists as a factor causing inflation because it increases the level of demand in the economy and leads to a higher PSBR.

Checkpoints

1 Fiscal policy refers to government policy on taxation, government spending and public sector borrowing requirement (PSBR).
2 The government's fiscal policy has a variety of social and economic objectives.
3 Taxation falls into one of two main categories: direct or indirect taxation. Both types have advantages and disadvantages.
4 The main direct taxes include income tax, capital gains tax, inheritance tax and corporation tax. Excise duties and value added tax (VAT) are the main indirect taxes.
5 Public spending refers to government's spending in the economy in order to improve the economic and social well-being of the population. Spending is mainly on social security and revenues come mainly from taxation.
6 Budgetary policy refers to the relationship between public spending and revenues. A budget deficit is made good by public sector borrowing.

Multiple-choice questions – 11

1   An indirect tax is one which is

     A   imposed on personal incomes
     B   paid to the Inland Revenue
     C   paid on company profits
     D   imposed on goods and services
     E   collected by local authorities

2   If the government received the following amounts from taxation, what percentage is raised from direct taxes?

	£ million
Income tax	400
Value added tax	300
Inheritance tax	150
Excise duties	150
total taxes	1000

     A   30%
     B   45%
     C   50%
     D   55%
     E   70%

3   The diagram below shows the relationship between the amounts paid in taxation and the level of income.

Which of the lines A, B, C, D, or E, illustrates a progressive tax?

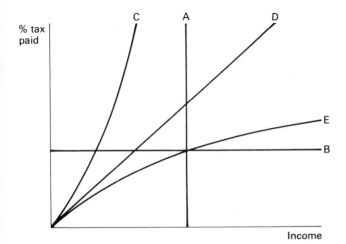

4   Which of the following is an example of an 'ad-valorem' tax?

    A   income tax
    B   motor vehicle excise duty
    C   excise duties on cigarettes and alcohol
    D   corporation tax
    E   value added tax

5   It would be consistent with a deflationary fiscal policy if the government lowered

    A   income tax
    B   valued added tax
    C   sales of Treasury bills
    D   interest rates
    E   government spending

6   The marginal rate of taxation is applied to the

    A   amount of tax payable after allowances have been taken into account
    B   proportion of tax paid on an increase in income
    C   proportion of tax paid on total income
    D   tax paid by very low income earners only
    E   tax paid by very high income earners only

7   Which of the following is most likely to be progressive?

    A   poll tax
    B   value added tax
    C   inheritance tax
    D   excise duties
    E   motor vehicle tax

8   A budget deficit is one

    A   where public spending is greater than the amount of revenue
    B   where public spending is less than the amount of revenue
    C   where public spending is equal to the amount of revenue
    D   where mistakes made by the government mean that government revenue is less than government spending
    E   where the budget leaves most people with less disposable income

9   Which of the following fiscal measures would be *least* likely to reduce the level of unemployment in the economy?

    A   less income tax
    B   less public borrowing
    C   less value added tax
    D   increased subsidies
    E   increased regional aid

10 Which of the following measures would the government take to finance its public sector borrowing requirement?

        A sell ordinary shares
        B sell bills of exchange
        C sell gilt-edged securities
        D buy Treasury bills
        E buy debentures

Answers on page 328.

Data response question 11

Tax rates and allowances					
Before the budget			After the budget		
Taxable income (£)	Rate (%)	Cumulative tax (£)	Taxable income (£)	Rate (%)	Cumulative tax (£)
0–17 900	27	4 833	0–19 300	25	4 825
17 901–20 400	40	5 833	Over 19 300	40	
20 401–25 400	45	8 083			
25 401–33 300	50	12 033			
33 301–41 200	55	16 378			
Over 41 200	60				

The information above applies to the 1988 budget.

(a) What is the marginal rate of taxation for someone earning £50 000 per annum
   (i) before the budget?
   (ii) after the budget?
(b) Describe the income tax changes introduced by the budget.
(c) Is the tax rate structure after the budget more or less progressive? Explain your answer.
(d) Assuming all other things remain equal, describe the effects of these income tax changes on
   (i) personal disposable incomes
   (ii) the poverty trap
   (iii) aggregate demand
(e) What do you think were the objectives of the Chancellor of the Exchequer in introducing these income tax changes?
(f) What other information would you require before deciding whether the overall impact of this budget was reflationary or deflationary?

12 The Stock Exchange

The meaning of the Stock Exchange

'The Stock Exchange is a market for second-hand securities.' A security may be in the forms of government (gilt-edged) stocks, local government securities, PLC shares or debentures. The Stock Exchange is a market where buyers of securities are in contact with the sellers of securities. It is a place where the necessary exchanges can take place. The securities are second hand because they have already been issued. New issues of stocks and shares are first sold on the *new issues market*.

The new issue market may take the form of disposing of new issue shares in one of the following different ways:

(a) *The public issue* The issuing house (usually a merchant bank, see page 195) will act as an agent for the company wishing to sell new issues of shares. It will prepare a prospectus which must be advertised in at least two national newspapers (see page 74). The advertisement will invite members of the public to take up some of the shares. If the share issue is oversubscribed (ie, too many investors wish to purchase the shares), each applicant will receive a proportion of their initial application for shares. If the share issue is undersubscribed (ie, too few investors wish to purchase the shares), then the issuing house will be left with unsold shares. However, the shares are probably underwritten. An underwriter agrees, for a commission, to take up any unsold shares. It is a kind of guarantee against not being able to sell the shares.

(b) *Offers for sale* In this case the issuing house itself purchases all of the shares and then proceeds, on its own behalf as the principal (and not the agent), to sell the shares. It assumes all the risks and expenses of selling the shares.

(c) *Placings* The issuing house attempts to place shares with particular shareholders. They will probably be offered to large institutional investors such as pension funds, insurance companies and investment trusts.

(d) *A rights issue* The company contacts existing shareholders and offers them the chance to purchase the new issues in proportion to their existing shareholding. They have 'rights' to purchase the new issues.

(e) *Issues by tender* Here new issues of shares are sold to the highest bidders, ie, those shareholders willing to pay the highest price.

It is only after shares have been sold on the new issue market that it is possible to buy and sell them on the Stock Exchange.

Examples of stock exchanges

The London Stock Exchange is at the centre of a network of stock exchanges throughout the British Isles. Stock exchanges are divided into units which are closely linked to the London Stock Exchange. The Scottish unit in Glasgow links Aberdeen, Dundee and Edinburgh. Dealers in these stock exchanges have detailed knowledge about local companies and their shares.

The London Exchange dates back to the second half of the seventeenth century, and the development of joint stock companies. The buying and selling of shares took place in numerous London coffee houses. Eventually, Old Jonathan's Coffee House and later New Jonathan's Coffee House, became the centre of dealings and the first real Stock Exchange. The present exchange is housed in a 26 storey building in London and was opened in 1973. The London Stock Exchange has close contact by telex, telephone and cable with all the major world stock exchanges such as the Bourse (Paris), Wall Street (New York) and Tokyo. It deals with securities from all over the world and not just United Kingdom securities.

Why do investors buy stocks and shares?

Investors purchase securities for the following reasons:

(a) *The security will earn a dividend* A dividend is a payment from the company's profits to shareholders. It is expressed as a percentage of the *nominal* or *par value* of the security, that is, the original or face value of the security. For instance, if a share with a par value of £1 receives 10 pence dividend then the percentage dividend is

$$\frac{10}{100} \times 100 \text{ which equals } 10\%$$

Therefore percentage dividend $= \dfrac{\text{dividend}}{\text{par value of security}} \times 100$

(b) *The security will earn a yield* This is perhaps even more important than the dividend because it represents what the security holder actually receives. It is calculated by expressing dividend as a percentage of the market value or current value of the security.

$$\text{Yield} = \frac{\text{par value of security}}{\text{market value of security}} \times \text{dividend per cent}$$

For example a share with a par value of £1 earns a dividend of 10%. However, the market value of the share is now £2. What is the yield?

$$\text{Yield} = \frac{100}{200} \times 10 = 5\%$$

(c) *The security may increase in price* As we have seen the market price of a security need not be the same as its nominal or par price. Shares originally bought for £1 may have a market price of £2. Thus this share could be sold at a *premium*, and a profit (or capital gain) could be made by selling these shares. However, the share could drop in price from a par price of £1 to a market price of 50 pence. This share would be sold at a *discount* and a capital loss would be made if the shareholder decided to sell this share.

Another reason why shares are bought is that it might enable the purchaser of shares to gain control of the company. This could be so if the shareholder purchases ordinary shares which carry a vote. Thus ordinary shares might be bought if one company was making a 'take-over' bid for another company.

Brokers and market-makers

After 'Big Bang' in 1986 (when the Stock Exchange became much more competitive and new technology was introduced) the traditional role of stock-brokers and stockjobbers was replaced by a new system of *broker-dealers*.

There are two types:

(a) Those who continue the role of the broker acting on behalf of their clients. They buy and sell to market-makers acting in the interests of their client. They arrange the transfer of shares, register changes of ownership and obtain share certificates. They advise customers regarding investments and send price lists and prospectuses to clients. These brokers receive a commission for services based on the value of the transaction involved.

(b) Market-makers who deal not only as brokers but also as dealers in shares. They tend to specialise in one type of security. Market-makers are found on the floor of the Stock Exchange and do not deal with members of the public but with brokers. They make a profit by buying at a lower price and selling at a higher price – this is known as the 'dealer's turn'.

'Big Bang' broke the monopoly of the stockjobbers and stockbrokers and allowed commercial banks and merchant banks to take on the role of either brokers or market dealers. This has ensured more competition for investors' business.

How shares are bought and sold

Assume an individual wishes to purchase shares. The transaction will take the following form.

A broker is contacted and the individual gives precise details of what shares and how many shares he or she would like to buy. The broker then contacts a market-maker about the shares which the individual wishes to purchase, not revealing whether he wishes to buy or sell.

The market-maker quotes two prices. The lower price is the one at which the market-maker buys and the higher price is the one at which the market-maker is prepared to sell. The broker may not be satisfied, in which case another market-maker will be asked for a quotation.

When both the broker and market-maker agree, they both make a note of the purchase and the bargain is checked next day. The motto of the Stock Exchange is 'My word is my bond' and therefore both parties to the business will honour the contract.

The broker then sends the individual who wishes to purchase shares a contract note which shows the number of shares bought, the price of the shares, the broker's commission, and the amount of the contract stamp and transfer stamp (in the case of a purchase), which are duties due to the government. The contract note should be kept by the individual in order to assess his liability for capital gains tax (see page 224).

The individual does not have to pay anything until the settlement day (or accounts day) arrives. Settlements must take place on settlement day and not at any other time. There are 24 settlement days in the year, mostly two weeks apart. The individual may therefore receive up to two weeks' credit before he pays any money if the previous settlement day has just passed.

The settlement of deals is completed by *Talisman* which is a computer network. It is concerned with recording all business and the movement of shares between buyers and sellers.

If the individual wished to sell shares, the broker would sell the shares to the market-maker at the agreed price and eventually pay the individual the money due to him.

Types of security which can be bought and sold on the Stock Exchange
The 9000 stocks officially listed on the Stock Exchange include a variety of different securities. Investors are given plenty of choice about what type of security to purchase. These are the main types of stock.

Company shares
We have already examined the different types of company share which can be bought and sold on the Stock Exchange. (These are discussed on page 75.) They include ordinary shares, preference shares, cumulative preference shares and participating preference shares.

Company debentures
(These are discussed on page 76).

Gilt-edged securities (or gilts)
These are securities issued by the government to finance the borrowing required to meet its expenditure requirements on defence, health, education and social services. Gilt-edged securities are so called because they are backed up by the resources of government. They pay a fixed rate of interest which is guaranteed by the government. They are repayable at face value at some future date. Their market price tends to fluctuate according to interest rates. There is a difference between 'bonds' and 'stocks'. Bonds are usually issued in units of £100, whereas stock can be bought in any amount.

Local authority stocks and bonds
These are similar to gilt-edged securities and they represent the borrowing of local authorities. Such investments are usually considered to be very safe carrying a fixed rate of interest and a guaranteed payment.

Investors are, therefore, faced with a choice between several types of security which they could purchase. What securities the investor does, in fact, purchase will depend on what his requirements are. If he wants to make a large profit with the necessity of some risk he may purchase ordinary shares. If, on the other hand, he wants a regular and safe but low return he may purchase gilt-edged securities or company debentures. Of course, it is not only individuals who purchase shares. Indeed, most of the shares are bought by institutional investors (as discussed on page 76).

'Bulls', 'bears', and 'stags'

Speculators are shareholders who buy and sell shares with a view to making profits. There are three main types of speculator: 'bulls', 'bears', and 'stags'.

Bulls

Bulls are optimists. They hope that share prices will rise and therefore they purchase shares now, at a low price, hoping to sell them later at a higher price. The market is said to be *bullish* when share prices are rising. A typical transaction would be as follows. A bull might buy shares and the usual contract note is made. No money is due before the next settlement day. Within the account period the price of the shares rises and the bull sells the shares at the new higher prices. On settlement day the bull receives money from the sale of the shares and then pays the money for the purchase of the shares. The bull pays the broker commission and government duties and the remainder is profit.

Of course there is a risk involved in this business. The bull could purchase shares and the price may fall in the account period rather than rise as anticipated. The bull may arrange a *contango* whereby he will carry over his position and not pay for the shares he has bought until perhaps the next settlement day. He will have to pay compensation to the seller of the shares who expected payment.

Bears

Bears are pessimists. They hope that share prices will fall and therefore they sell shares now at a higher price hoping to buy them back later at a lower price. The market is said to be *bearish* when share prices are falling.

A bear can make a profit by selling shares which he does not yet have. He will receive no money before the next settlement day. Before the next settlement day the price of the share falls and the bear will buy at these new lower prices. On the settlement day the bear pays for the shares bought and receives money for the same shares sold. The bear pays the broker's commission and government duties, and the remainder is profit.

Again there is a risk involved for the bear. The risk is that the price of the share rises rather than falls which means a loss on the business. To avoid this the bear may agree to make a payment called *backwardation* (similar to a contango). This is when the bear will carry the position and not give the buyer of the shares the shares expected until perhaps the next settlement day. The bear will have to pay compensation to the buyer of the shares who expected to receive them.

What the financial pages tell you about shares

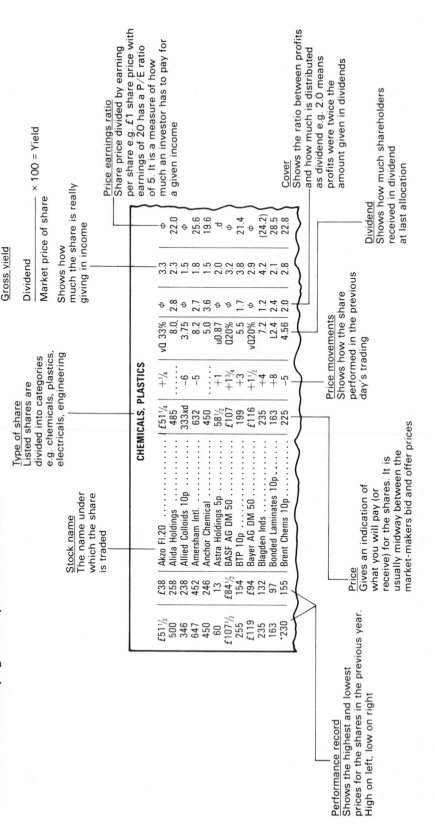

CHEMICALS, PLASTICS

High	Low	Stock name	Price	Price movements	Dividend	Cover	Gross yield	P/E ratio
£51½	£38	Akzo Fl.20	£51¼	+¼	vQ 33%	φ	3.3	φ
500	258	Alida Holdings	485	.....	8.0,	2.8	2.3	22.0
346	238	Allied Colloids 10p	333xd	−6	3.75	φ	1.5	φ
647	452	Amersham Intl.	632	−5	8.2	2.7	1.8	25.6
450	246	Anchor Chemical	450		5.0	3.6	1.5	19.6
60	13	Astra Holdings 5p	58½	+1	u0.87	φ	2.0	.d
£107½	£84½	BASF AG DM 50	£107	+1¾	020%	φ	3.2	φ
255	154	BTP 10p	199	+3	5.5	1.7	3.8	21.4
£119	£94	Bayer AG DM 50	£116	+1½	vQ20%	φ	2.9	φ
235	132	Blagden Inds	235	+4	7.2	1.2	4.2	(24.2)
163	97	Bonded Laminates 10p	163	+8	L2.4	2.4	2.1	28.5
*230	155	Brent Chems 10p	225	−5	4.56	2.0	2.8	22.8

Gross yield

Dividend / Market price of share × 100 = Yield

Shows how much the share is really giving in income

Price earnings ratio
Share price divided by earning per share e.g. £1 share price with earnings of 20 has a P/E ratio of 5. It is a measure of how much an investor has to pay for a given income

Cover
Shows the ratio between profits and how much is distributed as dividend e.g. 2.0 means profits were twice the amount given in dividends

Dividend
Shows how much shareholders received in dividend at last allocation

Type of share
Listed shares are divided into categories e.g. chemicals, plastics, electricals, engineering

Stock name
The name under which the share is traded

Price
Gives an indication of what you will pay (or receive) for the shares. It is usually midway between the market-makers bid and offer prices

Price movements
Shows how the share performed in the previous day's trading

Performance record
Shows the highest and lowest prices for the shares in the previous year. High on left, low on right

Stags

Stags specialise in buying new issues of shares. The stag hopes that a new share issue will be oversubscribed (ie, too many shareholders chasing too few shares) and thus the market price of these shares will rise. The stag attempts to buy as many shares as possible and then sell them later, at a profit, on the Stock Exchange.

'Bulls', 'bears' and 'stags' are often criticised for bringing about the change in share prices which they require by acting together. For example a group of 'bears' could sell a particular share and thus force down its price. They will then begin to purchase the same share at the lower price. The bears will have made a profit. Thus speculators are often criticised for bringing the Stock Exchange into disrepute (see page 244).

Movements in share prices

We have already discussed the fact that the par value (nominal value) of a share may differ from its market value. The market value of a share may fluctuate from day to day. The price of a share, like any other price, is determined by the supply of, and demand for, that share. If the demand for the share declines then the price of the share will drop. On the other hand if demand for the share increases then its price will increase.

Supply of, and demand for, shares can be influenced by several factors. Firstly, the annual results of the company. An individual investor, who is thinking of purchasing shares of a particular company, will pay attention to the company's balance sheet, how much profit the company made last year and how much of this profit was paid to shareholders in the form of dividend. The investor will also consider the yield on the shares.

Secondly, the investor will pay attention to rumours and newspaper articles which might apply to the company. For instance, if he reads an article suggesting that the company has just won a big export order to the USA then he might be optimistic about the future profitability of the company. In this case the investor might consider purchasing shares.

Thirdly, the overall economic and political situation in the United Kingdom and the world will be considered. The investor will pay attention to economic indicators such as the level of unemployment, the rate of inflation and industrial relations. If these indicators are relatively good then he might purchase shares. Similarly he will consider political factors such as the state of the world, whether there is a world crisis and the political situation of the United Kingdom government. If these factors are favourable then, again, the investor might be optimistic and buy shares.

When the investor wishes to find the price of the shares he has bought he will probably look in the *Financial Times* or, for the full list, consult the *Stock Exchange Daily Official List* which contains the names and prices of nearly 10 000 quoted securities. The Financial Times – Actuaries All-Share Index is issued daily and it is a guide to how share prices are moving on the Stock Exchange. The Index takes a sample of share prices and if it increases this signifies that share prices in general are probably increasing. If the index number decreases then share prices in general are probably decreasing.

Other important indices include the FT-SE 100 Index which is published daily in the newspapers. It is an average measure of the price movements of 100 key and leading ordinary shares. It started on 3 January 1984 and was given a base index number of 1000.0. The FT 30-Share Index is an average measure of 30 blue chips (first-class ordinary shares).

What are the advantages and disadvantages of the Stock Exchange?

The Stock Exchange is often described by its critics as being little more than a casino where speculators can force prices up or down to satisfy their own profit-making requirements. Indeed, there are periods when share prices have been forced artificially high only to suffer disastrous declines once the speculation subsides. Examples of such collapses of share prices include the Wall Street Crash in 1929 and the so-called 'black Monday' in October 1987.

The supporters of the Stock Exchange do not deny that speculation for profit takes place. However, they maintain that the vast majority of business on the exchange represents valid and genuine investments and not the search for profits. They say that the Stock Exchange performs several valuable functions:

(a) It provides a market where buyers and sellers of securities are in contact with each other. It therefore encourages investors to purchase securities because they know that they will be able to sell the shares when they so wish.

(b) It enables PLCs, local authorities and the central government to raise finance. Investors will be prepared to purchase these securities, knowing that they can be sold again. Without the Stock Exchange, United Kingdom firms and the United Kingdom government might run short of finance.

(c) Shareholders can follow their investments by looking at the *Stock Exchange Daily Official List* or in the *Financial Times*. Share prices are advertised, and changes easily followed. It also allows prospective shareholders to make a more rational decision about which shares to purchase.

(d) Brokers and market-makers, who are specialists in the Stock Exchange, can stabilise prices. For instance if the price of a share is falling too low according to the market-maker's experience, they may purchase these shares and therefore keep the price relatively stable. They can avoid large fluctuations in share prices.

(e) If a share is quoted on the Stock Exchange it means that the company has been investigated by the Stock Exchange council. It is a guarantee of honesty, and shareholders can be confident that the share represents a genuine company.

(f) The Stock Exchange provides a 'barometer' of the well-being of the economy. If the Financial Times 30-Share Index is rising, this might mean that confidence is prevailing in the economy and it is regarded as a good indicator. On the other hand, a falling Financial Times 30-Share Index will illustrate that there is pessimism about the state of the economy and it is regarded as a bad indicator.

Checkpoints

1 The Stock Exchange is where existing securities are bought and sold. New issues are sold on the new issues market. There are different methods of selling new issues such as offers for sale and placing.
2 Investors may buy securities to earn a dividend (or yield) or to speculate about the market price.
3 Since the Stock Exchange 'Big Bang' there are two types of dealer on the market: broker-dealer and market-makers.
4 There are a variety of securities bought and sold on the stock exchange including shares and debentures of PLCs, gilt-edged securities and local government securities.
5 There are three main types of speculator to be found on the Stock Exchange: bulls, bears and stags.
6 Share prices move up or down according to supply and demand. Share price movements are indicated by the FT Share Indices.
7 The Stock Exchange is often criticised for being a casino but supporters argue that it performs a number of useful functions such as being a place where PLCs and government can raise finance.

Multiple-choice questions – 12

1 A PLC issues half of its authorised capital of £200 000 and only requires 75p per share to be paid up. How much is its issued capital?

    A £ 50 000
    B £ 75 000
    C £100 000
    D £150 000
    E £200 000

2 Which of the following types of security would normally have voting rights?

    A ordinary shares
    B debentures
    C gilt-edged securities
    D Treasury bills
    E cumulative preference shares

3 The Stock Exchange is a market for all the following except

    A shares in retail co-operatives
    B gilt-edged securities
    C debentures issued by PLC's
    D local authority bonds
    E shares in public companies

4 If a company's shares are quoted on the Stock Exchange it means that

    A the company has been granted unlimited liability
    B the Stock Exchange council will fix the share price
    C the Stock Exchange guarantees shareholders against loss
    D the Stock Exchange underwrites all the company's shares
    E the company may issue shares to the general public

5 A shareholder receives a dividend of 5% on the shares which he purchased for £100. The nominal value of the shares is £200. The amount of dividend the shareholder actually receives is

    A £ 5
    B £10
    C £20
    D £25
    E £50

6 When shares in a limited company have a market value of £95 and a nominal value of £100 then

    A the company must have made a trading loss

B the shares are said to be at a premium
C the broker has made a loss of £5
D the shares will pay a low dividend
E the capital of the company remains the same despite a fall in the price of its shares

7 Which of the following can be used to calculate the yield of a share?

A $\dfrac{\text{nominal value} \times \text{dividend}}{\text{market price}}$

B $\dfrac{\text{nominal value} \times \text{market price}}{\text{dividend}}$

C $\dfrac{\text{market price} \times \text{dividend}}{\text{nominal value}}$

D $\dfrac{\text{nominal value} + \text{dividend}}{\text{market price}}$

E none of these

8 A person who buys shares on the Stock Exchange hoping their price will fall is known as

A an optimist
B an institutional investor
C a stag
D a bear
E a bull

9 Which of the following is *not* put forward as an advantage of the Stock Exchange?

A it is a place where the government can raise capital
B it is a place where local authorities can raise capital
C it encourages speculation in buying and selling shares
D it is a place where public companies can raise capital
E it is a barometer of the economy

10 'Blue chips' are

A gilt-edged securities
B first-class ordinary shares
C debentures
D new issues
E cumulative preference shares

Answers on page 328.

Data response question 12

THE MARKET
Speculators retire hurt

INITIALLY hard hit by fears of new hostilities in the Middle East, shares and gilts were pounded again later in the session when the money statistics showed a big jump in bank lending.

Speculators retired hurt in many recent favourites and, although there was some bargain-hunting at the lower levels, the indices suffered a sharp setback.

The FT 30 Share index, which was 34·3 lower at 2 pm, ended 27·3 down on the day at 1889·6, while the FTSE 100 Index finished 28·0 off at 2400·7, after 2390·8.

GEC slipped to 243p at the outset but buyers quickly reappeared on hopes of major acquisition news and the shares closed 4 better on balance at 251p. **ICI** also managed a small net gain at £15·13, while **Great Universal Stores "A"** picked up from the day's low of £14·20 to close 28 off at £14·34 on support ahead of Thursday's results.

However, there was little relief for **Hawker Siddeley,** 17 down at 585p, or **Lucas Industries,** 18 off at 761p.

The retreat in gilts saw falls extending to £1¼ at one stage but the market steadied at the close and losses were cut to a maximum of £1, albeit without much enthusiasm for a further rally.

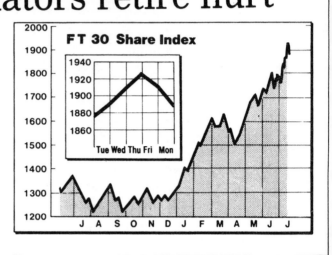

(a)   Why, in the economic sense, does the Stock Exchange qualify as 'a market'?

(b)   (i) What was the value of the FT 30 Share Index at its lowest point in the day?

   (ii) At what price did the GEC share price finish the day?

   (iii) On what day in the previous week did the FT 30 Share Index reach a maximum?

   (iv) During which two months during the previous year did the FT 30 Share Index reach its lowest points?

   (v) Why did Great Universal Stores 'A' shares pick up from the day's low of £14.20?

(c)   (i) What is a gilt?

     (ii) Apart from gilts name three other types of security which are bought and sold on the Stock Exchange.

    (iii) What is a 'blue chip' share?

(d) The article refers to speculators.

     (i) Explain what types of speculator can exist on the Stock Exchange

    (ii) Explain the meaning of the statement 'speculators retire hurt'

(e)   (i) What two reasons explain the fall in share and gilt prices during the day?

    (ii) Explain why these events had such an adverse impact

(f) Explain the difference between the FT 30 Share Index and the FT-SE 100 Index.

13 **The population**

Population facts and figures

The population of the United Kingdom in 1984 was 56.4 millions which makes the United Kingdom's population the 15th largest in the world. The United Kingdom consists of four different countries: England, Scotland, Wales and Northern Ireland.

UK Population statistics 1984

	Surface area (sq km)	Population (mills)	Density per sq km
England	130 439	46.8	359
Wales	20 768	2.8	135
Scotland	78 775	5.2	66
Northern Ireland	14 120	1.6	113
UK	244 102	56.4	231

Note: Great Britain consists of England, Scotland and Wales only. The density of population in the United Kingdom is one of the highest in the world with 231 people per square kilometre which is about the same as West Germany and India. Statistics are gained from registration of births and deaths and every decade a population census takes place.

The population census
The first official population census took place in the United Kingdom in 1801 although there were estimates and studies even before that date. A census has been held every first year of a decade ever since. There has been only one exception to this, in 1941, due to war. The last census was held in 1981.

The purposes of holding a census
A census helps the government to adequately plan the nation's resources for the next decade. The government wants to know:

(a) how many houses it needs to build;
(b) how many schools and colleges should be built;
(c) how many old and sick people there are;
(d) what the age distribution of the population is;
(e) how much public transport needs to be provided;

(f)   where most people are living and any changes in this distribution.

The gathering of statistics from the census helps the government to answer many questions about the nature and pattern of the United Kingdom's population and to plan accordingly for future needs and requirements.

Factors affecting the size of population

There are basically three factors which determine the size of population:

(a)   birth rate;
(b)   death rate;
(c)   migration patterns.

If birth rate exceeds death rate then there is a *natural increase in population*. If death rate exceeds birth rate then there is a *natural decrease in population*. *Emigration* is when people leave a country to live elsewhere. *Immigration* is when people enter a country to live in that country. *Net emigration* means that more people have left the country than entered, and *net immigration* means that more people have entered the country than have left. What is happening to net migration will affect the size of population.

Birth rate

The birth rate is a statistic which shows the number of births per thousand of the population in a certain country in a certain year. The birth rate is now lower than at the beginning of the twentieth century.

Birth rate per thousand population

1900–02	1930–32	1950	1961	1971	1978	1983	1985
28.6	16.3	15.9	17.6	16.3	12.3	12.8	13.1

The birth rate declined during the inter-war period due to more and better birth control and lower family sizes caused by the inter-war depression. Since 1945 the birth rate has fluctuated somewhat. For instance, in 1947 the birth rate increased to 20.5 per thousand of population and in 1961 it increased to 17.6 per thousand of population. However, the general trend has been for the birth rate to decline and in 1978 the birth rate was 12.3 per thousand of population (although it rose again by 1985). The birth rate depends on the following factors.

The number of women of child-bearing age

The critical child-bearing age group among women is between the ages of 15 and 44. The more women there are in this age group then the greater the likelihood that there will be a higher birth rate. The number of women in this age group can be predicted over periods of about 20 years by estimating how many females are currently below 15 years of age and how many will leave the group within the same period.

The number of marriages

Most children are born to married people but there are still children who are born outside marriage. The greater the number of marriages and the earlier people marry then the greater the probability of a higher birth rate.

Ideas of family size
If the trend is to have large families, as in Victorian days, then this will mean a higher birth rate. If, on the other hand, married couples do not wish, for whatever reason, to have large families this will curtail the birth rate. Ideas of family size will themselves be determined by the married couples present and hoped-for standard of living, by the size of child benefits, whether the woman wishes to carry on working and on attitudes towards birth control.

The death rate
The death rate is a statistic which shows the number of deaths per thousand of the population in a certain country and in a certain year. The death rate has continued to decline throughout the twentieth century.

Death rate per thousand of population

1900–02	1930–32	1971	1978	1979	1983	1985
17.3	12.2	11.6	11.9	12.1	11.8	11.8

The decline in the death rate has been a major contributory factor in the increase in population since 1900. A major element in the declining of the death rate has been the decline in the *infant mortality rate* (see page 255).

The death rate also determines a person's life-expectancy, and average life expectancy has increased for both men and women. At the beginning of the twentieth century a man could expect to live to 49 and a woman to 52. In 1985 a man could expect to live to 71.4 and a woman to 77.2 years.

Factors which have tended to decrease death rate include:

(a) *improvements in the standard of living* Better diet, better clothing, more leisure time, better housing.
(b) *improved working conditions* Fewer accidents at work and better conditions to work in, such as fewer hours and a pleasanter environment.
(c) *the development of the Welfare State* The existence of more hospitals, doctors and nurses. Better care for babies, the old and the sick.
(d) *improved medical techniques* Many dangerous diseases no longer exist in the United Kingdom, for example cholera. Also, there are new and better methods in surgery such as transplants.
(e) *better public health and sanitation* Much legislation ensures that health and sanitation services are adequately provided in all localities.
(f) *better educated population* People now realise what is 'good' and 'bad' for them, and have better eating habits and a more sensible approach to possible health dangers in life. However, there are contradictions here in that some people continue to smoke, eat and drink too much.

The death rate is expected to continue to fall in the future with continued medical improvements.

Migration
Migration has an important effect on the size of population. The increase in the population is larger or smaller than the natural increase in population depending on whether there is net immigration or net emigration. The migration record of the United Kingdom is described below.

The nineteenth century
For much of this period there was net emigration as people emigrated to the USA, Canada, Australia, South Africa and New Zealand.

The early twentieth century
During this period there was marginal net immigration especially during the inter-war period as people came to the United Kingdom to escape the threat of the Nazis in Germany.

Since 1945
Between 1945 and the early 1960s there was net immigration, especially from the West Indies, India and Pakistan. However since the early 1960s there has been net emigration. Between 1973 and 1983 net emigration amounted to 365 000 people. On average 221 300 people have emigrated each year, offset by about 184 800 immigrants.

There have been two forces at work. The traditional emigration has taken place mainly to the USA, Canada and Australia. There has also been a new trend of immigration as people from India, Pakistan and the West Indies came to the United Kingdom. However the government has taken measures to restrict immigration into the country and future immigration depends on the political policies of future governments. The stricter enforcement of immigration legislation since the early 1960s has meant less immigration and helps to account for the net emigration in this period. However, in both 1984 and 1985 there has been net immigration. In 1985 there was net immigration of 59 000 people.

All these three factors – birth rate, death rate and migration – determine the size of population. Let us now examine how the population of the United Kingdom has changed over the years with an emphasis on population trends since 1945.

The population increase since 1945

Population of the United Kingdom (millions)

1951	1961	1971	1978	1985
50.2	52.8	55.5	55.9	56.6

The population of the United Kingdom continued to increase between 1951 and 1971 (by about 10%). It rose by only 0.6% between 1971 and 1974 and actually fell by 0.2% between 1974 and 1978. However, since 1978 population has steadily increased, with the exception of a slight fall in population between 1981–82 (see page 257). Let us examine the three determinants of the size of population at work since 1945.

Population and population structure: selected countries

	Estimates of mid-year population (millions)						Percentage[1] aged		Expectation of life at birth[1] (years)	
	1961	1971	1976	1981	1984	1985	Under 15	60 or over	Males	Females
United Kingdom	52.8	55.6	55.9	56.4	56.5	56.6	19	21	71.4	77.2
Belgium	9.2	9.7	9.8	9.8	9.8	9.9	20	19	68.6	75.1
Denmark	4.6	5.0	5.1	5.1	5.1	5.1	20	20	71.4	77.4
France	46.2	51.2	52.9	54.2	55.0	55.2	22	18	70.4	78.5
Germany (Fed. Rep.)[2]	56.2	61.3	61.5	61.7	61.2	61.0	17	20	70.2	76.8
Greece	8.4	8.8	9.2	9.7	9.9	9.9	22	17	70.1	73.6
Irish Republic	2.8	3.0	3.2	3.4	3.5	3.6	31	15	68.8	73.5
Italy	49.9	54.0	56.2	56.5	57.0	57.1	21	18	69.7	75.9
Luxembourg	0.3	0.3	0.4	0.4	0.4	0.4	19	18	66.8	72.8
Netherlands	11.6	13.2	13.8	14.2	14.4	14.5	22	16	72.7	79.3
Portugal	8.9	9.0	9.7	9.9	10.1	10.2	26	15	65.1	72.9
Spain	30.6	34.1	36.0	37.8	38.3	38.6	26	16	70.4	76.2
European Community[3]	281.5	305.2	313.7	319.1	321.2	322.1	..	..	..	..
Sweden	7.5	8.1	8.2	8.3	8.3	8.4	19	22	73.0	79.1
Turkey	28.2	36.2	41.1	45.4	48.3	49.3	39	5	53.7	
Australia	10.5	12.9	13.9	14.9	15.6	15.8	25	14	71.4	78.4
USSR	218.0	245.1	256.7	267.7	275.1	278.6	36[5]	13	64	74
Egypt	26.6	34.1	37.9	43.5	47.2	48.5	40	6	51.6	53.8
Tanzania	10.6	13.6	16.4	19.2	21.1	21.7	46	6	47.3	50.7
Zimbabwe	4.0	5.5	6.3	7.4	8.0	8.3	51	3	51.3	55.6
China	671.0	840.0	908.3	1,011.2	1,049.7	1,059.5	34	8	62.6	66.5
India	439.0	551.3	613.3	676.2	745.0	750.9	39	6	46.4	44.7
Japan[4]	94.0	105.7	112.8	117.6	120.0	120.8	23	14	74.2	79.7
Canada	18.3	21.6	23.0	24.3	25.1	25.4	22	14	71.9	78.9
USA	183.8	206.2	215.1	230.0	236.7	239.3	22	16	70.5	78.2
Brazil	71.8	95.2	109.2	124.0	132.6	135.6	38	6	57.6	61.1
Peru	10.3	13.8	15.6	17.8	19.2	19.7	41	5	52.6	55.5

1 Latest available year.
2 Includes West Berlin.
3 Includes United Kingdom, Irish Republic, Denmark, Greece, Portugal, and Spain throughout.
4 Includes Okinawa.
5 Under 20.

Birth rate

Refer to the table showing birth rates on page 251. Since 1945 the birth rate has fluctuated up and down but the general long term trend since 1900 has been for a lower birth rate. There have been two periods since 1945 when the birth rate has increased: the late 1940s and early 1960s. In the late 1940s the increase was undoubtedly due to the reunion of families after the 1939–45 war. The increase in the early 1960s was due to some extent to those people born in the 'baby boom' of the late 1940s, beginning to have their own children, and an improvement in standards of living since 1950 enabling people to afford to have children. There has been a small baby boom at the end of the 1970s and early 1980s as birth rates again increased slightly. Again this is due to those people born in the early 1960s having their own children, and a higher standard of living.

However, the trend has been for the birth rate to fall. There have been several factors put forward to explain this.

(a) Ideas of family size have changed. Large families are an exception.
(b) The desire by married couples to have fewer children and a better standard of living for themselves.
(c) Methods of birth control are available and better understood. Also abortion – owing to the 1967 Abortion Act – is legalised.
(d) Women prefer to work for a longer time and begin a career before starting a family.
(e) Although people are marrying at quite a young age they are not having as many children for the reasons that have already been outlined.

Death rate

The death rate has declined since 1900 and this trend has continued since 1945. In 1985 the death rate was 11.8 per thousand of population (see table on page 252). The decline in the death rate has been a major contributory factor in the increase in population. A major element in the decline in the death rate has been the decline in infant mortality rate (ie, the number of infants who die each year before reaching the age of one year per 1000 live births).

Infant mortality rates per 1000 live births

1900–02	1930–32	1971	1978	1980	1983
142	67	18	13.2	12	10.1

The infant mortality rate has declined quite dramatically due to better ante-natal and post-natal care, intensive care units, improved medical techniques, the introduction of the Welfare State, better health and diet of mothers, better education and a general improvement in the standard of living. However, there is still no room for complacency as there are still regional variations of infant mortality throughout the United Kingdom and the United Kingdom's infant mortality rate is still greater than countries such as Denmark (8.0), Japan (6.2) and France (8.9).

As death rates have declined, life expectancy has increased and in 1985 a man could expect to live to the age of 71.4 years and a woman to the age of 77.2. Indeed the United Kingdom has, what is called, 'an ageing population' (see page 259).

The reasons why the death rate has declined have been outlined on page 252 and these should be re-examined in the light of experience since 1945. However, there are some points worth further discussion. Medical science has developed to such an extent that many diseases, such as cholera and typhoid, are no longer found in the United Kingdom. Also, new surgical techniques have helped many people, for example new organ transplants such as kidney and heart transplants. Nevertheless, there is an alarming increase in deaths from heart disease and cancer. In 1983, the most common causes of deaths were heart disease (216 542 deaths), cancer (148 647 deaths), respiratory diseases (93 886 deaths) and road accidents (5790 deaths).

Natural increase or decrease in population since 1945
In nearly all the years since 1945 there has been a natural increase in population. This means that birth rate has exceeded death rate. The exception to this was in 1976 when there was a natural decrease in population. In that year 680 800 people died and 675 500 people were born. In 1985 the natural increase in population was 86 000 (659 000 deaths and 745 000 live births).

Migration
Between 1945 and the early 1960s there was net immigration. However, successive Immigration Acts have limited the amount of immigration by making it more difficult to become a citizen of the United Kingdom. Indeed, between 1973 and 1983 the population of the United Kingdom was reduced by nearly 365 000 by net migration. An average of 221 300 people have emigrated each year, offset by an average of 184 800 immigrants. Unusually, for both 1984 and 1985 there was net immigration into the United Kingdom. For instance in 1985 the total number of new residents in the United Kingdom was 232 000 and the number of departing residents 174 000 – a net gain of 59 000. Emigrants have tended to go to the USA, Australia, Canada and New Zealand. Some of this emigration has been in the form of a 'brain drain' – when highly skilled and well qualified people leave to live abroad. Immigrants have come from the West Indies, Pakistan and India. Many of these people have had difficulty in assimilation into British society. Moreover many British people have found it difficult to accept these immigrants. Thus there have been racial and social problems in many cities in the United Kingdom. However immigrants have contributed a great deal to the United Kingdom economy (doctors, nurses, and shopkeepers) and to a more cosmopolitan way of life in society. The United Kingdom has yet to cope successfully with the variety of social and racial problems which the post-1945 immigration has posed.

The effects of an increasing population

The population of the United Kingdom has increased since 1800 and this increase still continues today, although the population did decline between 1974 and 1978. The population of the United Kingdom by the year 2000 is expected to be about 58.4 millions. However, this is only an estimate based on present conditions and, like any estimate, it may prove to be wrong.

Population changes and projections in the United Kingdom (in thousands)

	Population at start of period	Average annual change				
		Live births	Deaths	Net natural change	Net civilian migration and other adjustments	Overall annual change
Census enumerated						
1901–11	38 237	1 091	624	467	− 82	385
1911–21	42 082	975	689	286	− 92	194
1921–31	44 027	824	555	268	− 67	201
1931–51	46 038	785	598	188	+ 25	213
Mid-year estimates						
1951–61	50 290	839	593	246	+ 6	252
1961–66	52 807	988	633	355	+ 12	367
1966–71	54 643	937	644	293	− 40	253
1971–76	55 907	766	670	96	− 37	60
1976–81	56 206	705	662	43	− 8	35
1981–82	56 352	722	669	53	− 99	− 46
1982–83	56 306	722	660	62	− 21	41
1983–84	56 347	718	652	66	+ 47	112
1984–85	56 460	745	659	86	+ 72	158
Projections*						
1987–91	56 891	804	647	157	− 17	140
1991–96	57 452	834	645	190	− 17	172
1996–2001	58 312	795	648	146	− 17	129
2001–06	58 957	732	654	78	− 17	61
2006–11	59 259	713	663	50	− 17	33
2011–16	59 422	736	677	59	− 17	41
2016–21	59 629	763	694	69	− 17	52

* 1985-based projections.

The concept of optimum population

Optimum population is that level of population where national income per head of population is maximised. This means that population is at its best size and is achieving a level of national income (or output) which is at its best given that level of population. If a country is overpopulated it means that there are too many people with too few resources to provide a level of national income which maximises national income per head. If a country is underpopulated it means that there are too few people to make use of the resources available to increase national income and maximise national income per head.

The size of optimum population may increase (or decrease) if there is a change in the technology or resources available. If technology improves or new resources are developed then the size of optimum population will increase. If, on the other hand, technology is diminished (perhaps by a war) or resources are used up, then the size of optimum population will fall.

The advantages of an increasing population

(a) If the existing population is below optimum size then an increase in population will have the advantage of increasing national income and national income per head will increase. Thus the standard of living will improve.

(b) A larger population will, all other things remaining equal, increase the demand for goods and services in the economy. This will stimulate investment and output and create more jobs and incomes. Moreover, it will stimulate new inventions and new technology.

(c) A larger population may have the effect of increasing a country's international prestige. The larger a country's population then (often) the greater its influence in world affairs.

(d) It will mean that there is a greater demand in the economy, more division of labour can be introduced and the economies of large-scale production can be employed in many industries.

(e) If the increasing population is mainly to be found in the working population (see page 263) this will mean there will be more workers to develop resources and more goods and services will be produced. Moreover they can pay more taxes to improve benefits for the dependent age groups – the very young and very old.

(f) If the increasing population is mainly in the younger age groups this will mean that the population is more mobile and flexible. Moreover, these people will be less traditional in their outlook on the economy and society.

The disadvantages of increasing population

(a) If the increase in population means that that population exceeds its optimum size then there will be too many people in the country. National income per head will be lower than it should be because there are not enough resources available. Thus a country will have a lower standard of living.

(b) Where a country is chronically overpopulated an increase in population may mean severe hardship, poverty, malnutrition, and high death rates.

(c) An increasing population will put a great strain on a country's social, health and educational facilities. There may be overcrowding in houses, shortages of doctors, shortages of medicine, shortages of schools and teachers, and food shortages.

(d) If the increasing population is to be found mainly in the dependent age groups this will increase the burden on the working population. The dependent age groups are the very young (0–16 years) and the very old (65 + years). These people do not contribute to the economy in the sense that they are not part of the working population (see page 263), and do not help develop resources. Thus the working population will have to produce more goods and services and pay higher taxes to support social benefits such as child allowances and old-age pensions.

(e)   A country may have balance of payments difficulties because it may have to import more food and raw materials to satisfy the needs of its increasing population and industries.

Thus there is no easy answer to the question about whether an increasing population is good or bad. A great deal depends on the existing level of population relative to its present stock of resources (ie, whether the country is overpopulated or underpopulated. Moreover, much depends on which age group is accounting for the population increase. In the short term, at least, having a lot more babies in the economy will not have many economic benefits.

The age distribution of population

Look at the statistics for the age and sex structure of the population of the United Kingdom on page 261. Since 1900 there have been changes in the age distribution of population. The long-term trend has been for there to be proportionately fewer people in the age group 0–16, roughly about the same proportion in the age group 16–64, and a greater proportion of people in the age group 65 + . It is extremely important for the government to know the present and estimated age distribution of population so that it can plan how many schools it needs, how many old people's homes are required, how much old age pensions will cost, and how many maternity clinics are required.

The United Kingdom's ageing population
The United Kingdom has an ageing population. This means that on average people are living longer and that the average age of a person in the United Kingdom is higher.

The United Kingdom has an ageing population for two main reasons. Firstly, the death rate has declined so that people are living longer. Secondly, there has been a decline in the birth-rate which has caused a decline in the proportion of people in the age group 0–16 years.

What are the effects of an ageing population?

(a)   *There will be an increasing burden on the working population* (see page 263). Those people over the age of 65 are part of the dependent population. This means that they rely on the working population to produce goods and services they require and to pay taxes to finance old people's homes and old age pensions. Thus an ageing population puts an increased burden on the working population. Of course, the working population could be increased by lowering the school-leaving age and by raising the age of retirement to above 65 years. However, both these developments are extremely unlikely for social and political reasons (eg, unemployment would be increased).

(b) *Changes in consumption*
Old people demand different goods and services compared with younger people. Young people demand pop records, clothes and entertainment. Old people spend most of their income on food and fuel. Moreover, old people tend to save more of their income than young people. Thus an ageing population will mean changes in demand patterns. The government will also need to know that there is an ageing population because they will need to spend more on old people's homes, pensions and perhaps the health service in general.

(c) *Immobility of labour*
As people become older they become less geographically and occupationally mobile. This may have a bad effect on the economy, as the new expanding industries will find it difficult to recruit suitable workers whereas the declining industries will make people unemployed who then do not move to another job or another area.

(d) *Society will become more conservative*
Older people tend to be more conservative and cautious in their views on politics, society and ways of living. Thus an ageing population might mean less dynamism and innovation in the United Kingdom.

The United Kingdom is expected to continue having an ageing population at least until the end of the twentieth century. This is because the death-rate is expected to continue to fall with further medical achievements. However, the proportion of total population formed by the ageing population will depend on what happens to the birth rate and this is determined by factors such as ideas of family size, the standards of living and age of marriage.

The sex distribution of population

In 1985 there were 27.6 million males and 29.0 million females in the United Kingdom population. Therefore, there are more females than males in the population and this obviously has consequences for the nature of the labour force, patterns of consumption and expected birth-rate (since one factor which determines birth-rate is the number of women between 15 and 44).

However the sex distribution is more complicated than simply stating that there are more females than males. This is because up to the age of approximately 50 years males exceed females, then after the age of approximately 50 years females exceed males in large numbers. These facts are illustrated in the table of statistics for the United Kingdom opposite.

These figures show that in age groups up to about 50 years there are more males than females. In the older age groups there are more females than males and the ratio of females to males gets larger in these older age groups.

Why are there more males than females in the younger age groups?
There is a slight excess of male births over female births. For every 106 male babies born, 100 female babies are born. With improvements in care for babies, and better ante-natal and post-natal care, there has been a drop in infant mortality

Age and sex structure of the population of the UK (in millions)

	0–4	5–14	15–29	30–44	45–59	60–64	65–74	75–84	85+	All ages
Census enumerated										
1901	4.4	8.0	10.8	7.5	4.6	1.1	1.3	0.5		38.2
1911	4.5	8.4	11.2	8.9	5.6	1.2	1.6	0.6		42.1
1921	3.9	8.4	11.2	9.3	7.0	1.5	1.9	0.7		44.0
1931	3.5	7.6	11.8	9.7	8.0	1.9	2.5	1.0		46.1
Mid-year estimates										
1941	3.4	6.8	9.2	10.3	8.5	2.3	3.2	1.3		44.9
1951	4.3	7.0	10.2	11.2	9.6	2.4	3.7	1.8		50.3
1961	4.3	8.1	10.3	10.5	10.6	2.8	4.0	1.9	0.3	52.8
1971	4.5	8.9	11.8	9.8	10.2	3.2	4.8	2.2	0.5	55.9
1976	3.7	9.2	12.4	10.0	9.8	3.1	5.1	2.3	0.5	56.2
1981	3.5	8.1	12.8	11.0	9.5	2.9	5.2	2.7	0.6	56.4
1983	3.6	7.6	13.1	11.1	9.4	3.2	5.0	2.8	0.6	56.3
1984	3.6	7.4	13.3	11.2	9.3	3.3	4.8	2.9	0.7	56.5
1985										
Males	1.9	3.7	6.8	5.7	4.6	1.5	2.2	1.0	0.2	27.6
Females	1.8	3.5	6.6	5.6	4.7	1.7	2.8	1.9	0.5	29.0
Total	3.6	7.3	13.4	11.3	9.3	3.1	4.9	2.9	0.7	56.6
Projections*										
1987	10.7		13.5	11.6	9.2		8.0	3.8		56.9
1991	11.0		12.9	12.1	9.5		7.9	4.0		57.5
1996	11.7		11.6	12.6	10.5		7.7	4.2		58.3
2001	12.0		10.8	13.2	11.0		7.6	4.4		59.0
2006	11.7		11.0	12.6	11.6		7.9	4.5		59.3
2011	11.1		11.7	11.3	12.1		8.8	4.5		59.4
2015	10.8		12.0	10.6	12.6		9.1	4.5		59.6

* 1985-based projections.

rates. This has especially benefited male babies who, contrary to the opinion that they are the stronger sex, suffer a higher death-rate at birth and soon after birth. Thus more males are now surviving into childhood and adulthood.

However, as the death-rate among males is greater than females in virtually all age groups, the excess of males over females diminishes for each successive age group. As we have seen after the age of 50 years there are more females than males.

Why are there more females than males in the older age groups?

(a) Women can expect to live longer than men. Several factors have been put forward to explain this; women are physically stronger than men, men do more dangerous work, men smoke and drink more, men indulge in dangerous sports and men suffer more stress at home and at work.

(b) More men were killed in the two World Wars, especially the 1914–18 war, which would help explain why there are more females than males in the older age groups.

In the future it is likely that the excess of females over males will diminish in the total population. This is because the generation affected by the 1914–18 War, when there were many male deaths, is now passing out of the statistics. Also, continued improvements in medical techniques will proportionately beneficially affect males more than females, in all age groups, since the death rate for males is at the moment greater.

Geographical distribution of population

A knowledge of the geographical distribution of population is important to the government to enable it to plan the allocation of resources in a particular region. How many roads will be required? How many schools, hospitals and old people's homes will be needed?

If you refer to the table on page 250 you can see that the bulk of the United Kingdom's population live in England (46.8 million) which has a density of 359 people per sq km.

Most of the population is situated in the South East of England and the Midlands

There has been a drift south of people from the old and declining industrial areas of Wales, Scotland and Northern England. Most of the United Kingdom's new and expanding industries such as chemicals, electrical and manufacturing industries are situated in the southern half of the country. Therefore people have moved to find work. This drift south reverses the trend of migration seen in the Industrial Revolution when people moved north and into Wales to the coalfields where the traditional industries were situated.

Most of the population live in cities

About 80% of the United Kingdom's population live in cities (ie urban areas).

London itself has a population of almost 8 million people. There are 19 cities in the United Kingdom with over 250 000 inhabitants. Moreover there are seven large conurbations in the United Kingdom where about one-third of the United Kingdom population lives. A conurbation is an area of urban sprawl and is a built-up area comprising various cities and towns which may stretch for miles. The seven conurbations are: Merseyside, Birmingham, Manchester, Leeds, Newcastle, London and Glasgow. The density of population is particularly high in these conurbations. The reasons why people live in cities are mainly traditional. The city was the place where work was available and where the factories were situated. Thus people left their rural areas in the Industrial Revolution to find work in the cities.

The decline of inner cities and growth of new towns
The inner city areas of large cities tend to be areas where there is overcrowding, slum housing, poor social infrastructure, few hospitals, and few leisure amenities. Living conditions are very squalid indeed in these areas. The government has built several new towns (eg, Crawley, Welwyn Garden City, and Telford) and has encouraged people, especially those in the inner city areas, to leave the cities and move to the new towns.

Moreover there has been a migration of people from the inner city areas into the suburbs of cities as new housing estates have been erected.

Older people moving to the South Coast and South West
An interesting development in recent years has been the movement of older people to live on the South Coast. Such people have moved to towns like Eastbourne and Worthing where a high percentage of people are over 65 years. One reason for this is that the climate is pleasanter in these areas. This movement of older people has consequences for the local authority provision of old people's homes, hospitals and leisure facilities. A great strain may be felt by ratepayers (and, by 1990, poll tax payers) in these areas.

It is expected that the present trends of geographical distribution of population will continue into the future.

The occupational distribution of population

The meaning of the working population
In 1985 the population of the United Kingdom was 56.6 million. The working population (excluding those in HM Forces) numbered 27.6 million in June 1985.

The working population is made up of all those over the age of 16 years in the following categories:

	Employees in employment
plus	Employers
plus	Self-employed
plus	HM Forces
equals	EMPLOYED LABOUR FORCE

Population changes and projections : by region and country

United Kingdom

Average annual change 1971-1985 a

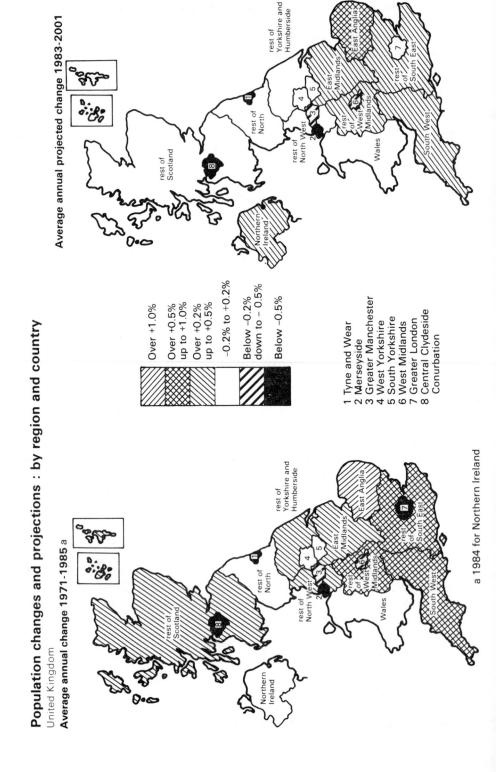

Average annual projected change 1983-2001

Over +1.0%

Over +0.5% up to +1.0%

Over +0.2% up to +0.5%

−0.2% to +0.2%

Below −0.2% down to − 0.5%

Below −0.5%

1 Tyne and Wear
2 Merseyside
3 Greater Manchester
4 West Yorkshire
5 South Yorkshire
6 West Midlands
7 Greater London
8 Central Clydeside Conurbation

a 1984 for Northern Ireland

plus	Benefit claimants (ie unemployment benefits, supplementary benefits)
plus	Those on government training schemes
equals	WORKING POPULATION

It includes people in paid employment who are over retirement age (65 for men, 60 for women) and part-time workers. It does not include children under 16 years, full-time students, house-persons not seeking work, prisoners, people incapable of work and people not seeking work (ie, not claiming benefit) and those men over 60 who may be claiming benefits but need not sign on at an unemployment benefit office.

The size of the working population will be affected by any changes in the school-leaving age, the proportion of people pursuing full-time education after the age of 16, the number of women who wish to work, how many people past retirement age carry on working and, indeed, if the retirement age is changed. For instance, if school-leaving age is raised from 16 to 17 years this will have the effect of reducing the size of the working population as would a decrease in the age of retirement from 65 to 60 years for males. These measures would also reduce the level of unemployment.

The future size of working population is difficult to estimate because it will depend on government policies towards early retirement and school-leaving age as well as the attitude of married women to work. The numbers of people in the age group 16–65 years is expected to remain fairly static so, therefore, all other things being equal, the size of working population should remain roughly the same.

The size of working population is important to the economy because it is these people who produce the goods and services for all people in the community. They also support the dependent age groups by paying taxes which finance child benefits and old age pensions as well as government spending on hospitals, schools and roads. It is interesting to note that, in June 1985, 27.6 million of the United Kingdom population were actually in the working population (and not all of these were in employment) and they carry the burden of providing for the dependent groups in the economy.

At the beginning of the twentieth century the economic activity rate among women was very low. There were very few jobs open to them, except domestic service, and married women especially were not expected to work in employment. However, since 1945 women have formed an increasing proportion of the working population. Women are found mainly in clerical and administrative work in all industries, in textiles and clothing, metal-using trades, distributive trades, various light industries (such as food, drink and tobacco), nursing, teaching and catering.

The proportion of women finding employment is increasing for various reasons:

(a) There has been a change in society's attitude towards women at work.
(b) The decline in the birth-rate and lower family size.
(c) Desire by families to have a higher standard of living.

Distribution of working population of the UK (in thousands)

	Unadjusted								Seasonally adjusted	
	Working population [1,2,3]	Un-employed excluding students [2]	Employed labour force [1,3]	Employees in employment [3]			Self-employed persons (with or without employees) [3]	HM Forces [4]	Working population [1,2,3]	Employees in employment [3]
				Total	Males	Females				
1978	26 342	1 343	24 999	22 777	13 389	9 388	1 904	318	26 372	22 762
1979	26 609	1 234	25 375	23 157	13 476	9 682	1 903	314	26 646	23 138
1980 At June	26 819	1 513	25 306	22 972	13 306	9 666	2 011	323	26 873	22 950
1981	26 718	2 395	24 323	21 870	12 547	9 323	2 118	334	26 788	21 849
1982	26 663	2 770	23 894	21 400	12 203	9 197	2 170	324	26 749	21 380
1983	26 586	2 984	23 602	21 059	11 948	9 111	2 221	322	26 680	21 040
1983 September	26 961	3 167	23 793	21 178	12 005	9 173	2 290	325	26 810	21 099
December	26 986	3 079	23 906	21 222	11 937	9 286	2 359	325	26 939	21 183
1984 March	26 978	3 143	23 835	21 081	11 857	9 225	2 428	326	27 078	21 208
June	27 094	3 030	24 065	21 242	11 905	9 337	2 496	326	27 191	21 224
September	27 484	3 284	24 201	21 349	11 989	9 360	2 523	328	27 337	21 274
December	27 519	3 219	24 299	21 422	11 963	9 459	2 550	327	27 469	21 380
1985 March	27 459	3 268	24 191	21 288	11 888	9 400	2 577	326	27 557	21 414
June	27 569	3 179	24 391	21 460	11 749	9 511	2 604	326	27 666	21 442
September	27 831	3 346	24 485	21 525	11 991	9 533	2 635	326	27 688	21 452
December	27 847	3 273	24 574	21 586	11 958	9 627	2 665	323	27 805	21 543

Sources: Department of Employment
Department of Economic Development (Northern Ireland)

1. The working population consists of the employed labour force and the unemployed (claimants); the employed labour force includes employers, self-employed and HM Forces as well as employees in employment.

2. From April 1983, the figures of unemployment reflect the effects of the provisions in the Budget for some men aged 60 and over who no longer have to sign at an unemployment office.

3. Estimates of employees in employment up to June 1984 take account of the results of the 1983 and 1984 Labour Force surveys. Estimates for later periods include an allowance for continued undercounting (see the article on page 114 of the March 1985 *Employment Gazette*). Estimates of the self-employed up to mid 1984 are based on the results of the 1981, 1983 and 1984 Labour Force surveys. The provisional estimates from September 1984 are based on the assumption that the average rate of increase between 1981 and 1984 has continued subsequently. A detailed description of the current allowances is given on page 114 of the March 1985 *Employment Gazette*.

4. HM Forces figures, provided by the Ministry of Defence represent the total number of UK service personnel, male and female, in HM Regular Forces, wherever serving and including those on release leave. The numbers are not subject to seasonal adjustment.

(d) Women are more career-minded.
(e) Labour-saving devices in the home, such as vacuum cleaners and washing machines, have given women more time to work.
(f) The effects of recent legislation like the Equal Pay Act and the Sex Discrimination Act (see page 290).

Economic activity rates[1]: by sex, EC comparison, 1985			Percentages
	Males	Females	All
United Kingdom	59.6	38.3	48.7
Belgium	52.6	33.0	42.6
Denmark	61.5	49.5	55.4
France	51.6	35.4	43.3
Germany (Fed. Rep.)	58.5	33.8	45.6
Greece	55.2	27.3	41.0
Irish Republic	51.7	21.7	36.7
Italy	55.2	28.1	41.3
Luxembourg	56.1	29.3	42.3
Netherlands	53.2	27.6	40.3
Portugal	53.9	35.6	44.5
Spain	50.6	21.2	35.7

1 The total working population (including the armed forces) expressed as a percentage of the total population.

Changes in the occupational distribution of population
A large decline in the proportion of the working population in primary industries

(a) Employment in agriculture, forestry and fishing has declined due to increasing mechanisation.
(b) Employment in mining and quarrying has declined due to increasing mechanisation and competition from other countries and other fuels.

An increase in the proportion of the working population engaged in tertiary industries

(a) There has been a large increase in the numbers of people employed in the public services provided by national and local government. Thus there are more doctors, nurses, teachers, Civil Servants etc. This has been due to greater government spending on education, defence and the Welfare State. However since 1980, the total of employees in the public sector has declined (see page 87 for statistics).
(b) The proportion of people employed in insurance, finance, banking, distributive services and commerce has increased. This has been due mainly to a greater demand for these services from manufacturing industry which

has become more sophisticated. Also, the standard of living has improved in the United Kingdom, therefore people are spending more of their incomes on leisure services.

There are services which have declined, for instance the proportion of people employed in domestic service is now negligible, whereas in 1900 quite a high percentage of the working population, especially women, were employed in domestic service. Moreover, the proportion of people employed in transport and communications has declined mainly due to the increasing private ownership of the motor car since 1945.

The proportion of the working population involved in secondary industries remained much the same between 1945 and 1980

Since 1980 employment in secondary industries has been in decline. There has been a decline in the old, traditional, staple industries of textiles, shipbuilding and steel. However, there are some new and expanding industries which employ a greater proportion of the working population, for example, electrical and engineering products. Finally, employment in the construction industry has declined since 1900 due to increased mechanisation. Since 1980 employment in manufacturing has declined.

The trends that have been outlined in the occupational distribution of the working population are expected to continue. Employment in primary industries is expected to continue falling. Employment in service industries, ie, tertiary industry, is expected to continue expanding as standards of living improve. Employment in the secondary industries is expected to decline but there will be expanding industries and declining industries.

Checkpoints

1   The size of population is affected by birth rate, death rate and migration.

2   Birth-rate is determined by the number of females of child-bearing age, the number of marriages and ideas of family size. The natural increase of population refers to the excess of births over deaths.

3   Death-rate is determined by factors such as diet, standard of living, medical techniques and education. Infant mortality rate is the number of infants less than one year of age per 1000 live births who die.

4   Migration is influenced by the numbers of emigrants and immigrants.

5   In the 1970s and 1980s in the United Kingdom both death-rate and birth-rate have fallen but there has (usually) been a natural increase in population which exceeds net emigration. There has been net immigration in 1984 and 1985.

6   Optimum population is that level of population where national income per head of population is at a maximum. An increasing population may be either an advantage or disadvantage depending on whether the population is at present above or below optimum size.

7   The United Kingdom has an ageing population, due to the decline in death-rate, and this will have consequences for patterns of demand and the burden on the working population.

Employees in employment in the UK: by industry¹ (in thousands)

	1971	1976	1981	1983²	1984²	1985²		
						Males	Females	Total
Agriculture, forestry, and fishing	432	393	352	349	340	253	85	338
Metal goods, engineering, and vehicle industries	3 705	3 330	2 919	2 637	2 608	2 073	539	2 612
Energy and water supply industries³	797	721	709	659	634	531	82	613
Extraction of minerals and ores other than fuels, manufacture of metal, mineral products, and chemicals	1 278	1 157	934	817	798	651	148	799
Other manufacturing industries	3 102	2 794	2 367	2 155	2 136	1 237	885	2 122
Construction	1 207	1 252	1 138	1 012	989	849	121	970
Distribution, hotels, catering, and repairs	3 678	3 964	4 166	4 174	4 337	2 042	2 428	4 470
Transport and communication	1 550	1 456	1 423	1 326	1 311	1 035	269	1 304
Banking, finance, insurance, business services, and leasing	1 336	1 494	1 740	1 823	1 887	1 009	963	1 972
Other services	5 036	5 975	6 121	6 109	6 202	2 269	3 997	6 266
All industries and services	22 122	22 543⁴	21 870	21 059	21 242	11 950	9 517	21 467

1 As at June each year.
2 Estimates of employees in employment take account of the results of the 1983, 1984, and 1985 Labour Force surveys.
3 Includes coal mining.
4 Includes 8 700 employees who were not allocated to individual industry groups.

8   There are more women than men in the United Kingdom although the number of men exceeds the number of women in younger age groups.

9   In the United Kingdom most people live in urban areas and live in the Midlands and south east of England. These areas provide most of the employment opportunities.

10   The occupational distribution of population in the United Kingdom is such that most people work in the tertiary (service) sector, followed by secondary (manufacturing) and finally the primary sector.

11   The working population is defined as all of those persons over the age of 16 years who are in employment or are actively seeking employment (ie, they are registered as unemployed).

Multiple-choice questions – 13

1 A rise in the death rate is likely to

    A increase the size of the dependent population
    B have no effect on patterns of demand
    C increase the level of national income
    D reduce government spending on old age pensions
    E increase the size of the working population

2 The working population of the United Kingdom is defined as

    A everybody who earns an income
    B trade union members
    C everybody between the ages of 16 and 65 years
    D total employed labour force plus claimants for unemployment benefit plus people on government training schemes
    E all those people in work

3 Which of the following would *not*, other things remaining equal, increase the size of a country's population?

    A an increase in the birth-rate
    B an increase in immigration
    C a decrease in emigration
    D better diet and medical improvements
    E an increase in the infant mortality rate

4 Which of the following is most likely to increase the size of the working population?

    A stricter immigration laws
    B an increase in school-leaving age
    C an increase in retirement age
    D government spending cuts reducing nursery education
    E an increase in old age pensions

5 A natural increase in the population means

    A birth rate is less than death rate
    B death rate is less than birth rate
    C infant mortality rate is increasing
    D total population is greater than the optimum size
    E immigration exceeds emigration

6 Optimum population is defined by the economist as the level of population at which

    A death rate equals birth rate

     B productivity is maximised
     C immigration equals emigration
     D national income is at a maximum
     E national income per head is maximised

7 Which of the following would *not* lead to a decrease in the size of population?

     A improved methods of contraception
     B immigration is less than emigration
     C death rate is less than birth rate
     D a rise in the average age of marriage
     E higher levels of infant mortality

8 There has been a drift of population to South-east England for all the following reasons except

     A the attraction of higher wages
     B new industries do not need to be near coalfields
     C there are more job opportunities
     D the standard of living is higher
     E government regional aid to the South East

9 In which of the following industries has employment risen?

     A coal mining
     B shipbuilding
     C textiles manufacture
     D motor vehicles manufacture
     E banking and finance

10 Which of the following statements about the United Kingdom population is true?

     A there has been a drift of population into inner city areas
     B women do not live as long as men
     C the average age of the population is falling
     D the number of old age pensioners is increasing
     E the proportion of the labour force working in manufacturing industries is expanding

Answers on page 329.

Data response question 13

Those who care

Growing numbers of people now live to a great age. Lots of them need to be looked after. Those who care for them should get more help

Lord Shinwell, the Labour politician, died recently at the age of 101. That would once have made him a rarity. No longer: the number of Britons over 100 rose ninefold between the 1951 and 1981 censuses. Thanks to economic prosperity, better nutrition and medical frontiersmanship (probably in that order), lots more people are living into old age. Since 1981, the population of pensionable age has increased by nearly 2%. But the number of over-75s has risen by 10% and of over-85s by nearly 14%. The change has been dramatic, and has not finished yet. In 1931, only 2.1% of Britons were 75 or over. By the time of the 1981 census, the proportion was 5.7%. By the year 2021, official projections put the figure at 7.7%.

Britain, like other industrial countries, is moving into the age of the four-generation family. Even now, lots of grandparents are still around for their grandchildren's weddings. Increasingly, they will be able to sip a glass of wine at their great-grandchildren's christening. It sounds touching. But there is a catch: as people grow older, they grow frailer. Thus, while only 8% of all old people over 65 cannot go downstairs without help, the proportion rises to 31% among those who are over 85.

Who provides the help they need? Few of the elderly live in hospitals (just over 1%, according to 1981 figures) or in special homes (some 2%). A great many old people—53% of women aged 85 and over—live alone. But as people grow older, more of them (32% of women of 85 and over, for instance) are forced to move in with younger relatives. And as more and more old people need some care, a growing number of families find themselves doing the caring.

Most of these carers are women; and so are most of the cared-for. An Equal Opportunities Commission (EOC) study in 1982 found that about three-quarters of all those caring for dependent relatives were women. Daughters were four times as likely to be looking after elderly parents as sons. "It is clear", concluded the EOC, "that the responsibility for looking after an elderly dependant usually falls to the nearest female relative".

Nobody knows for sure how many people are looking after elderly relatives. The EOC guessed perhaps 750,000; today, the figure may be nearer 1m. Some old people need far more time and attention than others. A survey for the Policy Studies Institute (PSI) in 1982 found that the average amount of care needed each day by an elderly or handicapped person was a little over three hours. Some needed far more.

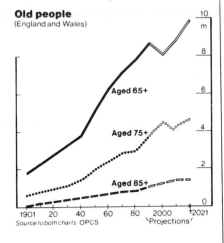

Old people
(England and Wales)

Aged 65+

Aged 75+

Aged 85+

1901   20   40   60   80   2000   2021

Source to both charts OPCS   'Projections'

(a)   (i) What proportion of the total population was over 75 years of age in 1931?

(ii) What was the percentage increase since 1981 of those aged 85 years and over?

(iii) According to projections what proportion of the population in 2021 will be aged over 75 years?

(b)   What three factors does the article suggest are the main causes of this ageing population? Explain these factors in more detail.

(c)   (i) How does the sex distribution of the population aged 65 years and over differ from the 0–15 years age group? (This information is not provided in the stimulus material.)

(ii) Discuss the causes of this difference.

(d)   Why is the Equal Opportunities Commission concerned about the ageing population?

(e)   Discuss the wider effects of an ageing population for the economy as a whole.

14 Labour

Unemployment: by duration[1]

United Kingdom

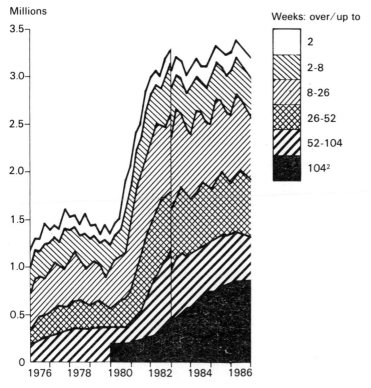

Millions

Weeks: over/up to
- 2
- 2-8
- 8-26
- 26-52
- 52-104
- 104[2]

1 Figures up to October 1982 relate to the registered unemployed.
From October 1982 the figures are on the new basis (claimants).
From April 1983 some men aged 60 or over did not have to sign
on at an Unemployment Benefit Office to receive the higher rate
of supplementary benefit and national insurance credits. Between
March and August 1983 the number affected was 162 thousand,
of whom about 125 thousand were in the over 52 weeks
category.
2 Data are only available from October 1979.

Unemployment

The unemployment problem is of concern to the government because it means
that a scarce factor of production (ie, labour) is lying idle and being wasted.

Moreover, there is the cost to the tax payer of paying taxes to finance social security and unemployment benefits for the unemployed. Unemployment can also lead to social problems such as violence and hooliganism as well as being a cause of social and personal distress.

Between 1945 and 1973 unemployment was at a fairly low level due mainly to prosperity in the international economy and determination by United Kingdom governments to operate monetary and fiscal policy to ensure full employment. Thus a high level of demand existed in the economy and unemployment rarely rose above 2 or 3%. However, unemployment was worse in the assisted areas of Wales, Northern England, Scotland and Northern Ireland. These regions had specialised in the industries of shipbuilding, coal, steel and textiles which have been in decline for many years. Since 1973 unemployment has dramatically worsened due to the world recession and in some measure to government deflationary policies to fight inflation which have caused lower demand and higher unemployment.

Indeed unemployment in the 1980s is often compared with the mass unemployment of the 1920s and 1930s, a period known as 'The Depression'. In that period unemployment reached over 3 million and, at its worst, 25% of the working population were unemployed.

The meaning of unemployment

There is some controversy about what exactly is meant by unemployment. It was once defined as all those people between the ages of 16 and 65 who were willing and able to work but were without a job, that is, all those registered as unemployed (not just claimants) expressed as a percentage of employees in employment and registered unemployed only. However the official definition (as at 1987) is now calculated from the number of people registered as unemployed *and* claiming unemployment benefit on the day of the count. It is calculated as a proportion of the working population including employers, self-employed and HM Forces. (See page 263 for a definition of working population.) Critics argue that this leads to a lower total of unemployed persons because the following groups may be excluded.

> people not registering or receiving benefit, like house persons and old people. They may not be eligible for benefits (like many house persons), although they are seeking work

> males over the age of 60 who receive benefits but need not register at a benefit office

> young people who are over the age of 16 and on a YTS scheme

> school leavers who may not have been unemployed long enough to qualify for benefits

> students claiming benefit but returning to full-time education

However, some people may be included in the statistics who have already found employment by the time the statistics are published. Also, some of those registered as unemployed and receiving benefit may, in reality, be retired or sick or disabled.

The new method of calculating unemployment certainly leads to a lower figure. This has led to the claim that the government has fiddled the statistics. What do you think?

The meaning of seasonal adjustment

Many statistics look at raw and sharp fluctuations over short periods. Interpretation of trends can often be made easier by extracting known seasonal elements. Seasonal adjustment removes seasonal distortions which are considered to have no significance in terms of underlying economic trends.

Seasonal adjustment is used in many statistical series; for instance, gross domestic product, consumers' expenditure, unemployment, average earnings, money supply and balance of payments are published in both original and seasonally-adjusted form.

Unemployment statistics are influenced greatly by seasonal factors such as weather, holidays and Christmas. Unemployment tends to be higher at the beginning of the year. Moreover, school leavers are excluded because their numbers vary from year to year and the end of term date varies which may affect statistics on the day of the count.

Removing seasonal effects gives a clearer guide to an underlying trend.

What do we mean by full employment?

In the United Kingdom full employment was defined (in a White Paper on Employment Policy of 1944) as a situation where the recorded unemployed falls below 3% of the working population. Thus full employment does not mean that there is absolutely no unemployment at all. There are always some people who are unemployed at any one period of time. Some of these are included in the following categories.

(a) *Residual unemployed* These are those people who, because of physical or mental handicaps, cannot find a job.

(b) *Voluntary unemployed* These are those people who because of strikes or even due to a desire not to work find themselves out of work.

(c) *Seasonally unemployed* These are those people who depend on casual employment at certain times of the year, such as deck chair attendants, and will be out of work at any one time.

(d) *Frictionally unemployed* These are those people who are at the moment out of work but are looking for vacancies.

(e) *Structurally unemployed* These are those people who are at present out of work because the industry in which they work is in decline. This problem is worsened by immobility of labour which means that these people find it difficult to move to get another type of job.

Thus it is almost impossible to have a situation of 100% employment. In consequence full employment is taken to mean a politically acceptable percentage of unemployment (between 2 and 3%).

The mobility of labour

The mobility of labour refers to the ability of labour to move. There are basically three types of mobility, *industrial mobility*, *geographical mobility* and *occupational mobility*.

Industrial mobility
This term refers to the ability of labour to move from one industry to another industry without any need to change occupation or area.

Geographical mobility
This term refers to the ability of labour to move from one geographical area to another, either to do a similar job or another job.

Occupational mobility
This term refers to the ability of labour to move from one occupation to another occupation.

Labour is generally accepted to be *immobile*. This means that labour finds it very difficult to be industrially, geographically and occupationally mobile.

Geographical immobility of labour
This is an important characteristic of many types of unemployment, such as structural unemployment and frictional unemployment. Labour finds it difficult to move area for the following reasons:

(a) People's unwillingness to move away from the area where they presently live due to family ties. Also, people might like the area where they live because of the recreational and cultural activities available.
(b) People's fear of the unknown.
(c) People may not want to disturb their children's education, especially if their children are at a crucial stage of the education process, ie, taking exams.
(d) People may find it difficult to find accommodation in the new area. For instance, a council house tenant will probably have to join a queue in the new area. A person owning their own property has to go through the expense and effort of finding a new house, with solicitor's fees, estate agent's fees and a new mortgage to pay.

Occupational immobility of labour
This again is an important characteristic of unemployment because people are unable to get jobs if they do not possess the skills and training which are required. Moreover, people may not want to do certain dangerous or dirty jobs or may be ignorant of re-training schemes.

The government has attempted to overcome the geographical immobility of labour in many ways. It operates a regional policy which 'takes the work to the workers' since the workers are reluctant to move to the work. There are some inducements to persuade people to move to a new area, including boarding allowances available for 12 months if dependants remain in the present area, and removing barriers to getting accommodation, such as giving priority on housing lists. However, this policy is largely unsuccessful and instead regional policy attempts to persuade firms to move into the area where the unemployed live.

The government has attempted to overcome occupational immobility of labour by setting up government training centres and giving grants to firms attracted to the area to help meet their retraining costs. The government has also encouraged people to move jobs by offering lump sum redundancy payments. There are various schemes which attempt to alleviate youth unemployment such as the Youth Training Scheme (YTS) whereby unemployed school leavers are given training more fitting to industry's requirements, with the aim of making them more employable.

Types of unemployment

There are various different types of unemployment each having different causes and characteristics.

Cyclical (or mass) unemployment
This is associated with the trade cycle (hence the name), the alternate booms and slumps in the level of industrial activity particularly prevalent in the 1930s. The economist, Keynes, advocated that mass unemployment, which is due to a general deficiency in demand throughout the economy, should be remedied by reflationary fiscal and monetary policies which will stimulate demand in the economy which in turn will stimulate output and employment, the so-called 'demand-side' policies.

Frictional unemployment
This is characterised by geographical and occupational immobility of labour. It occurs when a person may have been made unemployed in a certain area but vacancies exist in the same occupation in another area. However, people do not want to move (see Immobility of labour, opposite). This might be due to ignorance of opportunities elsewhere or because of the several factors already discussed as causes of immobility. This is sometimes referred to as transitional (or normal) unemployment.

Structural unemployment
This is closely associated with frictional unemployment and again is characterised by immobility of labour. There are always changes and re-adjustments needed in the economy. When this re-adjustment does not occur quickly enough there may be severe pockets of unemployment in areas, industries and occupations in which the demand for labour is falling faster than the supply. This is structural unemployment and occurs in the declining industries of shipbuilding, textiles, coal and steel.

Regional unemployment

Structural unemployment tends to be concentrated in those areas of the country which have specialised in these now declining industries. These are the assisted areas of Wales, Scotland, Northern Ireland and Northern England. Thus this has caused a phenomenon called *regional unemployment* which is unemployment in certain regions which is above the national average.

Technological unemployment

Structural unemployment may also be due to the introduction of more automated processes. In this case people may be displaced by machines. This is often called *technological unemployment* and has been increasing in recent years.

The main problem with structural, regional and technological unemployment is that they are characterised by immobility of labour. Thus labour tends to remain unemployed, in the short run at least.

Seasonal unemployment

Many seasonal workers are out of a job for anything from a few weeks to several months (for example those who work in the building, catering and fruit-picking industries) although some will seek full-time work. Much of this seasonal and casual employment is therefore done by house persons and students.

Voluntary unemployment

Some degree of unemployment will always exist because some people do not want to find work owing to idleness or their chosen way of life (eg, tramps). This type of unemployment is closely associated with the natural rate of unemployment views of some economists (see page 206).

Residual unemployment

There will always be a category of unemployment consisting of people who, because of physical or mental disabilities, find it very difficult to find work. Many firms attempt to employ a certain percentage of workers from this group, but by no means are enough opportunities being given.

Government policies to alleviate unemployment

We have already discussed some government policy on page 279 in the discussion on attempts to overcome the problem of geographical and occupational immobility of labour. For instance, to overcome geographical immobility, the government operates a regional policy to attract 'work to the workers' in the assisted areas. To overcome occupational immobility of labour the government has set up retraining centres, and financed the Youth Training Schemes.

The Youth Training Scheme (YTS) was introduced in April 1983, providing up to 12 months training and planned work experience as an introduction to working life. Between April 1985 and March 1986 there were almost 399 000 entrants to YTS. In April 1986 the scheme was extended to provide two years of work-related training for 16 year old school leavers and one year for 17 year old school leavers, with opportunities for all trainees to gain recognised vocational qualifications or credits towards such qualifications. The estimated cost of the scheme in 1986–87 is approximately £900 million.

Youth Training Scheme leavers: by destination[1]

Great Britain				Thousands and percentages
	YTS members leaving in			
	Apr–Sept 1984	Oct–Mar 1985	Apr–Sept 1985	Oct–Mar 1986
Leavers[2] (thousands)	236	132	281	133
Destinations (percentages)				
Full-time work				
Same employer	27	17	31	22
Different employer	31	33	24	27
Part-time work	1	1	4	4
Full-time course at				
college/training centre	4	1	4	1
School	—	—	—	—
Different YTS scheme	5	9	5	11
Other	2	2	7	4
Unemployed	30	36	26	32

1 Destination relates to the leavers' activities at the time of the survey. Surveys are conducted monthly some 3 months after leaving YTS.
2 Notified to Manpower Services Commission at the end of March 1986.

However, the government can influence the level of unemployment in the economy by its operation of fiscal and monetary policy. A deflationary fiscal and a deflationary monetary policy will have the effect of reducing demand in the economy which will increase unemployment. Reflationary fiscal and reflationary monetary policy will decrease unemployment by increasing demand (demand-side policies):

(a) A reflationary fiscal policy would involve higher government spending and lower taxation. This will create a budget deficit (ie, increased PSBR) which will have an expansionary effect on output and employment.
(b) A reflationary monetary policy would involve lower interest rates, availability of credit and easy HP facilities.

Such a policy was advocated by Lord Keynes in his famous book *The General Theory of Employment, Interest and Money* which was first published during the 1930s depression. However, Keynesian policies have been blamed for causing too much inflation by stimulating too much demand (ie, overheating the economy). The Conservative governments of Margaret Thatcher have moved away from Keynesian policies and have instead adopted supply-side measures (see page 320) such as lower income tax, retraining of workers, educational initiatives (YTS, GCSE, TVEI and CPVE) and privatisation. The aim of the policy is to increase output (supply) and thereby increase employment.

Unemployment and inflation

Traditionally it has been believed that high inflation and high unemployment could not exist at the same time. This was because unemployment is characterised by a lack of demand whereas inflation is characterised by a high level of demand. Moreover if there is full employment then trade unions are in a strong bargaining position, they achieve high wage increases which are then passed on to consumers in high prices.

An economist called Phillips constructed a curve (known as the Phillips' Curve) which related high wages (and hence inflation) to a low level of unemployment. However, in the 1970s and early 1980s the United Kingdom economy, like many other economies, suffered from high inflation rates and high unemployment rates. This phenomenon became known as *stagflation* or *slumpflation* and was partly due to high oil prices. The higher oil prices had an inflationary effect causing higher transport costs, higher petrol prices, higher heating and fuel costs which is passed on in higher prices. At the same time high oil prices had a deflationary effect for two reasons. Firstly, more expensive oil meant that countries throughout the world had less to spend on manufactured goods causing unemployment in the United Kingdom's export industries. Secondly, firms faced with high oil prices attempted to curtail costs elsewhere. Thus labour was shed in an attempt to cut costs of production.

The deflationary fiscal and monetary policies of the Thatcher Conservative governments were also blamed, by some critics, for the worsening unemployment in the 1980s. Such policies may have helped reduce inflation, but at the cost of higher unemployment. This was because the level of demand in the economy was held down.

However, some economists refer to a natural rate of unemployment where both inflation and unemployment can exist together. Attempts to reduce unemployment by expansionary fiscal and monetary measures will cause inflation but lead to no long term fall in unemployment (see page 206).

Wages

Terminology used in wage discussions

We assume that wages are the reward for all forms of labour varying from the managing director to the worker on the factory floor. There are subtle distinctions between some of the terms used in discussions on wages which can cause some confusion.

The distinction between wages and salaries
Wages tend to be paid weekly usually in the form of cash in a wage packet. Wages can be paid either by time rate or piece rate or some combination of the two. Time rates and piece rates are discussed on page 285. Wages on the whole tend to be paid for manual work.

Salaries tend to be paid for non-manual work usually at monthly intervals in the form of a cheque. Unlike wage earners it is quite possible for a salary earner to earn the same salary irrespective of the length of time actually worked. For example, a person may have to work late at the office at regular intervals or may have a day or so off due to illness. However, there is no clear distinction between wages and salaries and to the economist they are both wages.

Wage rates
The wage rate (or basic wage rate) is the rate of wages paid for a specified period, usually an hour or a day.

The distinction between wages and earnings
Earnings are different from wages because earnings will also include overtime payments or bonuses for good time-keeping and so on. Figures on earnings may be expressed after income tax and national insurance have been taken away or expressed before income tax and national insurance are subtracted. Real earnings take inflation into account. If earnings increase more than inflation then real earnings have increased.

The distinction between gross wages and net wages
Gross wages are the complete wage paid to an individual including basic wage and

Annual percentage increases in prices and earnings, 1964-84

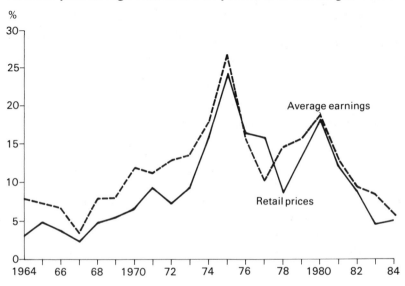

overtime. Net wages are what the person actually takes home after income tax, national insurance and superannuation have been deducted. Net wages are sometimes called take-home-pay or disposable wages (disposable income).

Real disposable income takes inflation into account. If disposable incomes increase more than inflation then real disposable income has increased.

Wage drift
Wage drift is the difference between basic wage and earnings. Thus certain groups of workers often disguise wage increases in the form of guaranteed overtime payments or other allowances. Wage drift is often blamed for being inflationary because it means that workers are taking home more money although their basic wages may not have changed that much.

Fringe benefits or perks
Some workers may receive perks such as low interest loans, a company car, commission, a company house or long holidays. Again, these are not calculated in basic wage rates and can disguise wage increases.

The distinction between money wages and real wages
Money wages are often termed *nominal wages* and are wages in terms of money. *Real wages* are wages in terms of the amount of goods and services which can be bought. Thus real wages take into account inflation and the real value of wages. For instance, a person may have a 10% increase in money wages but if prices have risen by 20% in the same period then real wages have declined and that person has a lower standard of living.

Converting raw money statistics into real terms
To convert a raw money statistic into *real terms* the money statistic needs to be *deflated* by an appropriate index number to compare it with a base year (which is given the value of index number 100). For instance, to calculate money income in 1987 into real terms we choose a base year (say 1980) and give it a value of 100. Then deflate the money statistic by the formula:

$$1987 \text{ money income} \times \frac{100}{\text{RPI in 1987 (assuming base year is 1980 and given a value of 100)}}$$

We can then calculate 1987's money income in terms of 1980's constant prices and we can compare it with all other years in terms of constant prices. Real incomes can, thus, be compared.

This method can also be used to convert earnings into real earnings, disposable income into real disposable income and GDP into real GDP.

Of course, if we can see that earnings are increasing more than inflation, then we can simply state that real earnings have increased.

Productivity agreements

A productivity agreement is when the trade union agrees with the employer that a wage increase should be related to some increase in productivity. Productivity refers to output per person per period of time (usually an hour). Thus any increase in wages is dependent on an increase in output per hour.

Wage comparability and relativity

Wage comparability refers to a situation where workers, perhaps in different industries, doing broadly similar jobs, having similar qualifications and possessing the same degree of responsibility receive comparable (ie, roughly the same) wages. The difficulty here is that some jobs are very difficult to compare with other jobs. How do you compare the work done by a teacher or a nurse with other groups of workers?

Wage relativity is a similar idea. This is when a certain group of workers have always received a wage which is relatively the same or perhaps a proportion more or less than another group of workers. Groups of workers are very concerned to maintain their *relativities* or *differentials* as they are often called. If a worker's differentials are being eroded, this is only painful in the sense that the wage relativity compared to other groups of workers has diminished.

Methods of wage payment

Time rate

Where time rates are in operation all employees engaged in similar work are paid an agreed sum per hour. Good, bad and indifferent workers receive equal payment if they work the same hours. This system involves time checks (clocking in and out) and supervision to see there is no slacking.

Piece rates

Here wages are dependent on work done with an agreed payment per unit produced.

Advantages

(a) It is easier for an employee to see whether he or she is getting the correct amount.
(b) Quicker workers receive more than others.
(c) Costs of supervision decreases, slower workers are just paid less.
(d) Output increases therefore it is an incentive to work.

Disadvantages

(a) It is only applicable for certain jobs. It may be applicable for jobs like apple picking but one could not pay a bus conductor on the same basis because the number of passengers on the bus is out of the conductor's control.
(b) There will be a decline in quality of work as workers speed up.

(c) The firm may have to employ quality inspectors which will lead to a rise in costs.
(d) Workers may impair their health by working too hard.
(e) There may be difficulties over whether workers are being credited with correct amounts.

Bonus rate

This is an inducement to make workers work harder. Generally a production target is set and a worker could receive a bonus if he or she reaches the target before time or for work done above the target. This is often a complicated system of payment.

Profit sharing

Profit sharing is an attempt to give employees a more direct interest in the prosperity of the firm. Workers hold a number of shares and receive a share in profits (above wages). ICI, for example, pursue such a scheme. This system may produce increases in output, because the worker (as a shareholder) will benefit from the success of the firm. Less supervision is needed for this system and it may promote good labour relations.

However, this system may not really work because profit sharing usually only takes place once a year. There will be a time lag between workers putting in the effort and gaining the reward.

Explaining wage differences

It is obvious that all workers in the economy do not receive the same wages. For instance, pop stars and footballers earn far more than factory workers. Barristers and surgeons earn more than teachers and nurses. Miners earn more than agricultural workers.

Explaining differences in wages between different occupations

The main factor which determines the level of wages in a particular occupation is the *interaction of demand for labour and supply of labour involved in that occupation.* If demand is high for a category of labour then it is likely that wages will rise and vice versa. If supply of a certain category of labour is limited then, again, it is likely that wages will rise and vice versa.

Factors affecting demand for labour

(a) *The marginal revenue product of labour* If a unit of labour produces a certain physical amount of a good which sells at a particular price (marginal revenue product) then the employer cannot afford to pay the worker a wage greater than the MRP. Thus the demand for labour is greatly affected by the value of its MRP. The higher the MRP of labour then the greater the demand for labour and the higher will be wages going to labour.
(b) *Elasticity of demand for labour* If demand for a particular type of labour is

inelastic then the likelihood is that labour will receive higher wages. Demand for labour will be inelastic when other factors cannot easily be substituted for it, when the demand for the good it produces is inelastic and if labour forms only a small percentage of the entrepreneur's total costs. If labour has a high MRP and demand for its services is inelastic then the probability is that wages for that labour will be high. Thus labour in expanding industries will probably earn more than labour in declining industries because they will have a high MRP and demand for their services will be inelastic. Moreover, skilled workers, compared to unskilled workers, will also have a high MRP and inelastic demand so again their wages will tend to be higher.

Factors affecting supply of labour
The supply of labour in a particular occupation depends on the following factors.

(a) *The skills and ability required* If a relatively rare ability is required, as with pop stars or footballers, then supply will be restricted and wages higher.

(b) *Qualifications and training required* If a job requires specific qualifications or training then supply of labour will be reduced and wages higher. For instance, barristers and doctors need good qualifications and a long period of training which limits the number of people who are able to do these jobs.

(c) *The ability of trade unions and professional bodies to restrict entry into the occupation* If trade unions and professional bodies, such as the British Medical Association, can limit entry into certain occupations by apprenticeships and the need to pass exams then supply will be limited and wages higher. The strength of a trade union to achieve higher wages will also be a considerable factor determining the level of wages to a particular occupation.

(d) *The mobility of labour* If labour is geographically and occupationally immobile then skilled workers in certain occupations may earn high wages because the supply of labour to these occupations will be limited.

(e) *Dangerous or dirty jobs* Sometimes the supply of labour to a particular occupation may be limited because the job is dangerous or dirty. Such occupations may command higher wages, as for miners or steeplejacks. Other jobs, such as teaching, or the Civil Service, have pleasant working conditions, job security and good pension schemes. Consequently, such jobs may earn lower wages. Other jobs may have a great many perks and fringe benefits and the money wages may be lower because of these advantages.

(f) *The valuation of leisure relative to income* If workers value leisure time more than income the supply of labour to an occupation may be limited. Normally, however, we assume that as wages increase so will the supply of labour.

(g) *Assisted areas and declining industries* If the area has a large pool of unemployed people because of declining industries then the supply of labour to many occupations may be high and may make for lower wages. In an assisted area, such as South Wales where unemployment may be above the national average, there will be a pool of available labour which may mean the average wages are lower than elsewhere.

(h) *The more limited the supply of labour to a particular industry the greater the likelihood of higher wages.*

Explaining differences in wages within the same occupations

There are other factors which help explain *the differences in wages within the same occupations.* For instance, some teachers earn more than other teachers, some miners earn more than other miners, and so on. These factors include:

(a) *Regional differences* In areas such as London where particular skills are extremely scarce and where the cost of living is very high, then wages may be higher to compensate. For instance, in London many workers earn an additional allowance. Also, wage drift may occur owing to the limited supply of certain workers.

(b) *Women's wages* Women's wages still tend to be lower than men's. For a fuller discussion on this see page 290. However there are many occupations such as teachers and doctors, where women and men earn the same wages.

(c) *Non-monetary benefits* Some people will have achieved a higher degree of seniority in a job, others will have been doing the job longer and earned more incremental increases (increments) over the year. Other people will have greater opportunities to work overtime or receive a variety of perks or fringe benefits. All of these factors could help explain why even within the same occupations some people achieve higher wages.

Women's wages

Reasons why women's wages tend to be lower

We have already made the point that in many occupations, such as teaching, medicine, and the law, women doing the same job as men earn exactly the same wages. However, this does not disguise the fact that in general women tend to earn lower wages than men. Why? One answer can be found by looking at the interaction of demand and supply of women's labour.

The demand for women's labour

This may be lower than the demand for male labour because:

(a) Women's marginal revenue product tends to be lower because it is suggested that they are weaker and less flexible in the number of jobs they can do, less willing to work overtime, less well-qualified and absent more frequently than men. It is further suggested that married women with a family are particularly to be criticised on many of these points. Moreover, it is maintained that a high proportion of the labour force prefers to work for a man rather than a woman. Thus women do not attain well-paid posts involving responsibility.

(b) Women are not as highly trained and well qualified as men. This may be because they married and had children at crucial stages in their careers. Thus fewer women achieve the higher paid jobs.

Distribution of gross weekly earnings[1] of employees[2] in selected industry groups: by sex, April 1985

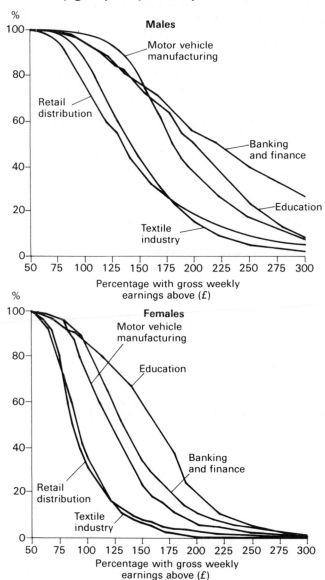

1 Includes overtime, shift premiums, bonus, and other payments. Recent pay awards not incorporated in earnings for the April survey pay-period will not be covered.

2 Full-time employees on adult rates whose pay for the survey pay-period was not affected by absenc

The supply of women's labour

(a) Women can do fewer jobs than men because of their lack of physical strength and qualifications. Thus they are able only to do a limited number of jobs. The supply of women to these jobs is such that wages will be low because of the large pool of female labour available to employers. This is particularly true of catering and unskilled jobs in manufacturing.

(b) Women are quite prepared to earn lower wages because many regard their earnings as only a supplement to the family income. It is often maintained that women's unions, or unions dominated by large proportions of women, such as health workers and nurses' unions, are less militant and not as well organised as male-dominated unions. Thus wages will be lower than male wages.

Many of these ideas are questionable. However, by tradition and custom (and prejudice) the feeling in many sectors of industry is that men are more productive and more reliable than women. Moreover, women can do fewer jobs and are quite prepared to work for lower wages. Thus men's wages tend to be higher.

Equal pay for women
There has been legislation passed since 1970 with the objective of achieving equal pay for women. The following are the main Acts.

The Equal Pay Act 1970
This required that women should be paid the same as men for 'work of the same or of a broadly similar nature'. The criticism has been that employers do not correctly interpret work of a similar nature.

The Sex Discrimination Act 1976
This required that women should not be discriminated against in employment opportunities either in job advertisements, opportunities for promotion and training or in dismissals.

The Employment Protection (Consolidation) Act 1978 (previously called the Employment Protection Act)
This laid down some provisions for the payment of maternity pay and job reinstatement within a certain period of having a baby if the woman so wishes.

What have been the results of this legislation?

(a) It is argued that much of the legislation has been ineffectual because there are too many loopholes. For instance, what is meant by similar work? Employers, not unnaturally, interpret the legislation to their own advantage. Moreover, employers still do not train women for the better-paid jobs.

(b) The increases in wage costs have fuelled inflation in the 1970s.

(c) More women have gone back to work causing unemployment among men.

(d) Women are having fewer children and in consequence the birth-rate is declining. There has been an increase in nurseries to look after the children while the women go to work.

(e) An improved standard of living for many families because the women are bringing home better wages.

(f) Some men suggest that their wages have been depressed by women. Since there are more women available for work the supply of labour has increased forcing lower wages throughout the labour force.

(g) Increased female membership of trade unions.

(h) More women are concentrating on their careers thus eventually there will be more women holding well-paid jobs with responsibility.

(i) Women will continue to storm other traditional male-dominated strongholds. Women have even been known to enter the members' pavilion at Lords cricket ground and the Church of England regularly discusses whether women should be ordained as priests.

Many of these ideas are mere interpretations of what some people believe has happened, or indeed will happen, as a result of equal pay for women. What do you think?

Income and wealth

Distinguishing between income, wealth and capital
Income is a flow of money going to a factor of production, or the owner of a factor of production, over some specified period of time. The income of each factor of production has been discussed on pages 4–8. The flow of income to the factor of production called labour is termed *wages*.

Wealth is a stock of assets which have a market value at any one given moment. The ownership of wealth can generate income. Wealth may include ownership of a house, stocks, shares, consumer goods and capital goods.

Capital is that form of wealth which can contribute to production, such as factories and machines (capital goods).

The creation of income and wealth
Incomes are created by the factors of production, or the owners of the factors of production, hiring out the factor in return for a flow of income. For instance, landowners hire out their land for rent.

The creation of wealth is when value is added by an economic activity to inputs of materials. The production process, as described in Chapter 2, consists of three main sectors – primary, secondary and tertiary. Any activity involved in the production process is creating wealth.

The distribution of income and wealth
The distribution of income within the United Kingdom is unequal. In 1983, 25% of the total pre-tax income earned went to the top 10% of income earners. The bottom 10% of income earners accounted for only 2.3% of total income earned.

This means that high income earners, although relatively few in number, account for a large proportion of total income.

The distribution of wealth is also unequal in the United Kingdom. Two-thirds of all personal wealth is owned by 10% of the adult population, half of all personal wealth is owned by 5% of the adult population, a quarter of all personal wealth is owned by 1% of the adult population. This represents a more unequal distribution of wealth than in any other Western European country.

Factors which may influence the distribution of income and wealth

Factors which influence income distribution

(a) *distribution of wealth ownership* Since wealth generates income, the more wealth an individual owns then the more income he/she will have.
(b) *taxation and government spending* A progressive tax system and transfer payments (ie, pensions, unemployment benefits etc.) will reduce inequalities in income distribution.
(c) *differences in wages paid to different occupations* Some jobs receive higher wages (see pages 286–8).

Factors which influence wealth distribution

(a) *historical accumulations of wealth and inheritance*
(b) *taxation and government spending* A progressive tax system, such as an inheritance tax and even a wealth tax, would redistribute wealth from the rich to the poor. Government spending on transfer payments and social capital (schools, hospitals and old people's homes, for example) would also lead to a more equal distribution of wealth.
(c) *incomes* If incomes are made more equal then wealth accumulation would be made more equal.

Trade unions

The growth of trade unions

Trade unions have their origins in the trade clubs of the eighteenth century. The early trade unions were persecuted by the governments of the late eighteenth and early nineteenth centuries who feared an English version of the French Revolution which occurred in 1789. However, by the 1860s skilled workers were forming trade unions (the new model unions) and towards the end of the nineteenth century unskilled workers also formed trade unions (New Unionism). The government's view on trade unions at this time was somewhat undecided. Some legislation was passed which encouraged the formation of trade unions whereas other legislation penalised trade unions. Trade unions became respectable after their efforts in helping the United Kingdom fight the 1914–18 war. However, the fortunes of trade unions slumped during the inter-war depression of the 1920s and 1930s when there was mass unemployment. Between 1945 and 1979 trade unions became increasingly powerful and membership increased dramatically, so much so that some governments attempted to curb the power of trade unions by the introduction of various pieces of legislation.

By the end of 1984, 11.1 million people in the United Kingdom belonged to a trade union, 17% fewer than in the peak year of 1979 when membership stood at 13.3 million. Prior to 1979 membership had increased for many years.

Another interesting development is that due to successive amalgamations between trade unions, there are now fewer, but larger unions, the biggest of which is the Transport and General Workers Union (TGWU).

However, in general the size of many trade unions has declined since 1979. (For example, the TGWU had 2 086 000 members in 1979 and only 1 035 000 in 1987.)

Trade unions: numbers[1] and membership[1] in the UK

	Number of unions	Total membership (thousands)	Percentage change in membership since previous year
1974	507	11 764	+ 2.7
1975 [2]	501	12 193	+ 3.6
1975	470	12 026	
1976	473	12 386	+ 3.0
1977	481	12 846	+ 3.7
1978	462	13 112	+ 2.1
1979	453	13 289	+ 1.3
1980	438	12 947	− 2.6
1981	414	12 106	− 6.5
1982	408	11 593	− 4.2
1983	394	11 337	− 2.2
1984	371	11 086	− 2.2

1 As at December each year.
2 Thirty-one organisations previously regarded as trade unions are excluded from 1975 onwards because they failed to satisfy the statutory definition of a trade union in Section 28 of the *Trade Union and Labour Relations Act, 1974.*

The objectives and purposes of trade unions

Trade unions have four main objectives each of which can be divided into many parts.

Trade unions exist to promote the interests of their members

(a) *Improving pay* Trade unions negotiate wages, piece rates, bonuses etc.

(b) *Improving working conditions* Trade unions negotiate holidays and improvements in the physical environment at work.

(c) *Safeguarding jobs* Trade unions become involved in discussions about redundancies and personal grievances. Trade unions aim to achieve full employment.

(d) *Offering monetary benefits* Trade unions provide sickness and accident benefit, unemployment pay, strike pay and pensions. Many of these benefits have become less important with the development of the social security and state administered welfare payments.

Trade unions exist to promote the economic prosperity of the country
Trade unions aim to achieve full employment and at the same time to achieve increases in national income. Thus they aim to achieve an increase in each individual citizen's standard of living. Moreover, trade unions want a more equal distribution of income and wealth through improved social services and social security schemes. Trade unions attempt to co-operate with government in the formation of economic policy.

Trade unions exist to improve conditions in society
Trade unions strive for improvements in education and indeed run many educational courses and offer university places at Ruskin College, Oxford. They require more leisure time for citizens and better facilities for adequate use of leisure. They require a reduction in class differentials and the reform of 'bad' laws. Trade unions will also take up the interests of groups in society whom they consider to be ill used (eg, senior citizens).

Trade unions participate in organisations which have political, social or economic objectives
Trade unions are represented on such bodies as the Monopolies and Mergers Commission, consumers councils and the Workers' Educational Association. Moreover, the trade union movement is closely associated with the Labour Party. Indeed, a proportion of a trade union's funds (received from subscription from members) might be used to help finance the Labour Party. Individual trade unions will also sponsor MPs and have votes at the Labour Party conference.

Types of trade unions

There are four main types of trade unions:

(a) *craft unions*;
(b) *general unions*;
(c) *industrial unions*;
(d) *white collar unions*.

Craft unions
These unions are some of the oldest of the trade unions. Many can trace their origins back to medieval guilds and regard their traditions and privileges as

precious. They represent skilled workers and tend to be very small. They can sometimes have members from many different industries because workers with a particular skill see themselves as having more in common with each other than with other workers in the same industry. Some craft unions may allow semi-skilled workers to join to compete against the large general unions. An example of a craft union is the Amalgamated Engineering Union (AEU).

General unions

These unions attract workers from a variety of different industries and from those who perform different jobs. Some of the general unions can be very large, such as the Transport and General Workers' Union (TGWU) and the National Union of General and Municipal Workers (NUGMW). These unions trace their origins back to the development of the unskilled workers' unions (New Unionism) in the 1880s. The general unions have the advantage of large memberships and therefore some of them are very wealthy. Also, it means that a worker can remain in the same union even if the job changes. However, such unions have been criticised for complicating the structure of trade union membership and because they cannot represent the interests of a variety of different workers. Owing to amalgamations the number of general unions has declined but some are very big, such as the TGWU.

Industrial unions

These are unions which attempt to include all of the workers, skilled and unskilled, in a particular industry. Their development has been held back by the unwillingness of the industry's skilled workers (who probably belong to a craft union) to give up their traditions and privileges. Also, such skilled workers fear that their interests will be swamped by the interests of unskilled workers as, for example, with ASLEF which has opposed joining with the National Union of Railwaymen (NUR) to form a single trade union in the railway industry. However, there are some examples of industrial unions such as the National Union of Mineworkers (NUM) and the Union of Communication Workers.

Sometimes different unions in a particular industry may keep their independence but form a confederation which will meet employers and negotiate on behalf of all the unions in the industry.

White-collar unions

These are developing rapidly and represent the professions, government Civil Servants, scientists and clerical and administrative workers in industry and local government. These are called white-collar workers because they probably go to work in a jacket and tie (as opposed to blue-collar workers). They have developed since increasing numbers of the middle class wish to organise themselves to negotiate better wages and conditions. Examples of white-collar unions include Manufacturing, Science, Finance (MSF) (formed from a merger between ASTMS and TASS), the National Union of Teachers (NUT) and the National and Local Government Officers Association (NALGO).

The internal organisation of trade unions

Trade unions do not have a common organisation. This is because each individual union developed separately over the years and may have differences in their internal organisation. However, there are certain common characteristics.

The shop steward

The shop steward is probably one of the workers on the shop floor (factory floor) and has direct contact with the shop-floor workers. The shop steward collects union dues, gives out union information, makes sure union rules are observed, ensures agreements are carried out and may have to deal with any differences between workers and management. A convenor is the main shop steward in a large factory.

The branch

Every member of a trade union belongs to a particular branch and is eligible to attend branch meetings. The branch admits new members, elects delegates to conference, discusses local and national agreements and grievances and elects union officers. Attendance at branch meetings tends to be low because affairs can be tedious and time consuming. Consequently, many branches tend to be run by a few dedicated people. The branches will elect representatives to sit on district or area committees which control the local branches.

The conference

Branches elect delegates to represent them at the annual union conference. The conference is the policy-making body of the union but since it meets only once a year it finds it difficult to enforce its decisions.

Full-time officials

These are the full-time and paid officials of the union who help shop stewards, branches and districts. They advise and help in the interpretation of union policy and whenever disputes or problems occur. They can either be appointed by the general secretary of the union or elected by its members. Many of these officials have shop-floor experience and some may be experts in a particular aspect of union affairs.

The general secretary

The general secretary is the most important full-time official and can be a nationally known figure. Normally elected by a ballot of union members, the general secretary may keep the post until retirement age. The general secretary is responsible for the day-to-day running of the union and may personally conduct national negotiations with employers.

The national executive

The general secretary is a member of the national executive which is the leadership of the union. Members are either elected by conference or by regional ballots. Only the national executive has the power to call an 'official strike' (ie, a strike sanctioned by the union).

The TUC, trades councils and employers' organisations

The Trades Union Congress (TUC)
The TUC was formed in 1868 and it is the central body of the trade union movement. The TUC conference is held annually at a seaside resort.

The functions of the TUC

(a) Although not all trade unions belong to the TUC it purports to represent the views of the trade union movement as a whole.
(b) It mediates in disputes between unions or even between a union and an employer.
(c) It represents the trade union movement in discussions on economic policy with the government. It can also sometimes represent the views of the government to unions and vice versa.

Criticisms of the TUC

(a) It has no real power over individual trade unions and can only hope to persuade or influence union attitudes. Individual unions jealously preserve their independence and there is no obligation to obey TUC general council pronouncements.
(b) It does not represent all trade unions.
(c) The TUC is too bureaucratic with a General Secretary and a General Council which is the executive body. The general council consists of general secretaries of individual unions. Much of the work is delegated to committees.

Trades councils
Individual unions can meet on a local basis in the trades councils. There are over 500 of these spread throughout the United Kingdom and include the members of different trade union branches in the locality. They organise meetings and activities in the locality and spread the policies of the TUC.

Employers' associations (or federations)
These represent the employers in a particular industry and are on the opposite side to trade unions as regards wage and work conditions agreements. An example is the Engineering Employers Federation. Although there are about 100 employers' associations they are more difficult to organise compared to trade unions, because employers are in a situation of competition against each other.

The Confederation of British Industry (CBI)
This was founded in 1965 and represents industry in discussions with the government and TUC. It is headed by a Director-General and run by a council which delegates work to committees. The CBI works closely with the TUC and

represents the views of industrialists and employers to both the government and TUC. Like the TUC it has only a very loose influence on its individual members.

Collective bargaining and the settlement of disputes

What is collective bargaining?
This is when the trade unions will bargain or negotiate with the employers to determine their members' wages and working conditions. The objective is to reach a mutual agreement on wages, conditions of work, hours, safety, health, and so on. Both parties are left to decide these issues by themselves without government interference (such as an incomes policy, see page 215).

Negotiation
This is the first stage in the collective bargaining process. Negotiations normally take place at a national level between the national executive of the trade union and the employers' federation. However, negotiations can also take place at a local level between individual employers and shop stewards at a particular plant. Such local negotiations will take into account local conditions and traditions but they must still conform to any national agreements.

The process of voluntary negotiation has been helped by an element of government action. Previous governments set up Joint Industrial Councils and Wages Councils.

Joint Industrial Councils
These were established in 1916 and consist of representatives of trade unions and employers in the industry. They meet regularly to discuss most aspects of wages, conditions of work and procedures to be followed in the case of dispute. They are not forced on any particular industry but there are about 200 in existence.

Wages Councils
These consist of representatives of the trade union and employers. They fix minimum wages and holidays and give advice on problems affecting the industry.

The settlement of disputes
Negotiations may break down and some form of industrial action may be taken either by the union (see page 300 for a list of alternative actions) or in the form of a *lock-out* by the employer. A 'lock-out' is when the employer closes the gates and refuses to allow workers into the factory to work. There are two main stages in dealing with a dispute.

Conciliation
This is when a third party is brought in to solve the problem by bringing both sides back together. In 1974 an independent Advisory Conciliation and Arbitration Service (ACAS) was set up, consisting of people experienced in industrial relations. This service can offer to provide conciliation between the trade unions and employers. Sometimes a Court of Inquiry may be set up, headed,

perhaps, by an academic, which makes a report on the causes of the problem and puts forward possible solutions.

Arbitration

This is when both sides agree to allow a third party (an arbitrator) to investigate the problems and put forward a solution. Normally both sides will agree to abide by the verdict, but there is no legal compulsion for either side to do so. ACAS offers an arbitration service as well as a conciliation service.

It is usual after conciliation or arbitration that the problem will be solved and the industrial unrest will abate. However, sometimes one side refuses to go to arbitration or perhaps refuses to accept the verdict of the arbitrator. In such cases negotiations either begin again or the industrial unrest continues until one side emerges as the victor.

Criticisms of trade unions

Many of the 'problems' associated with trade unions have been the subject of recent government legislation (see Employment Acts 1980 and 1982 and the Trade Union Act 1984 on pages 305–6).

There are several aspects of trade union behaviour which have been the subject of criticism.

The operation of restrictive practices

There are several restrictive practices which are criticised.

The closed shop

This is when all workers in a factory (or shop) have to be a member of a particular union. Thus if a person refuses to join the union or is dismissed from the union then he or she also loses his or her job. This is seen as a threat to individual liberty because the person must join the union to gain the job. However closed shops are supported on the grounds that they increase the strength of the union and make negotiations easier for employers (they know agreements will be binding on all workers). The problem of closed shops was addressed by the Employment Act 1980. (See page 305.)

Demarcation disputes

Certain jobs can only be done by members of a particular union. The idea is that it protects the jobs of skilled workers from being undermined by unskilled workers. The problem is that a simple task might require several different workers from different unions to finish it. A dispute could occur if workers attempt to do a job reserved for a member of a particular union.

Restrictions of labour supply

Jobs can be made more secure by ensuring that long apprenticeships have to be served. A closed shop also restricts labour supply to members of a particular union.

Refusal to operate new machinery
Fearing that their jobs will be at stake unions may sometimes oppose the use of new machinery. They will also encourage over-staffing to protect members' jobs.

Time wasting
Some workers attempt to waste time, especially at break time, to ensure that a job continues for a longer time. They may also engage in a 'go-slow' or 'work-to-rule' (abiding by every rule of the company) to prolong certain work.

Mates
Certain skilled workers might insist on having an unskilled mate at their side even though there may be little or no work for the mate to do.

Unnecessary overtime
This is where overtime is not really necessary but is allowed in order to maintain a certain level of wages. Workers may restrict output to ensure that as much overtime as possible may be taken.

Kangaroo courts
This is where a union will impose its own discipline on its members irrespective of the employer's attitude. This takes place in the branches and is, again, a threat to individual liberty.

All of these restrictive practices may reduce the productivity of industry in the United Kingdom and restrict economic growth (see page 140).

Strikes and industrial action
There are various forms of industrial action including all-out strikes, one-day token strikes, overtime bans, working to rule, go-slows, sympathetic action with another group of strikers and sit-ins (or work-ins). The success of the action depends on factors such as the amount of disruption which can be caused, the strength and resources of the union and its members and, to an extent, public sympathy for the action.

Strikes
The strike is a complete withdrawal of labour and should be considered as a last resort measure although it is being used immediately in some cases. There are two types of strike: the *official strike* and the *unofficial strike*. The official strike is sanctioned and recognised by the union. Unofficial strikes are usually called at a local level by a shop steward and are not sanctioned by the union. Unofficial strikes (also called 'wild cat' strikes) can later be made official. A frequent criticism was that the United Kingdom suffered from far too many days lost through industrial action and strikes. The problem appeared not to be official strikes but unofficial strikes. The pattern of strikes in the United Kingdom was that they were mainly short lived, unofficial and small in scale. However, they did tremendous damage and many days were lost through this type of action. It would be a mistake to believe that the United Kingdom's strike record was very much

Industrial disputes — working days lost and number of stoppages

United Kingdom

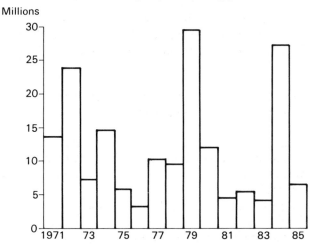

Working days lost during year

Millions

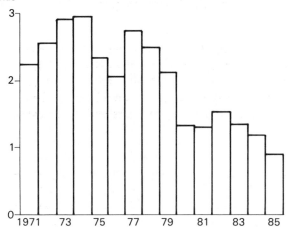

Work stoppages in progress during year

Thousands

worse than in other countries. Indeed, the number of days lost in the United Kingdom through strikes was not as bad as it is in some other countries.

Since the Trade Union Act 1984 (see page 306) secret ballots have been necessary before a lawful trade dispute. Moreover the Employment Act 1982 (see page 305) defines what types of dispute are unlawful and makes the union liable for damages in the case of unlawful trade disputes.

Picketing

Picketing was also criticised. Picketing is when strikers attempt to persuade fellow trade unionists not to enter the factory or cross the picket lines. This picketing should be peaceful but very often was quite violent with fighting and the police were often called in to restore order. Secondary picketing, which was the picketing of suppliers or customers of the firm, was also criticised on the grounds that it was not picketing the strikers' place of work. The Employment Act 1980 has banned secondary picketing and set limits on numbers of pickets (see page 305).

It is worth noting what is meant by a 'blackleg' and 'blacking'. A 'blackleg' is a person who continues to work even though the rest of the workforce is on strike. Such a person will be criticised by the strikers because he or she will enjoy the hoped-for fruits of the strike (higher wages) without suffering the hardships. 'Blacking' is when a particular firm's goods will not be handled by the workers in another firm, probably because the workers in the blacked firm are on strike.

Union democracy

The criticism here was that many trade unions were not democratic organisations and infringed on personal liberties. For instance, the operation of a closed shop did not accord with the principles of democracy and individuals being allowed to follow their own conscience about whether to join a trade union.

Moreover, in the elections of officials, many unions used to have a show of hands in the branch meetings. This sometimes allowed intimidation of members to take place and, in any case, very few of the members attended branch meetings. The 'show of hands' system allowed decisions to be made by a few activists, many of whom had left-wing political views and were in a position to pursue their ideas through the union. Often shop stewards were elected who had quite left-wing views and this may have led to more unofficial strikes. The large number of unofficial strikes was also undemocratic because they were unconstitutional and not sanctioned by the national executive.

Trade unions were also criticised for the 'show of hands' procedure in mass meetings of workers when deciding on a strike. Again this left members open to intimidation and the meetings were often infiltrated by outside activists. Since the Trade Union Act 1984 (see page 306) *secret ballots* have been necessary for union election and before lawful trade disputes. This has made trade unions appear to be more democratic to some of their critics.

However, even at union conference and the TUC Conference there was and is a procedure called the '*card vote*' or '*block vote*' whereby many thousands of members' votes can be cast by a single individual at the conference. Indeed, even at the TUC Conference the large unions can cast over one million votes by holding up a single card. The criticism remains that there may be many individuals in the union membership who do not agree with the way in which their votes have been cast.

The structure of trade unions

There are many criticisms levelled at the structure of trade unions.

(a)   There are too many trade unions and they are not organised on an industrial basis.
(b)   Trade unions are very conservative, dominated by antiquated procedures and rules. Moreover, they jealously protect their privileges and traditions.
(c)   Too much power is in the hands of shop stewards many of whom do not have the ability or qualifications to perform their role effectively.
(d)   There is little contact between the national executive and the shop floor.
(e)   Trade unions together with management have been accused of fostering the 'them' and 'us' attitude which embitters industrial relations in the United Kingdom and hinders economic growth.

Recent government legislation regarding the trade unions

The Donovan Report 1968
This report recommended:

(a)   clearly defined powers for shop stewards who should receive training.
(b)   more full-time union officials to improve relationships between the union leadership and the shop floor.
(c)   a reduction in the number of unions by means of voluntary mergers.
(d)   setting up machinery to deal with cases of unfair dismissal.
(e)   more emphasis on plant bargaining to take into account local conditions.
(f)   the setting up of a Commission for Industrial Relations (CIR) to investigate disputes.

The report did not recommend prohibiting closed shops, nor did it end trade union immunity from civil action in pursuit of a trade dispute, nor did it advocate secret ballots. The CIR was immediately set up.

In Place of Strife 1969
This was a Labour government White Paper based largely on the Donovan Report. The White Paper proposed:

(a)   a ballot of members before an official strike took place.
(b)   a 28 day conciliation pause before industrial action.
(c)   the CIR should investigate inter-union disputes and finance union mergers and shop steward training.
(d)   employers must recognise a trade union if so recommended by the CIR.
(e)   an industrial board should be set up to enforce these conditions with the powers to 'penalise' offending unions or employers.
(f)   the TUC should help the unions put their own house in order by encouraging union mergers, eliminating inter-union squabbles and demarcation disputes and increasing trade unions' subscriptions to enable more full-time officials to be appointed.

The White Paper never became law owing to the fact that the Labour Party lost the 1970 election. It was bitterly opposed by much of the union movement especially the reference to the penal clauses.

Industrial Relations Act 1971

This was passed by the Conservative government and laid down the following requirements:

(a) All collective agreements between unions and employers should be legally binding unless the parties do not wish them to be so.

(b) There should be a code of industrial relations practice to set down guidelines on many aspects of labour relations.

(c) Trade union rules were to be vetted by a registrar with whom trade unions had to register. If unions did not register then they lost their legal immunity from civil action.

(d) A National Industrial Relations Court (NIRC) was set up which could fine unions for unfair practices, grant a 60-day cooling-off period in the case of a dispute and enforce ballots of union members when strike action looked likely.

(e) Descriptions of unfair practices were laid down and compensation given to those injured by such practices.

(f) Workers had the right to belong or not to belong to a trade union. Indeed closed shops were replaced by agency shops whereby an employee could make a donation to a charity rather than a subscription to the union.

(g) Workers had safeguards against unfair dismissal and would receive compensation.

(h) The CIR assisted in the operation of the Act and investigated special cases.

The Industrial Relations Act was bitterly opposed by the trade union movement. Many days were lost through strikes and many unions refused to register with the Registrar or appear before the NIRC. The Conservative Party lost the 1974 election and was replaced by a Labour government.

The Trade Union and Labour Relations Act 1974

This repealed the Industrial Relations Act 1971 and restored the unions' position to what it was before that Act. It contained two additions:

(a) It was unfair to dismiss a person for belonging to a trade union.

(b) It was fair to dismiss a person for not joining a union (unless there were religious grounds) or who left a union which was operating a closed shop agreement.

The Employment Protection Act 1975

This Act introduced the following provisions.

(a) It set up the Advisory Conciliation and Arbitration Service (ACAS), as discussed on pages 298–9.

(b) Unions not recognised by an employer (called independent unions) could refer claims to ACAS.

(c) Employers were to disclose any information to a union which would help good industrial relations.

(d) Women who leave work to have a baby should receive maternity pay for six weeks and be entitled to return to work within 29 weeks of the birth.

(e) Union officials, including shop stewards, should receive paid time-off to pursue union activities.
(f) Where a person is laid off because of lack of work then he should receive a guaranteed weekly sum.
(g) Where a worker is unfairly dismissed he should be re-employed or receive compensation.
(h) Employers were to consult with (independent) unions before redundancies took place.

The Act has led to some differences of opinion between independent unions and employers as illustrated by the Grunwick dispute in 1976. This was when Grunwick, a film processing plant, refused to recognise the clerical union, APEX, during a dispute. This led to a prolonged and difficult dispute.

The Employment Act 1980
The Conservative Party won the election of 1979 and passed the Employment Act in 1980. This laid down the following conditions.

(a) It encouraged the use of secret ballots in trade union elections or when deciding on strike action by government funding.
(b) Picketing was to be peaceful picketing, the number of pickets was to be limited and secondary picketing was to be banned. Moreover, essential supplies of goods and services were to be maintained even during a dispute.
(c) The closed shop was to continue but a code of practice was to be published to protect individual workers' rights. The code of practice was to include the following points. Firstly, the closed shop has to be voted for by a large majority of employees (ie 80% of those eligible to vote) in a secret ballot. Secondly, an employee can refuse to join the union if he/she 'genuinely objects on grounds of conscience'. Thirdly, the secret ballot on closed shops has to take place every five years.
(d) The burden of proof in cases of unfair dismissal is to fall on the employer.
(e) ACAS involvement in deciding the recognition of independent unions by employers was to be stopped.
(f) Unfair recruiting practices by trade unions was to be stopped.

The Act met opposition by trade unions mainly on the grounds that their picketing activities were severely restricted. However, some Conservative Party supporters said that the Act did not go far enough and left closed shops intact.

The Employment Act 1982

(a) This Act made unlawful any action aimed at encouraging employers to give employment only to union labour.
(b) The Act made unlawful any political strikes, for example strikes against privatisation.
(c) Unions were made liable for damages up to £250 000 from any person whose business was damaged by unlawful industrial action (ie, not defined as a lawful trade dispute).

The Trade Union Act 1984

(a)   Secret ballots were made necessary for union elections.
(b)   Secret ballots were made necessary before lawful trade disputes.
(c)   Secret ballots were made necessary before the union could have a political fund in favour of the Labour Party.
(d)   This Act extended government funding for secret ballots.

Checkpoints

1   Unemployment has been a major economic problem during the 1970s and 1980s. It is defined as the number of people registered as unemployed and in receipt of unemployment benefit.
2   A problem with some types of unemployment is that they are characterised by geographical and occupational immobility of labour.
3   There are several types of unemployment such as mass, frictional, structural and regional unemployment.
4   Government policies to reduce unemployment may be either demand-side and/or supply-side policies.
5   The natural rate of unemployment idea suggests that unemployment and inflation can exist together.
6   Wages are different from earnings and there is much terminology involved in wages discussions, eg wage drift, productivity agreements. Wages are usually paid by time rates or piece rates.
7   Wages differ between occupations as determined by the demand and supply of labour for a particular purpose. The demand for labour is determined by its marginal revenue product. Wages differ within occupation and women's wages tend to be lower than those of men. There has been some legislation to help towards more equal pay.
8   Trade unions have objectives such as improving the pay and conditions of their members.
9   There are four main types of trade union: craft, general, industrial and white collar.
10   The internal organisation of most trade unions includes shop stewards, branches, conference, full-time officials, the general secretary and national executive. The TUC is an important trade union organisation to which most unions are affiliated.
11   In case of industrial disputes there is a machinery available to help, such as conciliation and arbitration.
12   Trade unions are often criticised for operating restrictive practices, strikes, closed shops, picketing and for being undemocratic.
13   There has been much government legislation to control the activities of trade unions, such as the Employment Act 1980.

Multiple-choice questions – 14

1 Which of the following is likely to hinder increases in wages in a particular industry?

    A when wages are a smaller proportion of the industry's total costs
    B a fall in the price of a substitute commodity
    C the industry increases its profits
    D machines cannot be substituted for labour
    E an increase in demand for the industry's product.

2 Real income is best defined as

    A income in terms of its purchasing power
    B take-home pay
    C wages plus overtime
    D all earned and unearned income
    E wages in money terms less taxes

3 A textile worker is unemployed because of a fall in demand for United Kingdom textiles caused by cheap foreign imports.
   This is described as

    A cyclical unemployment
    B seasonal unemployment
    C structural unemployment
    D frictional unemployment
    E technological unemployment

4 The government's deflationary fiscal policy reduces the level of demand, and unemployment increases throughout the economy.
   This is described as
   (select from A–E in Question 3.)

5 In order to reduce the level of unemployment the government may

    A reduce money supply
    B increase interest rates
    C reduce government spending
    D restrict bank credit
    E budget for a fiscal deficit

6 In order to increase the labour force from 5 to 6 workers the employer has to increase the weekly wage from £100 to £110. The marginal cost of employing the additional worker is

    A £ 50
    B £ 60

C £100
D £110
E £150

7 Which of the following does *not* reinforce geographical immobility of labour?

    A house prices are higher in regions of relative prosperity
    B children's education may be disrupted
    C higher wages in those regions where labour is in short supply
    D people may be ignorant about job opportunities in other regions
    E people are reluctant to move away from family and friends

8 Which of the following will be most likely to achieve a more equal distribution of income and wealth?

    A progressive taxation
    B less government spending on old age pensions
    C the introduction of a poll tax to replace rates
    D the abolition of child benefit
    E value added tax increases

Questions 9 and 10 refer to the following table showing the production of a firm.

No. of workers employed	Marginal physical product (units)	Marginal revenue product (£)
1	2	50
2	10	250
3	20	500
4	32	800
5	46	1150
6	40	1000

9 Diminishing returns to scale begin to set in after the number of workers employed is

    A 2
    B 3
    C 4
    D 5
    E 6

10 The price of the product is

    A £ 5
    B £10

C £15
D £20
E £25

Answers on page 329.

Data response question 14

(a)   (i) Which country had the lowest level of unemployment in 1987?
    (ii) What was the United Kingdom's unemployment rate in 1987 (seasonally adjusted)?
    (iii) Which United Kingdom region had the highest level of unemployment in 1987?
    (iv) How many people were on government training programmes in 1987?
    (v) How is long term unemployment defined in the statistics?

(b)   How do government statisticians define unemployment? (Make reference to those groups who are included and excluded from these statistics.)

(c)   What is meant by 'seasonally adjusted unemployment'?

(d)   Why do some United Kingdom regions have higher unemployment than others? Give reasons for your answer.

(e)   How would you explain the increasing unemployment in the United Kingdom between 1979 and 1987?

(f)   What measures can the government take to reduce the level of unemployment in the United Kingdom?

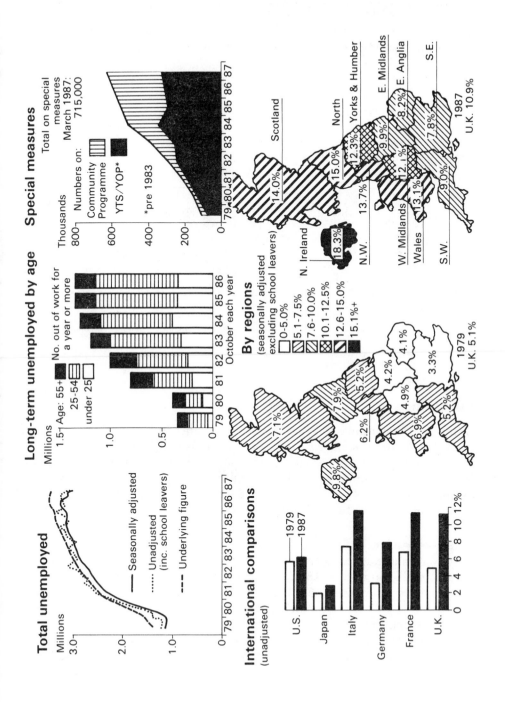

Total unemployed

Millions

— Seasonally adjusted
···· Unadjusted (inc. school leavers)
-- Underlying figure

79 80 81 82 83 84 85 86 87

Long-term unemployed by age

Millions

No. out of work for a year or more

Age: 55+
25-54
under 25

79 80 81 82 83 84 85 86

October each year

Special measures

Total on special measures
March 1987: 715,000

Thousands

Numbers on:
Community Programme
YTS/YOP*
*pre 1983

79 80 81 82 83 84 85 86 87

International comparisons

(unadjusted)

1979
1987

U.S.
Japan
Italy
Germany
France
U.K.

0 2 4 6 8 10 12%

By regions

(seasonally adjusted excluding school leavers)

0-5.0%
5.1-7.5%
7.6-10.0%
10.1-12.5%
12.6-15.0%
15.1%+

Scotland 14.0%
N. Ireland 18.3%
North 15.0%
Yorks & Humber 12.3%
N.W. 13.7%
E. Midlands 9.9%
W. Midlands 12.1%
E. Anglia 8.2%
Wales 13.1%
S.W. 9.0%
S.E. 7.8%

1987
U.K. 10.9%

Scotland 7.1%
N. Ireland 9.8%
North 7.9%
Yorks & Humber 5.2%
N.W. 6.2%
E. Midlands 4.2%
W. Midlands 6.9%
E. Anglia 4.9%
Wales 5.2%
S.W. 4.1%
S.E. 3.3%

1979
U.K. 5.1%

15 Economic problems of today

The UK economy 1979–1985							
	1979	1980	1981	1982	1983	1984	1985
GDP[1]	102.6	100.0	98.5	100.3	103.5	106.4	109.9
Index of prices	84.8	100.0	111.9	121.5	127.1	133.4	141.5
Average earnings	89.8	100.0	112.9	123.5	133.9	142.1	154.1
Unemployment (per cent)	5.1	6.0	9.3	10.9	11.9	12.4	12.9
PSBR[2] (per cent of GDP)	4.9	5.7	3.5	3.3	3.2	3.1	2.2
Visible balance	−3449	1233	3360	2331	−835	−4391	−2068
Invisible balance	2796	2002	2866	1701	3998	5953	5831
Sterling index	90.8	100.0	99.2	94.4	86.7	82.0	81.9

[1] At 1980 prices.
[2] The figures are for fiscal years.

Inflation

Every government since 1945 has faced the problem of inflation. Inflation may be defined as *the persistent increase in the general price level*. Inflation is not only a post-war phenomenon, it has existed at many times in the United Kingdom's history. However, in 1975 inflation reached the unprecedented rate of 25%. It has been the main economic objective of Conservative governments since 1979 to reduce the level of inflation. In 1987 inflation was approximately 4%.

The causes of inflation

Broadly speaking, economists agree that there are three main types of inflation. *Demand-pull inflation* is when demand exceeds supply (production) of goods and services, causing prices to rise. This excessive demand may be due to too much credit, over supply of money and excessive government spending. Closely associated with demand-pull inflation is the *monetarist* view that inflation is only due to increases in the money supply. *Cost-push inflation* occurs when costs of production increase, causing prices to rise. Increasing costs may be wages or the cost of raw materials. Economists disagree on which type of inflation has been most prevalent since 1945. Some economists feel that cost-push inflation is most prevalent. However, the Thatcher Conservative governments have seen monetarist inflation as the main type. There are now basically two schools of thought.

Consumer prices
% increase on previous year

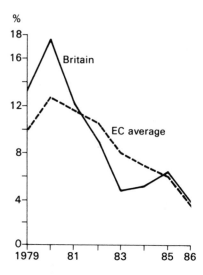

The monetarists
The supporters of Professor Milton Friedman believe that most inflation has been caused by over-issue of money. This then sets off an inflationary spiral of too much demand and higher prices.

Remedies
The basic remedy, it is argued, is to deflate the economy by taking the following actions.

(a) Reduce government spending and increase taxation, thus reducing the size of the budget deficit.
(b) Reduce money supply.
(c) Control bank lending.
(d) Impose restrictions on hire-purchase and credit.

The Thatcher Conservative governments employed deflationary monetarist policies during the early 1980s.

Problems
Critics of this idea say that the initial cause of inflation is not monetarist or demand-pull but cost-push influences. Anyway the cure could be worse than the disease since it will cause mass unemployment.

The Keynesians
The supporters of Lord Keynes blame inflation on cost-push forces. Import prices have increased and trade unions have achieved large wage increases.

Thus inflation is caused and the increase in money supply has fed the flames.

Remedies

(a) Implement prices and incomes policies (voluntary or compulsory).
(b) Control trade union power to achieve high wages.

Monetarists say that this is not attacking the real cause of inflation. There are problems with prices and incomes policies. What about special cases? What about collective bargaining?

What is wrong with inflation?

Inflation leads to

(a) Bad effects on fixed-income earners such as pensioners whose pensions fall in real value.
(b) Bad effects on the balance of payments since exports become more expensive.
(c) Bad effects on savings and investment since there is no incentive to save or invest.
(d) Bad political consequences such as those in Germany in the 1920s and 1930s. Extreme political groups may become popular as the public become disillusioned.

A more comprehensive discussion on inflation can be found in Chapter 10.

Balance of payments

Current Account

Britain's trade with the rest
of the world in goods and services

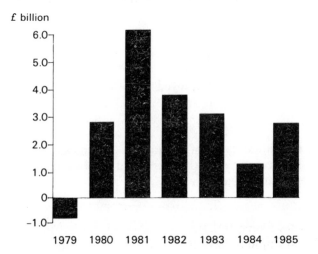

£ billion

1979 1980 1981 1982 1983 1984 1985

The balance of payments is the record of the United Kingdom's trade with other countries. Basically it consists of two parts: the *current account* which comprises visibles (the difference between imports and exports of goods, ie, balance of trade) and invisibles (import and export of services). *Investment and other capital flows* comprise the investments by the United Kingdom abroad and by other countries in the United Kingdom.

The United Kingdom's major problem has traditionally been with visibles as shown by balance of trade deficits during the 1970s. These deficits were due to inflation causing the price of the United Kingdom's exports to be too high and the dramatic increase in oil prices since 1973. Invisibles were (and are) usually in surplus. During the 1970s the United Kingdom was hindered by balance of payments deficits but during the 1980s a surplus on current account had a favourable impact on the overall balance of payments (see pages 154–7). However, by 1986 and 1987 the current account deficit had returned (£1.7 billion in 1987).

Why are governments concerned with balance of payment deficits?
Continuous deficits will have the effect of running down a country's reserves of gold and foreign currency. It will also mean that the pressure is put on the exchange rate and overseas investors will have no confidence in the economy. Therefore deflationary policies may have to be introduced which will have a bad effect on domestic output and employment.

Policies to overcome balance of payment deficits

(a) Increase interest rates and introduce deflationary policies, but any attempts to deflate the economy will damage industry and employment.
(b) Introduce protection, such as tariffs. However, this may result in problems such as retaliation.
(c) Devaluation of the pound, a last resort measure tried in 1949 and 1967. However, there are problems associated with this action because it may not always be effective (see page 163).
(d) Allow the pound to float downwards in value. However, this may fuel inflation.

During the 1980s the visible surplus became a deficit. This was due to an unprecedented deficit on manufacturing trade which was not outweighed by the continued surplus on oil trade. However, the current account remained in surplus due to the surplus on invisibles. By 1986 and 1987 the surplus on current account had been replaced once again by deficit.

The effects of North Sea oil and gas

In the 1970s the United Kingdom discovered new sources of energy in the North Sea – oil and gas. At a time of rising world energy prices this was of considerable benefit to the economy. Advantages included:

(a) *Benefits to balance of payments* The United Kingdom by 1980 had become self-sufficient in oil and gas and this meant that imports were reduced and exports increased. Thus the current account benefited a great deal. The

Gloom as trade deficit doubles

By Peter Rodgers and Mark Milner

Britain fell heavily into the red in May with a trade deficit in goods of £1.161 billion, more than double that in April.

The figure was far worse than expected and led to immediate fears in the City that the consumer boom was getting out of control, sucking in imports on a large scale.

Analysts warned that this could prompt tighter government policy and a rise in interest rates to curb the spending spree.

The poor figures led to the stock market's biggest ever one-day fall of £9.4 billion, with the gloom spilling into the foreign exchange markets, where the pound came under pressure.

Even when invisible trade in services and tourism is added the overall trade picture remains bad, with a current account deficit of £561 million in May, compared with a surplus of £96 million in April.

Pundits had been expecting the current account to be roughly in balance, with the trade in goods only £600 million or so in the red. There is also evidence that exports are not doing as well as expected.

Mr Stephen Lewis of Phillips & Drew, the brokers, said: "The numbers were just plain bad." He predicted that capacity shortages in British industry and rising demand would lead to a large jump in imports in the second half of the year, leading to a £1.5 billion to £2 billion deficit for the year.

---

investment and other capital flows aspect of the balance of payments also improved owing to overseas confidence in the United Kingdom economy caused by its development of oil and gas. Thus there was an inflow of capital investment. The balance of payments deficits of the 1970s were replaced by surpluses.

(b) The government benefited from oil taxation revenues which were imposed on oil companies in the North Sea in the form of petroleum revenue tax, corporation tax and royalties (abolished in 1988).

(c) Regions of the East of Scotland and the North East of England benefited from oil installations being built, and jobs being provided in ancillary industries such as oil rig construction. A regional multiplier effect took place. As people spent their incomes they provided other jobs for people throughout the regional economy.

However, certain qualifications have to be made to these advantages of North Sea oil to the United Kingdom in the early 1980s.

(a) The high sterling exchange rate caused by overseas confidence in the economy meant that exports became more expensive and imports cheaper which had an adverse effect on the exporting and manufacturing sectors of the economy. Also interest, profits and dividends had to be paid to investors in North Sea oil which had an adverse movement on invisibles.

(b) It is one matter to say that the government had more taxation revenue but it is another matter as to how these revenues were spent. Critics of government policy argue that North Sea oil revenues were wasted on giving income tax cuts and reducing the size of PSBR.

(c) In the mid-1980s oil prices fell. This was due to over-supply by producing nations, a decline in demand from oil-consuming nations caused by recession in the late 1970s and early 1980s and a weakening of the OPEC cartel. The effects of this on the United Kingdom were that sterling fell as confidence in the United Kingdom economy weakened, the balance of payments deteriorated as less oil revenue was forthcoming. To protect the pound and balance of payments, interest rates were kept at a historically high level.

The sterling exchange rate problem

There are two possible problems which may occur with the sterling exchange rate.

The sterling exchange rate may be too high

This problem has been discussed already in the previous section. Basically, due to North Sea oil and high interest rates prevailing in the economy in the early 1980s, the sterling exchange rate became relatively highly valued compared to foreign currencies. This had the bad effect of making exports more expensive and imports cheaper which seriously damaged the balance of payments current account, the manufacturing sector and employment. It can be said in favour of high exchange rates that low import prices had a deflationary effect on the economy and restricted inflation.

The sterling exchange rate may be too low

This should of course have the advantage of making exports cheaper and imports more expensive. Thus more exports and fewer imports should benefit the balance of payments. However, there are several disadvantages to a low exchange rate.

(a) High import prices may cause inflationary tendencies especially if trade unions ask for higher wages to maintain living standards.
(b) If demand for exports and imports is inelastic or supply of exports inelastic then the economy will not benefit from the low exchange rate.
(c) There may be pressure on the pound to go even lower as investors lose confidence in sterling and begin selling it. The onus will be on the government to support the pound on exchange markets which might lead to a drain in resources of gold and foreign currencies.
(d) There is a loss of prestige to the United Kingdom if the pound is allowed to fall too low.

Therefore the pound sterling can be either too high in value or too low in value compared to foreign currencies. Whether it is too high or too low depends on the present situation as regards inflation, employment, balance of payments and growth.

A fuller discussion of balance of payments and exchange rates can be found in Chapter 8.

Exchange rates

Sterling exchange rate index
Monthly average of daily rates 1975 = 100

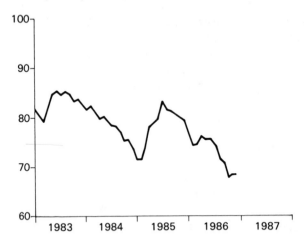

Economic growth

Economic growth is the term used to describe increases in a country's gross national product (GNP) ie, the total value of its production of goods and services. Growth refers to a percentage increase in GNP (or GDP) in any one year. For much of the post-1945 period the United Kingdom has had much lower growth rates than its main competitors, although in the mid-1980s the United Kingdom's economic growth was higher than that of many of its economic rivals.

The United Kingdom's standard of living, employment and exports are greatly determined by its growth. There are several possible reasons for the United Kingdom's poor growth during the period up to the mid-1980s.

(a)   Lack of investment.
(b)   Bad management.
(c)   Too many strikes.
(d)   Bad government.
(e)   Low productivity (ie, output per hour) among workers.
(f)   Out-dated capital and machinery still in existence.
(g)   Too much spent on non-marketable sectors such as services like health and education.
(h)   Taxation is too heavy.
(i)   The British may be a lazy workforce.
(j)   Attempts to solve balance of payments problems by deflation have affected economic growth.

It is likely that there is no one reason for low growth. Any attempts to stimulate economic growth may, in the short run, worsen balance of payments and

Britain: output per worker

Annual average % increase

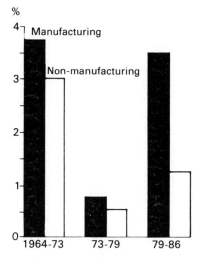

Unemployment

During the depression of the 1930s unemployment reached 3 millions (ie 20–25% of the working population). Since 1945 most governments in the United Kingdom have been determined that unemployment should never be so bad

inflation. Refer to pages 140–2 for more detailed information about economic growth.

Unemployment in Europe

Adjusted for different counting methods

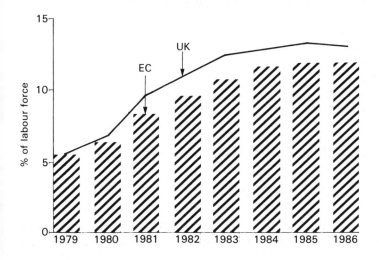

again. Their attitude was based on the Beveridge Report of 1942 which demanded the maintenance of full employment. Consequently since 1945 unemployment has rarely been above 1 million. However, in the 1970s unemployment worsened markedly and in the early 1980s stood at well over 3 million unemployed.

It was believed that unemployment and inflation could not exist in an economy at the same time. However, during the 1970s the United Kingdom had unemployment and inflation together and this situation is called '*stagflation*' or '*slumpflation*'. This resulted from the higher oil prices of the 1970s and 1980s causing inflation and also causing more unemployment. Also, Conservative government deflationary policies, for example the reduction in government spending, and the increasing use of technology, worsened the unemployment situation.

Unemployment 1960–86 (% of labour force)

ILO common definitions. Averages (rankings out of 12 countries in brackets)

	1960–69	1970–79	1980–86	1982–86	1960–86
UK	1.9 (4)	4.3 (7)	10.6 (10)	11.7 (10)	5.1 (4)
USA	4.8 (6)	6.1 (9)	7.8 (4)	8.1 (4)	6.1 (6)
Japan	1.3 (3)	1.7 (2)	2.5 (2)	2.6 (2)	1.7 (2)
EC	—	4.2	9.9	11.0	—
OECD	—	4.2	7.5	8.1	—

Policies to reduce unemployment
This is discussed on pages 280–2. The government can work on the demand side or on the supply side of the economy. Demand-side policies (aimed at increasing demand in the economy and therefore more jobs) would include increases in government spending and regional policy to the assisted areas.

The supply side (aimed at encouraging individuals and firms to produce more) would include income tax cuts, educational initiatives and YTS schemes, encouraging small firms and creating a better informed employment market.

Some politicians and economists have been concerned about the government's re-definition of the terms by which a person may be considered to be unemployed. They suggest that this re-definition means that unemployment figures are now significantly lower than the real number of unemployed and that the government has 'fiddled the figures'.

The decline of manufacturing industry in the United Kingdom since 1979

Since 1979 manufacturing output has declined although it has begun to increase again since the early 1980s. However, by 1987 manufacturing output was still at a lower level than in 1979. Moreover, in 1983, for the first time except in periods of war, the United Kingdom moved into a deficit on its trade in manufactured goods.

1980 : surplus on manufactures of £3 billions
1983 : deficit on manufactures of £4.9 billions
1985 : deficit on manufactures of £5.8 billions

This decline in manufacturing is also indicated by its declining proportionate share of GDP and employment (see page 269 for statistics).

Manufacturing output

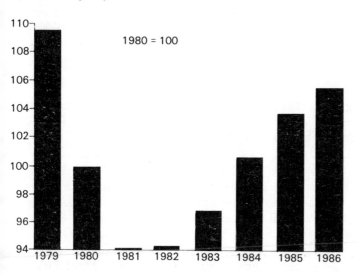

The causes of decline in manufacturing
The causes of the decline in manufacturing are as follows.

(a) A relatively high value of sterling exchange rates in the mid-1980s made United Kingdom exports uncompetitive and imports cheap.
(b) High United Kingdom interest rates led to a decline in investment in manufacturing in the United Kingdom.
(c) World recession since 1979 led to a decline in manufacturing exports.
(d) Government deflationary monetary and fiscal policies have reduced aggregate demand and harmed manufacturing. The government's main economic objective has been to reduce inflation and this has had adverse side-effects on the rest of the economy.
(e) The quality of United Kingdom manufactures is often less than competitors'.
(f) Prices of United Kingdom manufactures are higher than foreign manufactures. This may reflect low labour productivity (see page 7) and high levels of earnings.

The decline in manufacturing is very worrying. This is because traditionally the United Kingdom is known as a manufacturing country and one day North Sea oil will run out. This anticipates a serious balance of payments problem for the future. Some economists even talk of the United Kingdom as a 'doomed economy'. However, other economists argue that the United Kingdom has a comparative advantage in services, such as banking and finance, and these will compensate for the decline in manufacturing. Indeed, in 1987, services account for a large part of employment and GDP (see page 269) and for the United Kingdom balance of payments current account earnings.

Oil prices from 1973

There have been two major periods of dramatic increases in oil prices – 1973–4 and 1979–80. These higher oil prices were due to the policies of the Organisation of Petroleum Exporting Countries (OPEC) which demanded higher and higher prices for their supplies of oil. The effects were as follows.

Inflation
Countries purchasing oil had to pass these increased costs on to consumers in the form of higher prices. Moreover transport costs increased and trade unions demanded higher wages. These factors all fuelled inflation.

Unemployment
Unemployment worsened in the developed countries for two main reasons. Firstly, high oil costs led businesspeople to seek to reduce costs in other areas of their firms. Thus labour was shed in an effort to reduce wage costs. Secondly, demand for manufactured goods diminished as countries throughout the world spent more on oil. The United Kingdom was faced with declining markets for its products, causing unemployment. Thus oil price increases caused both inflation and unemployment at the same time. This phenomenon is called 'stagflation' or 'slumpflation'.

Balance of payments difficulties
Demand for oil tends to be inelastic. Therefore countries imported approximately the same quantity of more expensive oil. At the same time exports diminished. This caused balance of payments deficits amongst developed countries. To a certain extent the United Kingdom was cushioned from the oil price rises of 1979–80 by the development of its own North Sea oil.

Sterling problems
Many of the OPEC countries converted their new found wealth in the banking and financial centres of the world such as London. Much of this investment was, and is, short term, known as 'hot money'. Consequently any sign of weakness in the United Kingdom economy, such as high inflation or unemployment, caused this 'hot money' to flow out. This put a strain on the sterling exchange rate which became very sensitive and volatile. In 1976 the pound declined dramatically in what was called a sterling crisis.

Energy-saving and new sources of energy
The high oil prices caused most of the developed countries to save energy mainly

by the imposition of high prices to ration use of energy and by 'save it' campaigns. Also capital was invested in alternative forms of energy such as solar energy and nuclear power.

However during the 1980s oil prices fell. The reasons for and consequences of this are discussed on page 317.

Checkpoints

1 Inflation is a major problem facing governments. There are three main views about its causes. Firstly that it is caused by too much demand (demand-pull). Secondly that it is caused solely by increases in money supply (monetarism). Thirdly that it is caused by increasing costs (cost-push). The proposed remedies for it differ according to the assumed cause of inflation.
2 Balance of payments deficits were of great concern to United Kingdom governments of the 1950s, 1960s and 1970s. Deficits are regarded as undesirable and remedies included deflation, protection and devaluation. Since the discovery of North Sea oil in the late 1970s the United Kingdom has enjoyed surpluses on current account although the decline in manufacturing trade is still a cause for some anxiety.
3 The exchange rate of the pound is of concern to the United Kingdom government. If the pound is too high or too low it will bring problems.
4 Economic growth has been relatively poor in the United Kingdom since 1945 compared with similar countries such as France, Japan and West Germany. The possible reasons for slow growth are discussed.
5 Unemployment is a major problem of the 1970s and 1980s. Government policy must at all times be aimed at reducing the level of unemployment by either demand-side or supply-side policies.
6 A feature of the United Kingdom economy during the 1980s has been the decline in manufacturing industry in terms of proportionate share of employment, GDP and trade.
7 Oil prices are of concern to the United Kingdom. Before the 1980s the United Kingdom was an importer of oil, now she is a net exporter. Any change in oil prices has side-effects on the value of the pound, the balance of payments and even the level of taxation and borrowing.

Multiple-choice questions – 15

1　Each of the following has been an objective of government economic policy since 1979 with the exception of

　　A　a lower level of unemployment
　　B　a higher level of economic growth
　　C　a reduction in the level of inflation
　　D　an increased public sector borrowing requirement
　　E　a balance of payments surplus

2　Which of the following is part of government monetary policy?

　　A　open market operations
　　B　public sector borrowing requirement
　　C　income tax
　　D　old age pensions
　　E　privatisation

3　Economic growth may be achieved by which of the following measures?

　　A　increasing workers' paid holidays
　　B　increasing the exchange rate of the pound
　　C　increasing interest rates
　　D　purchasing more imports of foreign manufactures
　　E　a rise in the productivity of labour

4　Which of the following measures would probably be part of a deflationary fiscal package?

　　A　increased interest rates
　　B　lower deposits for hire-purchase finance
　　C　increased income tax
　　D　increased unemployment benefits
　　E　increasing special deposits

5　Which of the following will definitely occur after a fall in the value of the pound on foreign exchange markets?

　　A　a reduction in import prices
　　B　a reduction in export prices
　　C　an improvement in the terms of trade
　　D　a visible trade surplus
　　E　more employment in export industries

6　Which of the following would not improve the United Kingdom's balance of payments surplus on current account?

　　A　an increase in manufacturing imports

B an increase in the value of invisible earnings
C an increase in the value of the pound given inelastic demand for exports
D a fall in the value of the pound given elastic demand for imports
E a fall in oil prices

7 Demand-pull inflation is most likely to be caused by

A a decrease in bank credit
B an increase in interest rates
C a fall in labour productivity
D an increased budget deficit
E an increase in earnings above the level of inflation

8 Which of the following is most likely to reduce the level of unemployment in an economy?

A increasing government spending on regional aid
B increasing interest rates
C increasing the exchange rate for sterling
D reducing import duties
E reducing subsidies to public corporations

9 Between 1986 and 1987 the national income of Erewhon increased by 15%. At the same time the country experienced 5% inflation. Which one of the following index numbers represents the national income of Erewhon in 1987 at 1986 prices (1986 = 100)?

A 103
B 110
C 115
D 118
E 120

10 The slower rate of economic growth in an economy as compared with its main competitors can best be seen by changes in the

A balance of payments figures
B money national income
C real national income per capita
D unemployment statistics
E real earnings

Answers on page 329.

Data response question 15

Refer to these selected statistics for the United Kingdom economy.

UK economy: selected statistics 1981–85	1981	1982	1983	1984	1985
Inflation	*Retail prices (percentage increase on previous year)*				
	11.9	8.6	4.6	5.0	6.1
Earnings	*Average earnings (percentage increase on previous year)*				
	12.9	9.4	8.4	6.1	8.5
Unemployment	*Total unadjusted unemployment (in thousands)*				
	2520.3	2916.9	3104.7	3159.8	3271.2
Output	*Index of GDP at constant factor cost (1980 = 100)*				
	98.3	100.1	103.1	106.4	110.2
Investment	*Gross domestic fixed capital formation as a percentage of GDP at factor cost*				
	19.2	20.1	20.4	21.7	21.2
Savings ratio	*Personal savings/personal disposable income (per cent)*				
	13.6	12.8	11.5	12.1	11.9
Money supply	*Sterling M3 excluding public sector deposits (percentage increase on four quarters earlier)*				
	15.1	9.0	11.2	10.1	13.4
Interest rates	*Clearing banks' base rate (per cent, last Friday in December)*				
	$14\frac{1}{2}$	$10-10\frac{1}{4}$	9	$9\frac{1}{2}-9\frac{3}{4}$	$11\frac{1}{2}$
Balance of payments	*Current account (total for whole year, £ million)*				
	+6226	+4032	+3163	+1562	+3763
Exchange rate	*Sterling rate against US dollar*				
	2.025	1.749	1.516	1.336	1.298

(a) Define each of the following terms
   (i) inflation
   (ii) earnings
   (iii) GDP at factor cost
   (iv) sterling M3
   (v) clearing banks' base rate

(b) Which year had
   (i) the lowest level of inflation?
   (ii) the highest level of unemployment?
   (iii) the lowest surplus on balance of payments current account?
   (iv) the highest percentage level of investment (as % of GDP)?

(c) With reference to the statistics for inflation, earnings and unemployment, what happened to the standard of living for citizens of the United Kingdom between 1981 and 1985?

(d) What happened to economic growth between 1980–1985?

(e) 'There are lies, damned lies and statistics.' As a student of economics interpret this statement. Give reasons for your answer.

Answers to multiple-choice questions

Chapter 1

1	C	6	A
2	C	7	D
3	D	8	B
4	C	9	E
5	B	10	D

Chapter 2

1	A	6	C
2	A	7	D
3	E	8	A
4	B	9	E
5	D	10	C

Chapter 3

1	D	6	D
2	A	7	B
3	B	8	C
4	E	9	A
5	E	10	D

Chapter 4

1	B	6	E
2	D	7	D
3	E	8	B
4	A	9	C
5	C	10	C

Chapter 5

1	D	6	D
2	C	7	B
3	B	8	E
4	A	9	D
5	E	10	A

Chapter 6

1	D	6	D
2	C	7	C
3	E	8	E
4	A	9	D
5	D	10	B

Chapter 7

1	A	6	C
2	E	7	B
3	B	8	C
4	D	9	A
5	E	10	E

Chapter 8

1	B	6	B
2	E	7	B
3	C	8	E
4	A	9	A
5	D	10	A

Chapter 9

1	B	6	E
2	D	7	A
3	C	8	C
4	E	9	E
5	D	10	E

Chapter 10

1	B	6	C
2	C	7	B
3	A	8	E
4	E	9	D
5	A	10	A

Chapter 11

1	D	6	B
2	D	7	C
3	C	8	A
4	E	9	B
5	E	10	C

Chapter 12

1	B	6	E
2	A	7	A
3	A	8	D
4	E	9	C
5	B	10	B

Chapter 13

1	D	6	E
2	D	7	C
3	E	8	E
4	C	9	E
5	B	10	D

Chapter 14

1	B	6	B
2	A	7	C
3	C	8	A
4	A	9	D
5	E	10	E

Chapter 15

1	D	6	E
2	A	7	D
3	E	8	A
4	C	9	B
5	B	10	C

Index

Index